Suck A Rock

THE PERSONAL STORY OF ONE SOLDIER
WITH A WORM'S EYE VIEW FROM A FOXHOLE IN
WORLD WAR II

Daniel Collier Houston

Photographs provided by the Author. The Cover photo was taken somewhere in Europe, Spring 1940 and depicts the author wearing his tam o'shanter firing a Bren-Gun from a foxhole (the flash-hider makes the barrel look larger than it is).

Persons wishing to contact the author may do so through Trafford Publishing.

National Library of Canada Cataloguing in Publication

Houston, Daniel Collier, 1923-
        Suck a rock / Daniel Collier Houston.

ISBN 1-55369-375-2

        1. Houston, Daniel Collier, 1923- 2. World War, 1939-1945--Personal narratives, American. I. Title.

D811.H697 2002   940.54'8173   C2002-901447-6

TRAFFORD

This book was published *on-demand* in cooperation with Trafford Publishing.
On-demand publishing is a unique process and service of making a book available for retail sale to the public taking advantage of on-demand manufacturing and Internet marketing.
On-demand publishing includes promotions, retail sales, manufacturing, order fulfilment, accounting and collecting royalties on behalf of the author.

Suite 6E, 2333 Government St., Victoria, B.C. V8T 4P4, CANADA

Phone	250-383-6864	Toll-free	1-888-232-4444 (Canada & US)
Fax	250-383-6804	E-mail	sales@trafford.com
Web site	www.trafford.com	TRAFFORD PUBLISHING IS A DIVISION OF TRAFFORD HOLDINGS LTD.	
Trafford Catalogue #02-0188		www.trafford.com/robots/02-0188.html	

10   9   8   7   6   5   4

Suck A Rock: Table of Contents

FOREWORD: PAGE   V

CHAPTER 1: Somewhere in North Africa   PAGE   1
Southern Tunisia, February 1943

CHAPTER 2: Somewhere in Alabama   PAGE   3
Montgomery, Summer 1939

CHAPTER 3: Somewhere in Canada   PAGE   5
Ontario, Summer 1939

CHAPTER 4: Somewhere in Canada & Alabama   PAGE   8
Ontario & Montgomery, Late Summer 1939

CHAPTER 5: Somewhere in Virginia   PAGE   10
Naval Operations Base, Norfolk, Fall 1939

CHAPTER 6: Somewhere in Canada   PAGE   14
British Columbia to Nova Scotia, End of 1939 & Spring 1940

CHAPTER 7: Somewhere in the North Atlantic   PAGE   21
Late Spring 1940

CHAPTER 8: Somewhere in Great Britain   PAGE   24
Late Spring 1940

CHAPTER 9: Somewhere in England   PAGE   26
Early Summer 1940

CHAPTER 10: Somewhere in England   PAGE   29
Summer 1940

CHAPTER 11: Somewhere in England   PAGE   32
Summer 1940

CHAPTER 12: Somewhere in Scotland   PAGE   33
Summer & Fall 1940

CHAPTER 13: Somewhere in England   PAGE   36
Fall 1940

CHAPTER 14: Somewhere in Great Britain   PAGE   39
Winter & Spring 1941

Suck A Rock: Table of Contents

CHAPTER 15: Somewhere in Great Britain   PAGE   42
Winter & Spring 1941

CHAPTER 16: Somewhere in Great Britain   PAGE   47
Spring & Summer 1941

CHAPTER 17: Somewhere in Norway, Great Britain & Hebrides   PAGE   52
Summer & Fall 1941

CHAPTER 18: Somewhere in Great Britain   PAGE   57
Fall 1941

CHAPTER 19: Somewhere in Great Britain   PAGE   59
Winter & Spring 1942

CHAPTER 20: Somewhere in England & France   PAGE   63
Summer 1942

CHAPTER 21: Somewhere in England & Ireland   PAGE   69
Summer & Fall 1942

CHAPTER 22: Somewhere in Ireland   PAGE   72
Fall 1942

CHAPTER 23: Somewhere in Ireland, Scotland,   PAGE   77
England & North Africa
Fall 1942

CHAPTER 24: Somewhere in North Africa   PAGE   82
Fall 1942

CHAPTER 25: Somewhere in North Africa, Algeria & Tunisia   PAGE   85
Winter 1942-43

CHAPTER 26: Somewhere in North Africa, Tunisia   PAGE   89
February 1943

CHAPTER 27: Somewhere in North Africa, Algeria & Tunisia   PAGE   93
February 1943

CHAPTER 28: Somewhere in North Africa, Tunisia   PAGE   98
Winter & Spring 1943

CHAPTER 29: Somewhere in North Africa, Tunisia   PAGE 103
Winter & Spring 1943

CHAPTER 30: Somewhere in North Africa, Tunisia   PAGE 107
Winter & Spring 1943

CHAPTER 31: Somewhere in North Africa, Tunisia   PAGE 110
Winter & Spring 1943

CHAPTER 32: Somewhere in North Africa, Tunisia   PAGE 114
Spring 1943

CHAPTER 33: Somewhere in North Africa, Tunisia   PAGE 117
Spring 1943

CHAPTER 34: Somewhere in North Africa, Tunisia   PAGE 121
May 1943

CHAPTER 35: Somewhere in North Africa Algeria & Tunisia   PAGE 127
Early Summer 1943

CHAPTER 36: Somewhere in North Africa, Algeria & Tunisia   PAGE 132
Early Summer 1943

CHAPTER 37: Somewhere in North Africa, Algeria & Tunisia   PAGE 137
Summer 1943

CHAPTER 38: Somewhere in North Africa, Algeria & Tunisia   PAGE 146
Summer 1943

CHAPTER 39: Somewhere in North Africa, Algeria & Tunisia   PAGE 150
Late Summer & Early Fall 1943

CHAPTER 40: Somewhere in Italy   PAGE 155
Fall & Winter 1943-44

CHAPTER 41: Somewhere in Italy   PAGE 160
Winter & Spring 1944

CHAPTER 42: Somewhere in Italy, North Africa, The Atlantic Ocean   PAGE 164
& Virginia
Late Spring & Early Summer 1944

CHAPTER 43: Somewhere in Virginia   PAGE 168
Summer 1944

Suck A Rock: Table of Contents

CHAPTER 44: Somewhere in Virginia, Alabama & Florida   PAGE 173
Late Summer 1944

CHAPTER 45: Somewhere in Virginia & Pennsylvania   PAGE 178
Fall 1944

CHAPTER 46: Somewhere in Pennsylvania   PAGE 183
Winter 1945

CHAPTER 47: Somewhere From Pennsylvania to Alabama   PAGE 187
Winter 1945

AFTERWORD   PAGE 190

Dear Reader: This is a personal story of one soldier with a worm's eye view from a foxhole in World War II. At birth, my parents named me "Daniel Collier Houston" and always called me "Collier." The military insisted that I was Daniel C. Houston. The Canadians and British called me "Alabama." The Royal Navy called me "Lofty" (I am 6' 3" tall). I have also been called some nasty names on various occasions. As you read this book, you might notice that American soldiers started calling me Sergeant and later Lieutenant. Also, the French and other people could not pronounce "Collier" but everyone could pronounce "Daniel." For these reasons, it was necessary for me to use my full name on many documents.

Please understand; I am not a hero. My purpose, together with all the other soldiers during the war, was simply to survive. Writing this book gives me great pain. It is important that the next generation know about how the people of the United States and our Allied Nations worked and suffered in order to win this war. People worked in vast factories, on railroads, in coal mines, in shipyards, in steel mills and in so many other unnamed jobs to provide weapons of war, food, clothing and shelter for millions of military personnel. The U.S., all the countries of Europe and many others had rationing of food and other commodities. England was the only country in Europe that did not ration bread.

As an example of suffering caused by the war, it is certain that my parents suffered during these years. My mother, Caroline Lizabeth (Callie) Ramer Houston and father, Walter Howell Houston, had five sons and one daughter. Walter Ray Houston was serving in the United States Navy. Ruby Houston Lewis was married to Harvey Burton, now deceased, who went from the University of Tennessee to Randolph Field, Texas for pilot training and then to Maxwell Field in Montgomery where they met and were married. He was serving in the United States Army Air Corps when the war started. Samuel James Houston, deceased, was in the Signal Corps serving in my division (34th Infantry Division) in Africa and later in another division in France. Lenus Milan Houston, deceased, served in the United States Army Infantry (Alabama National Guard). William Howard Houston was serving in the United States Army Air Corps, (The name changed during the first part of the war to " United States Army Air Force").

Then there was me, the youngest. I served in the ARGYLL AND SUTHERLAND HIGHLANDERS (discharged underage at sixteen); UNITED STATES NAVY; 48th HIGHLANDERS, transferred to CANADIAN SCOTTISH; Detached Service, THE ROYAL SCOTS; 135th INFANTRY REGIMENT, 34th INFANTRY DIVISION, II CORPS, UNITED STATES ARMY in Africa and 5th ARMY in Italy. After the African Campaign, I was appointed a SPECIAL MILITARY POLICE OFFICER and served under the command of the PROVOST MARSHALL, MEDITERRANEAN BASE SECTOR. The Provost Marshall was ordered by his superiors at Allied Supreme Command Algiers, to organize, schedule and load American troops and supplies at the sea port in Bizerta for the invasion of Sicily. He also commanded all Military Police in Africa.

My parents prayed daily. It was my good fortune to have known both of my grandmothers. My parents, grandparents and great grandparents were born in Covington County, Alabama, which borders the State of Florida. They were descendants of early pioneers from Virginia, North Carolina, South Carolina and Georgia. Both grandmothers told me stories of the War Between the States and the Indian Wars in Alabama, Georgia, Mississippi and Florida, which involved General Andrew Jackson and Sam Houston. My paternal grandparents were Samuel James Houston and Missouri Clementine Olive Houston.

My maternal grandmother, Georgia Anne Meadows Ramer, was part Cherokee and a widow. Her husband Jacob Daniel Ramer (my grandfather) had been sheriff of Covington County, Alabama and was killed in a shootout in 1893. We would sit in the swing on the porch and she would talk to me while shelling peas, peeling peaches and the like. She told me how the Indians could run a hundred miles without food or water by sucking on a rock. That is why this book is named "SUCK A ROCK."

Because of censorship during the war, all military personnel letters would start with the phrase "Somewhere in ____." All letters from the U.S. to military personnel overseas would be addressed to (Army Post Office) A.P.O. ____ New York, New York for those to the east and A.P.O.____ San Francisco, Cal. for those to the west.

This book is written from memory (60+ years later) and without any research of time, places or names. Some names I remember, some names I do not remember, and some names have been changed because it is not my intent to harm anyone including family members or descendants. These are my personal experiences and an earnest effort has been made to be accurate. However, it is likely some errors will occur. There are some experiences not included because it is too difficult to remember and write all the things that happened during these five years. Also, some horrible things happened that I have tried to forget. I was sixteen when I left home and I spent my 21st birthday in an army hospital. My survival was certainly only because of the Grace of God. One wrong step in a minefield and I would have been gone. This is not a history book. It is the responsibility of "Honest" Historians to record World War II as it happened without mincing words because of National Origin, Race, Color, or Religion. People who reject the facts of history, the murder and torture of millions of people by Hitler, Mussolini, Stalin, Hirohito, and Mao Tse-tung make old soldiers like me cry in the wilderness. There are countless numbers of kind people who helped me during my journey; to them I will be eternally grateful. Many thanks are due to Becky McPherson for helping with the manuscript and to Barbara Reed for the superb cover design.

February 1943

We were double-timing, in single file, as fast as we could in the darkness without running into cactus or making noise. Following me was a 1st Lt. and a staff sergeant of combat engineers attached to H.Q. 34th Inf. Div., U.S. Army. My mouth was dry so I continued to suck on a rock. We had just blown up a German ammunition and supply dump with two satchel charges. I had found the dump the night before while on patrol alone.

Then it happened. A great ball of fire lit up the sky. I whispered "down" and we dropped to our faces on the ground. My mind was racing with hope. Hope that the other two American soldiers were trained well enough to know not to expose their faces, which would shine and they would know to try to keep their "night sight" the best they could. It takes twenty minutes of total darkness or closed eyes to gain night vision.

Seconds after the explosion, we heard the sounds and felt the shock waves shake the ground where we lay. There were secondary explosions as other stacks of Afrika Korps 88 millimeter shells went up in flames. When the sounds stopped and darkness returned, I whispered, "Go" and we started moving again.

It happened again, thunk. As soon as the shell hit the firing pin in the bottom of the mortar barrel, I knew it would be a flare. I whispered "Down" as we dropped. There is no other sound like a mortar shell coming out of the barrel and flying through the air. The sky lit up around us as other mortars fired flares.

Then I prayed. If we were spotted, we were dead. After the flares burned out and darkness returned, I whispered "Stay down, don't move, they will be searching for us in minutes." Minutes later, with our bodies pressed to the ground and our faces covered, we could feel their boots hit the ground as they were moving fast towards us. As they rushed past us, a boot missed my hand by inches.

My mind was racing and I sucked and sucked on my rock. It was a good rock that I had carefully selected before we left our line. The Germans were now between us and the American battle lines. Decision time. The Afrika Korps was the German Regular Army. They were well trained, experienced and the greatest enemy any Allied Soldiers would ever fight. Also, they would force the Italian Regular Army (Eyeties) to fight in front of them. They would be super-angry and some Germans would be executed for allowing some green Americans to slip past their sentries and blow up some of their ammunitions.

The best course of action for the Germans would be to send out several squads, not just the one that passed us, then stop, spread out and wait in ambush in order to kill us. With these things in mind, I guided us south, parallel to our American position so as to return to our battle line around the southern flank. Using the Highlanders marching pace, we would cover three miles per hour instead of the U.S. Army pace of two and one-half miles per hour. There was star shine and in about an hour and a half the moon would rise. Seeing some rocks that we could hide in, we stopped and plopped down. Fatigue was setting in. We pulled our canteens and drank some water. Then we smoked and talked. It was about 4:00 A.M. judging by the position of the Milky Way. The lieutenant and sergeant each had one can of C-Ration Hash, which they shared with me. All the combat infantrymen ever got was C-Ration Beans because they were at the end of all supply lines. I showed them my rock and told them how my grandmother had taught me that an Indian could travel one hundred miles in a day by sucking on a rock. The lieutenant's name was O'Farrel and he was a West Pointer. The staff sergeant's name was McDonald and he had enlisted before the war and by completing many of the Engineering School courses had received promotions.

It became obvious that they had some questions in their minds. There was no rank on my uniform and yet I was the leader. The lieutenant said, "Who in the hell are you?" Then I told them about how I had enlisted in the Canadian Army at the beginning of World War II and all the years of training and missions with Canadians and the Royal Army, the transfer in England to the U.S. Army, twice promoted to sergeant, which I did not want. They said they had noticed that I never stopped to look at a compass or watch. I explained that I did not have either, but used the stars instead. The lieutenant asked why I was not an officer. Laughing, I said "I am still a teen-ager and not old enough to be an officer." Explaining why I had turned south instead of heading straight to our lines, it was also necessary to explain another problem. It was certain that many of our soldiers had seen the flares and had seen and heard the explosions. They would all stay awake all night expecting an attack and have itchy trigger fingers. It would have been suicide to go straight in. When I went on patrol, I would come in singing, shouting and cursing so no one would shoot. We slept for an hour.

After awakening, we drank some water, smoked and took a leak. Heading west for an hour, we then turned north and arrived after daylight in the rear of the American lines. When the officers and enlisted men found out that we had blown up the German ammo dump, we received many "well dones." The lieutenant asked me if I would like a transfer to the combat engineers and he said that he would guarantee that I would be an officer when I was old enough. I said "Yes, Sir." We three shook hands and parted as friends and more than that we shared a bond that only soldiers have when they face death together. These were the good guys. Little did I know, soon both of them would be Killed in Action (K.I.A.) and I would find out what they had tried to do for me. Now I will explain how I arrived in these desolate, barren Dorsal Mountains.

Montgomery, Summer 1939

In the decade of the 1930's, World War II had already started. Mussolini, the Dictator of Italy, started building his empire by attacking and conquering Albania and threatening other Balkan countries, conquering Tripolitania, Libya and Ethiopia in Africa. He already had Italian Somaliland. Hitler, the Dictator of Germany had quickly conquered Poland and then attacked the Soviet Union. This caused the Western Allies to declare war on Germany and Italy who had become allies. The Western Allied nations consisted of France, Belgium, Holland, Norway, Great Britain (United Kingdom) and the British Commonwealth of Nations, Canada, Australia, New Zealand, South Africa, India, Burma and others.

During the Spanish civil war, which was now over having been won by the Dictator Franco, the Germans and Italians had supported Franco the Rebel by sending "military volunteers" and weapons including aircraft, tanks, artillery and the like. Russia sent "volunteers" to form the "Red Brigade" to support the Royalists of the King. Although the Red Brigade was communist, some Americans volunteered to fight with them. In the meanwhile Russia had formed the Soviet Union by conquest and had attacked Finland to expand Stalin's empire. The Finns fought tooth and nail against superior forces and the Soviet Communist never did really conquer Finland. Finland negotiated with the Soviets and Germany during the war, more or less becoming neutral.

While these wars were going on, there was another war in the Pacific. Emperor Hirohito of Japan, another dictator, and called by his people "GOD" had expanded his empire by conquering Korea, Manchuria and many parts of China. The Japanese were continually expanding their conquest of the massive nation of China by murdering thousands of innocent Chinese. One of their famous atrocities was the "Rape of Nanking." What amazed me at this time was the complacency of the American officials and people. The Nazi Germans were having grand parties in New York with the rich and famous Americans.

In the fall of 1939, I was a student at Lanier High School in Montgomery, AL and had turned 16 years old. My birthplace was 101 Cherry Street in Highland Park and I graduated from Highland Avenue Grammar School after starting school at St. Mary's of Loretta. Then I graduated from Baldwin Jr. High. No, I was not a dumb dropout. My mother and father never worried about my grades, usually all A's. Being the youngest of six children in the Great Depression, I did not want them to worry. When I was old enough, I learned how to duplicate both signatures and signed all my own report cards.

The point of all this was one of the factors that saved my life. At this time, it was not possible for me to understand what I had learned would be so important in my military service. My classes at Baldwin and Lanier included; Algebra, Geometry, Latin, History, Geography, R.O.T.C. and some special English courses. I was blessed with a photographic memory. I can still see the last page of the Gee-O-Me-Try Book. ($C^2 = A^2 + B^2$) (Pythagorean Theorem) and I am now 78 years old! However, now I can't tell you what I had for breakfast this morning.

Growing up with army brats at Maxwell Field, building model planes, boredom, and other thoughts came to me. Maxwell was for advanced training for pilots who had already become pilots at Randolph Field, Texas (the West Point of the Air). So, I started hitchhiking to Canada, thinking that I could join the Air Force and become a fighter pilot. Hitchhiking was easy in those days provided you were clean and dressed reasonably. People were kind and generous. Generally, I tried to travel by the main roads going north but would accept a ride if it would carry me a reasonable distance north. I was in Tennessee when a man in a truck offered me a ride north on a minor highway sort of parallel to the western side of the Smokey Mountains. Traveling through the hills, we could see women carrying shotguns.

We arrived at a very small town in Kentucky, which was the driver's destination. When I told people where I was from and where I was going, they thought that it was a great thing to do. I thanked the driver and he wished me good luck as I got out of the truck and headed a short distance to the highway going north. As I started hitchhiking again, some ladies were walking by and stopped to talk to me. My deep-south accent was a blessing. The truck driver had warned me not to mess around with honky-tonks, mountain folks and shine whiskey. They asked me where I was from and where I was going. One lady said "Boy are you in any trouble?" My response was "No Mam" and I answered their questions. The same lady said "Son, you must be hungry, my house is right over yonder, dinner (noon meal) is on the stove and I was fixin to get it on the table. Son, you need some fattening up before you go to war. My husband and son will be thar to eat. Son, you'll have some vittles with us." Picking up my small suitcase, I followed the lady. While washing my face and hands using the washbasin at the well next to the porch, the husband and son came in. Dinner was good southern cooking. The lady had some more sons and daughters, but they were working too far from the house to come home for dinner. She said that they had carried their dinners to work. I continued hitchhiking to Canada, crossing the border at Niagara Falls, Ontario. Filling station owners were very kind, giving me road maps, allowing me to use their bathrooms to wash up and also letting me sleep there when I needed to.

SUCK A ROCK 3: Somewhere in Canada

Ontario, Summer 1939

After crossing into Canada at Niagara Falls, the first person I met was a tall, distinguished looking customs officer and border guard. Obviously, he was a Scot. I had walked across the bridge and he saw me coming. He said, "Son, come into my office and wait, I'll be right back", as he went out to check people in vehicles. In those days there was very little traffic. He returned to his office and said "Son, why did you come to Canada?" Being wise, he already knew the answer. I said, "I have come to Canada to fight the war." He did not ask the usual questions such as: how much money do you have?, where are you going? and for how long? He gave me some kind of roll and asked if I would like some tea. When I told him, "Yes, thank you", he handed me a mug of tea. A vehicle pulled up and stopped and he went outside. This was my first "Hot Tea" and it was not good. In the Deep South we always drank "Ice Tea" and coffee. "Hot Tea" would be my drink for the next several years and I would forget the taste of "Ice Tea" and coffee. As a matter of courtesy, it was important to drink the tea. I drank the tea. When the officer returned he asked me questions while he was filling out a form. When finished, he looked and said "Son with your build and blue eyes, you are a Scot." He told me that the Argyll's, Headquartered in Hamilton, needed some more men. So I told him my aim was to join the Air Force and become a pilot. Of course I told him I was twenty-one when he asked for my age on the form (I lied a lot, I was twenty-one for five years). "In that case, you can go to Toronto to the Horse Palace which was part of the Canadian Exposition and has been converted for military use," he replied.

"The Air Force has an office in the Horse Palace and the 48th Highlanders are headquartered there. Wait here and I will get you a ride to Toronto." Soon, a car with an elderly couple in the front seat pulled up and stopped. He then came back in his office and told me that this nice couple was going to Toronto and would be glad to take me to the Horse Palace. On the way, the gentleman stopped at a restaurant and they insisted that I have lunch with them. They wanted to know all about me, so I told them. We arrived at the Horse Palace, a very large building (probably named that because they had horse shows there during the Canadian National Exposition).

The first thing that I noticed were the cars parked in rows in front of the building. Most of them had Texas license plates. I heard later that the cars belonged to American pilots who had driven them there to volunteer in the R.C.A.F. (Royal Canadian Air Force) and when they shipped out left them there for the duration. (I would later learn that they called themselves the "Texas Airforce" and they would save my neck). Inside the building, a part of the large area had been partitioned off to make offices. The offices of the Royal Canadian Air Force were easy to find. There was a sergeant on duty and I told him that I would like to volunteer for pilot training. He filled out a form, which I signed when it was completed. My name, address, education and so forth were correct. My birth date indicated that I was twenty-one. Since it was late in the day, he said they would send me in the morning to their doctors for a physical examination and after that they would give me a written exam. He gave me some blankets and said "there is a bunking area, mess area, and latrine for the airmen and soldiers who work here and are stationed here." After eating I looked around, met some airmen and soldiers, found an empty bunk and went to sleep.

The next morning, I showered, dressed, went to eat, then to the sergeant's office. There were two Canadians in his office signing up for the Air Force. These were hectic times for everyone. The Canadians never did have a draft. Everyone who joined their military forces was a volunteer for regular military forces and further they had to volunteer to go overseas. Canada was

5

now in a Great War and volunteers were signing up all over Canada. The sergeant gave each of us a form authorizing our physical exams. A corporal drove us to a doctors' building and waited to take us back to the "Palace." The nurses and technicians X-rayed us; took blood samples for laboratory tests; and we urinated in glasses for tests. Three different doctors with different specialties examined us from top to bottom. We then returned to the "Palace" and reported to the Air Force sergeant. The sergeant gave each of us the written exam test forms, pencils and the corporal led us to another room lined with small tables and one chair with each. The corporal stayed with us until we completed the tests and turned them in to him. The test was a good general knowledge type and must be passed in order to go to pilot training school. The sergeant informed us that the doctor's report would take about three days and would be hand delivered to the Commanding Officer. In the meanwhile, we could relax, but if we went off base we must check in with his office every four hours; here is the phone number. "By the way," he continued, "this office has someone on duty twenty-four hours a day, we are at war." After spending three days looking around the "Palace" and some of Toronto, the sergeant said that the medical report had arrived and the Commanding Officer had reviewed it and the written exam. While I waited in the sergeant's office, he reviewed all of the paperwork.

Finally, the sergeant said, "You made a good grade on the written exam and you are in good physical health, but we have a problem. The doctors have recommended to the Commanding Officer, and the Commanding Officer has agreed, that you are under age. Therefore, you have been disapproved for enlistment." I tried to protest, but there was not anyway that I could prove that I was twenty-one. The sergeant continued, "We have no choice, the pilot training school is very expensive and space is limited and if your family or anyone objected, we would have to discharge you immediately. Come back when you are old enough, we would like to have you." I thanked him and got my bag and left.

Tent Camp at Hamilton

Ontario & Montgomery, Late Summer 1939

When I left the Horse Palace, I remembered what the Customs Officer at the border had said about the ARGYLL AND SUTHERLAND HIGHLANDERS being Headquartered at Hamilton and needing some more men. I started hitchhiking to Hamilton and on arrival their headquarters was easy to find. Headquarters was in some old buildings and the main body of troops had constructed a camp just outside of town. They were living in British pyramid tents, which look similar to American Indian teepees.

This time it was very easy to enlist. A sergeant filled out papers, which I signed, (I told him I was twenty-one) and a first lieutenant carried me in his own car to a doctor's office for a medical exam. Everything was completed in about two days and I was taken to the office of the lieutenant colonel in command of the First Battalion. I was introduced to some officers, sergeant majors (warrant officers), and noncommissioned officers as a volunteer from Alabama. By telephone, I had already been assigned to a company and a platoon. A staff sergeant became my leader and I walked with him as he led the way.

The procedure seems simple, but it is not. What helped me the most was being in the Boy Scouts when I was twelve, R.O.T.C. at Lanier High School and summer camp where I completed the second course of four courses of the Citizens Military Training Corps at Fort McClellan, Alabama. This was a little known program to train young men to be army officers. In the 1930's I skipped the first course because I was already in the Reserve Officers Training Corps. Had I stayed in high school and completed the other two courses, one each summer, I would have been commissioned a second lieutenant in the U.S. Army Infantry.

The supply sergeant and his staff issued me a kilt uniform; boots, caps, steel helmet, all clothing and blankets, rifle, bayonet, combat pack, full field pack, shaving kit, and the like. Dog tags were stamped in Bakelite plastic (developed by Union Carbide for electrical switch plates, etc.) with my serial number and other information. Dog tags have a hole in them through which you thread leather bootlaces and tie each of the two together to wear around your neck. This is so that if you are killed, the bottom one can be cut off and turned in to the proper authority and the top one remains with your body for identification.

After all of these things were completed, I started military training with the other soldiers. Everyone had started calling me "Alabama." I was happy when I found out that Canadian soldiers were paid $40.30 per month whereas American soldiers were only paid $21.00 per month. After about six weeks, I was ordered one day to report to the headquarters tent. The battalion sergeant major marched me in to report to the lieutenant colonel. The Lt. Col. said: "Alabama, I have received a direct order from the Prime Minister to discharge you immediately because you are underage. The Prime Minister has received a request from the U. S. Secretary of State together with proof of your age from your parents." I said, "Sir, I don't want a discharge." The Col. replied, "We don't want to lose you, but there is no choice." The sergeant major filled out the discharge form and the Colonel signed it. It was an Honorable Discharge with the reason stated: "Irregular Enlistment, Under Age." I saluted, and then went around saying good-bye to everyone. This was a surprise to me. I had kept my parents advised as to my whereabouts and that I was O.K.

Leaving the camp after turning in all my equipment except my kilt uniform, I proceeded to one of the soldiers' homes. We had become friends and his parents had let me leave my suitcase containing my civilian clothes at their home. After changing to civilian clothes and packing my kilts in my suitcase, I thanked the kind people and started hitchhiking back to Alabama. The trip was smooth and easy because by now, I had become an expert.

When I arrived at my home in Montgomery, my parents and I had some good conversations. It was a natural thing for them to worry about me. Both of them had an above average education and they were good readers and writers. My parents were good friends of Senator Lister Hill and his brother, Dr. Hill, of Hill Hospital in Montgomery. These families, together with others, were the descendents of the pioneer families of South Alabama. They knew everybody. Also, I was a paperboy, starting at the age of twelve, working for the "Alabama Journal " and the "Montgomery Advertiser." When I delivered the paper at Senator Hill's home, the only way I could collect was to go to his office on Saturdays. It took me a while to figure this out, perhaps because I was so young and my brain was slow. He was an intelligent gentleman and I liked him and his number one secretary and other staff. They were always giving me something special to eat. I would always be ushered into the Senator's private office unless he was in Washington. He was picking my brain. We had a great rapport and he would ask me about family, friends, school, and what was happening in the neighborhoods. After all, he had to run for U.S. Senator every now and then.

My parents told me that they had called Senator Hill and some congressmen to get me discharged from the Canadian Army. Also, my oldest brother Ray had contacted Senator Walter F. George of Georgia to enlist his help. In any event, the United States Secretary of State, Cordell Hull of Tennessee, replied back to Senator Hill that this was the fastest transaction that had ever occurred between two nations.

After being home for a few days, I told my parents that I wanted to enlist in the U.S. Navy. The Navy had a program wherein someone could enlist at the age of seventeen with their parent's consent. It would be easy to say that I was seventeen. The enlistment would last until your twenty-first birthday and then you would be discharged unless you re-enlisted permanently for a career in the regular navy. The old timers called this a "Baby Cruise."

The petty officer at the Navy Recruiting Station in Montgomery gave me some papers to fill out and told me that since I was seventeen (I lied), my parents' signatures would be required and they would have to be notarized. After leaving, I signed for my parents and went to Senator Hill's office. After visiting with his secretary for a while, she received a phone call and went into another office to look up some information. Having seen her use her Notary Seal many times, I knew the exact drawer where she kept it. Quickly, my parents' signatures were notarized. When she returned to her office, I told her goodbye and left. Later, I filled out the rest of the forms, the date in the proper places and her signature in the space provided. The next day, I gave the forms to the petty officer and completed a written exam. After a preliminary physical exam, he explained the rest of the procedures. It seemed that the Navy was more concerned about teeth than anything else. You had to have a minimum number of teeth to enlist and since I had all of my teeth, that was no problem. As soon as there were enough recruits to form a group, we would all be sent by train to the Naval Operations Base (N. O. B.), Norfolk, Virginia, picking up other groups along the way. The petty officer also told me that my group would leave at a certain time two days later and for me to be at his office ready to go.

Naval Operations Base, Norfolk, Fall 1939

Our train left Union Station in Montgomery headed for Norfolk. The petty officer informed the group that I had been selected to be in charge of the group as well as the others we would pick up on the way. He gave me a packet containing all of our papers, which I was to deliver on arrival at N.O.B. and meal tickets were distributed. We stopped in Birmingham and some other cities where we were met by petty officers and added other recruits to our group. In each case, the petty officer in charge would give me a packet containing the other recruits' papers. By the way, it was never known why I was selected to be in charge. Most of the recruits were over eighteen and not on a "Baby Cruise." Perhaps it was my grade on the exam and previous military experience.

Upon arrival at the railroad station in Norfolk, Virginia, we were met by a petty officer who directed us to board a line of Navy busses. The busses carried us through the gate at N.O.B. and to a group of buildings serving as a process center. The Navy personnel were prepared to process us step by step without any waste of time. We were issued uniforms; went to the showers, packed our civilian clothes in our suitcases, stripped down after showers for physical exams by Navy doctors, given shots and fast haircuts (almost shaved). It was a hectic two days. After everyone was squared away, (In the Navy now, must use correct terminology.), the Navy formed us into a seventy-five-man platoon. This was the Navy Standard Operating Procedure (S.O.P.) at all three training stations. Other than N.O.B., Norfolk, this included Great Lakes and San Diego.

We were assigned a platoon number and barracks. Again, I was selected to be in command of the platoon, except this time it was official with certain duties and authority including orders for punishment for due cause. The powers that be had someone sew the insignia of a "Navy Chief Petty Officer" on the upper arms of all my jackets, including Pea Coat. This was the highest rank for a noncommissioned officer in the U.S. Navy, three stripes up and a rocker down. However, in the center where the usual insignia for all chiefs and petty officers appear, such as Signalman, Gunners Mate, Engineman and the like, my insignia was a Square Knot. Therefore, I became a member of a select group of Navy recruits called "Square Knot Admirals."

Our platoon was assigned our real navy commanders, a chief petty officer, retired, an old China hand with tattoos from A to Z, recalled from retirement, and a Lt., recalled from retirement. As we were squaring away in our assigned barracks, a petty officer 2nd class came and informed me that the chief and lieutenant would be there at a certain time. The entire platoon was put through two exercises in how to form up at attention. When the chief and the lieutenant approached our barracks, I gave the order to fall in, then "Attention." As they entered, I did a perfect about face, saluted, and said: "All present and accounted for, Sir." I think this caught them by surprise. The lieutenant then presented me with a "Certificate of Appointment, Recruit Chief Petty Officer." The lieutenant gave the order to me: "At ease" and I did an about face and gave the order. We were given instructions about the training and some rules and regulations.

There were some prerequisites that went with this certificate. All recruits were required to wear leggings, (this is why the Navy calls recruit training "Boot Camp"), except recruit chiefs. Recruit chiefs could pass the marine guards at the gates without a pass and go anywhere on base. Also, they had a private room and office in the barracks.

The barracks were permanent buildings and each platoon had a large rectangular shaped room with concrete floors (deck); a metal pipe (jack stay) running down the center of the longest sides for hanging sea bags; a cot for each man perpendicular to the walls (bulkheads) with a locker alongside; a private room and office at one end; and across from this was the lavatories, showers, and water closets (head). At each end of the barracks was an outside door and I posted a man on watch outside each door for two-hour shifts, twenty-four hours each day.

It was my duty to teach the manual of arms, close order drill, military courtesy and the like. It was important to me when scheduling all the various duties to be completely impartial. Duty schedules were posted on the bulletin board every evening before "lights out" so that each man would know and be prepared for his duty for the next twenty-four hours. When time permitted, I interviewed each man in order to select leaders and also, to know the ones who would need special help. This platoon had a great deal of talent, after all, each and every one were volunteers. For example, three of them had some service in the U.S. Merchant Marine. They told me that they had seen that the United States would soon be in the war and decided to join the regular navy. When a duty assignment involved several men, such as cleaning the head, cleaning the decks and the like, it was my policy to assign a leader in charge who reported to me when the job was done.

We continued our training. All of the men were doing their best, with sometimes a few minor gripes, but because they knew that if they did not graduate they would be held back and go through training again. The chief and lieutenant were not with us all the time. They would come by to see how we were doing. On the weekends, they probably went home to their families, which they certainly should have done. They had been recalled from retirement and did not live on base. One evening a group of men came to me with a problem. One of the men did not take enough showers or wash his clothes in a timely fashion. My advise was, take him and his clothes to the showers, and get his attention. Do not hurt him because we would have a problem if he had to go to sickbay. Just make sure that he understands that in the Navy we live in close quarters and further, if he were aboard a ship, the petty officers would send him to sickbay. It did work out.

At the training swimming pool, we found out that about thirty men could not swim well enough. That old saying, "Throw them in the water and they will learn how to swim" does not work and may cause an absolute fear of water permanently in some people. Having been a lifeguard at Oak Park Pool in Montgomery, (it paid $ 5.00 per week which was good money in the Great Depression), I had every man in our first training session demonstrate his swimming ability from the shallow end of the pool. Yes, I did show off by swimming some laps underwater. Then I demonstrated treading water and most importantly, taking a deep breath, and simply letting my body go limp. Of course, the body has buoyancy and as you curl up you float face down and all you need do is turn your head up and breathe again. During the entire training course, we spent about twelve one-hour sessions in swimming classes and every man was able to pass the minimum swimming requirements for survival.

N.O.B. Norfolk was loaded with ships of all types. You could board a destroyer which was moored to the dock and then walk across many destroyers moored alongside. The aircraft carrier, U.S.S. WASP (sister ship to the U.S.S. HORNET) was there. Many other ships were there that later became famous in World War II. Ships that needed major repairs went to shipyards. These ships were busy with minor repairs, refits, reloading and training more crews from Boot Camp. It was impossible for the U.S. Navy to not understand the impacts of war in Europe, war in the North Atlantic, almost to the shores of the United States, and the war in Asia. There must have been about one thousand recruits at N.O.B. at that time. The recruits were not only allowed, but we were also encouraged, to go aboard ships to watch movies and talk with the various specialties in the evenings or weekends when we were off duty. The recruits studied the navy specialties to decide which schools to attend after graduation. Some of the specialties were Signalman, Yeoman (clerks), Quartermaster (stands watches at the helm, steers the ship), Engineman, Gunners Mate, Corpsman (Medic), Boatswain's Mate (has the whistle and is the boss petty officer), and others.

The exercise that I personally liked the most was when all recruits went on ships for a two-day training period in the Atlantic Ocean. Cadets from the Naval Academy at Annapolis were there. My request to go aboard the aircraft carrier U.S.S. WASP was granted (another perk). When I told the Officer of the Deck (OD) that my real wish was to be an aviator and in the meanwhile be a striking boatswain mate, he gave me the privilege to be at the helm when aircraft were launched. The aircraft were old models with radial engines, not the Spitfires that I wanted to fly. My memory kicked in, when I was old enough my friend Senator Lister Hill would give me an appointment to any military academy. Also, I was with my family when I met President Roosevelt when he was on the steps of the Capital in Montgomery campaigning. At that time, I was thirteen and he asked me what I wanted to do. I said, "I want to be an aviator, Sir." He turned to my father and said, "Mr. Houston, when this lad is old enough, call my office and he will receive an academy appointment." So maybe I could be an aviator later on.

When the Japanese attacked the Pacific Fleet at Pearl Harbor, they also attacked the Philippines and the Asiatic Fleet in China. The aircraft carrier U.S.S.WASP was in the Asiatic Fleet and the heavy cruiser U.S.S.HOUSTON was the flagship. The U.S.S.WASP went down and the U.S.S.HOUSTON had joined up with ships of the Royal Australian Navy. One night these ships had steamed into the middle of a Japanese invasion fleet and started firing at close range. The HOUSTON went down with all guns firing. This was not known until the end of the war when a few survivors were found in a prisoner of war camp in Japan. The U.S. Navy kept silent about the loss of the WASP and built another aircraft carrier named "U.S.S. WASP."

One night as we were nearing graduation, the chief and lieutenant came to our barracks just before lights out. They had been drinking heavily and with slurred speech said they had come to do an inspection to see who could graduate. The men stood at attention alongside their cots. They started down the rows pulling blankets and everything off the cots to see if anything was under them and opening each locker to see if any unauthorized things were in them. They opened a locker and saw a woman's picture in it. Turning to the young man standing there, one of them said, "Get this damn two-bit whore's picture outta here." The young man started shaking and said, "Sir, that's my mother." One of them replied, "I don't give a G.D., she is still a two-bit whore." One of them responded, "You bastard, I'm gonna teach you not to argue with me," and hit the young man in the nose and mouth. Blood spurted from the recruit's nose and mouth as the other one joined in hitting him. The recruit was using his arms to ward off the blows, so one of them pinned his arms while the other one punched him. That did it. In their drunken state, they would kill him. I was hollering knock it off and pulled one of them back and hit him as hard as I could in the throat. He went down grasping for breath. Pulling the other one off, I hit him in the throat and he went down. Realizing what I had done, I knew I had to leave fast. The penalty for a sailor hitting a naval officer was an automatic twenty years in the federal penitentiary at Ft. Leavenworth when stood before a Captain's Mast (court-martial). I called one of my leaders into my office with me and as I grabbed my peacoat and a few other items told him to give me as much time as he could, at least twenty minutes, then call the hospital and say, "There has been a minor accident, please send a corpsman. Pass the word to all hands to tell the truth and that none of you were involved."

I ran outside and started walking until one of the navy busses, which traveled regular routes on the base, picked me up and carried me to the main gate. Outside the gate, I boarded a city bus that made regular runs to downtown Norfolk. When I left the city bus, I walked over to the bus station and bought a ticket on the next bus leaving. The ticket was to Emporia, Virginia. When the bus stopped in Suffolk, Virginia, I got off and bought a ticket to Richmond, Virginia. Soon I was on my way to Richmond. I wanted to be hard to find and my suitcase with my civilian clothes was in Baltimore. Earlier, we had been given a weekend pass and since there was not enough time to go to Montgomery, one of the guys invited me to go with him to his home in Baltimore. I accepted and he carried his suitcase home and I carried mine to leave with his parents. All of us had to do something with our suitcases and any personal belongings before graduation. Arriving in Richmond, I bought a ticket to Washington and upon arriving there; I bought a ticket to Baltimore. It was morning when I arrived in Baltimore. I ate some breakfast and caught a streetcar to my friend's home. Baltimore impressed me with its miles of row houses all joined together with most of them looking alike with small front and back yards. I told my friend's mother that I had been given leave and wanted to pick up my suitcase. I told her that everyone was doing fine at the base and we expected our group to graduate soon. I changed into civilian clothes, packed my uniform in the suitcase and returned to the bus station downtown. I bought a ticket to Rochester, N.Y. and upon arriving there bought a ticket to Buffalo. I mailed a letter to my parents while in Baltimore explaining briefly what had happened, I was O.K., and for them not to worry if I didn't write for a while. Again, I would cross the border into Canada at Niagara Falls.

British Columbia to Nova Scotia, End of 1939 & Spring 1940

Crossing into Canada, again at Niagara Falls, my thoughts were about how things happen, my responsibility for seventy-five good men and what would happen to them, my responsibility to my parents. In my heart, I knew that I had done the right thing and wondered if the same Canadian customs officer that I had met before would be on duty. The Lord was with me; there was a different customs officer on duty at the border and I gave him a fake name and address to write on his form. It was easy to catch a ride to Toronto and the Horse Palace. The cars were still parked there that belonged to the American pilots who had volunteered for the R.C.A.F., but now they were dusty, the tires were flat and they looked older.

My enlistment in the 48th Highlanders went smoothly. They did not know that I had been in the Argylls until later. After going through the enlistment process, including being assigned a new serial number, issued uniforms and so forth, I was informed that the battalion was in training at Camp Borden. About six of us new enlistees were sent by train to Camp Borden where we were assigned to our companies and platoons. All of the Canadian Regiments have a hometown base. The 48th Highlanders home base was Toronto; therefore, some of the professional hockey players of the Maple Leafs had volunteered with the 48th Highlanders. The most notable thing that I remember of these times was when we were given leave and a group of us went to Toronto. Of course, I knew nothing about hockey, Maple Leafs, or ice-skating. When I was growing up in Montgomery, we played a similar game on roller skates using tin cans and any kind of stick that we could find. Beat up tin cans would really cut if they hit you. We went to an indoor ice skating-rink and two of the Maple Leafs said they would teach Alabama how to ice skate.

There were many young people there and dance music was playing. We paid some money and then had to take off our boots and put on shoes with runner blades attached. These two soldiers, one holding me on each side, would skate me around the rink gradually building up speed, then release me. When there was enough speed, I was O.K., slowing down my ankles would wobble and I would fall on my butt. We kept on trying. When the other skaters started recognizing these soldiers, they stopped skating and formed a ring around the ice. I had crashed into some of them and I was starting to feel ashamed. The other soldiers were standing by and passed the word; the Toronto Maple Leafs were teaching the American volunteer "Alabama" how to ice skate. At first, there was a murmur, and then when we were flying around the arena, there was a great shout, "Go Alabama." I started to figure it out. I said, "One more time." When I was released at high speed, I slowed down some and then started pumping my arms and legs in the same method as roller skating, making a complete circle around the rink. Not knowing how to stop and stand on two blades, I simply dropped on my butt again. The applause was deafening!

When soldiers are on leave, they wish to do everything possible in the short period of time that they have. Whether it is to see their family, their girlfriend, wife, look around, or drink. Leaving the ice rink, we went to a place called "A Beer Garden." We selected some tables and everyone ordered a draft beer. Looking around, I could see many tables with beautiful girls and no guys. The waiters brought beers for everyone except me. Then one of the soldiers, a corporal, grabbed the arm of a waiter and said, "We are one beer short." The waiter said, "My boss says we cannot serve the young one because we would lose our license." Then there was an eruption; the soldier went to see the boss. Meanwhile, I stayed at our table while all these beautiful girls were winking at me. Everyone could hear the debate. The soldiers were saying to the boss, "You will serve "Alabama," or we take your place apart." The boss said, "I have called the police." The corporal said, "Have you not heard of The King's Rules and Regulations (K.R.&R.)? This soldier is entitled to a rum ration and age does not matter." Two police officers came in, and after hearing both sides of the debate, one of them said, "Give the soldier a beer." The other one said, "And the beer is on me," placing some money on the bar as they both left.

Canada never did have a draft system during the war. Members of their military forces volunteered to be in their regular military forces and also volunteered to go overseas. Those who did not volunteer, but were eligible, were assigned to twelve months universal military training in Canada only. One of the volunteers in the 48th Highlanders was married and lived in Toronto. Later on, he was K.I.A. and his wife wrote the song, "I'll Never Smile Again." One of the volunteers in the Winnipeg Rifles or the Regina Rifles (I've forgotten which) wrote the song, "Anniversary Waltz."

After I was with the 48th Highlanders for a few weeks, a notice was posted on the bulletin boards asking for soldiers who would volunteer for a transfer to the Canadian Scottish Regiment. In the Canadian and British Armies, no one really joined the "army." Everyone joined a "regiment." The 48th Highlanders had filled all of their required ranks and a few more. The Canadian Scottish needed a few more soldiers. Since about all of the soldiers in the 48th Highlanders were from the Toronto area and many more were long time friends or relatives, they naturally wanted to stay together. It did not matter to me, so a few others and I volunteered to transfer. Then the army found out that I had been in the Argylls and had a previous serial number. The Maj. told me that having two serial numbers was never allowed and mine was changed back to the original one. All of us transferring were processed out, given papers to carry and sent by train to the Canadian Scottish Regiment whose hometown base was Victoria, Vancouver Island, British Columbia. It was on this train ride that I met two solders that would become two of my three best friends of the entire war. Bruce Lewis was from Sault Ste. Marie, Ontario and Lornie Roussain was a French Canadian from Quebec.

Upon arriving at the Canadian Scottish in British Colombia, we three were assigned to the same company. Later on, I met my other best friend, Roy Palmer, who was in the same company. Roy's parents had immigrated from Sweden to British Colombia. His brothers and sisters were all born in Canada and Roy was born in the State of Washington; making him an American citizen. It was tough to make a living during the Great Depression, especially for immigrants. Roy's mother taught school for a period of time at Peace River which was the end of civilization in those days. His parents also homesteaded on Vancouver Island. Roy was about seven years older than I and had worked as a lumberjack, commercial salmon fisherman, trapper and anything to do in the great woods. He was a great mentor for me and certainly saved me many times. We were closer than brothers. He told about volunteering in the Canadian Scottish. He was in a line to enlist and when it was his turn to speak to the enlistment captain who was seated at a table writing down information on each man, Roy stated his name, birthplace and so forth. The Captain said, "Another square head." Roy never forgot that. He tried to conceal his Swedish accent, but I always thought it was great.

After training some more (we were always training), orders were received to pack up, we were going to Europe. It was necessary to carry everything with us. Some of the soldiers had acquired a Siwash Indian totem pole, which they would setup in front of our battalion headquarters. They carefully sawed the totem pole into sections and packed the sections in wooden crates, which they made, in order to carry it to Europe. They made wooden dowels to use when reassembling the totem pole. This totem pole is now on display at our sister regiment's museum, the Royal Scots Regiment, in Edinburgh, Scotland.

The Author with the Totem Pole

We boarded a specially assembled train to go from British Colombia on the Pacific Ocean completely across Canada to Nova Scotia on the Atlanta Ocean. All soldiers carried their packs and small arms and were assigned to passenger cars while other critical materials such as larger weapons; ammunitions and the like were loaded in secure mail cars. Offices were setup for the battalion commander and company commanders with records and wireless (radio) communications in a mail car. There were dining cars for the soldiers and Pullman and dining cars for officers. This was a long, long train with two locomotives and sometimes three in the mountains. The journey took two weeks and I cannot describe the beauty of the mountains, the

Great Plains and the Maritime Provinces. We passed through all kinds of different weather. The train would stop at all major cities and sometimes-small villages. The locomotives would take on coal and water. The dining cars would take on food and the train crews would be changed. While all of this was going on, all of the officers and men would jump out and fall in formation and with the pipers and drummers in the lead, we would march several blocks around the town. Also, we marched some at double time and did calisthenics to loosen up because we would get stiff on the long ride. Civilians, newspaper reporters and town officials would come to see us and talk with us. We could tell all the young men were gone or leaving for the war. The pretty girls gave soldiers pieces of paper with their names and addresses and asked the soldiers to write to them. Also, some of the soldiers gave the girls pieces of paper. The girls were intrigued by my Alabama accent. When we made stops in Quebec, my friend, Lornie, would tell some of the French girls (in French) about me being from Alabama and all that and they would say, "Ou la la la c'est bon" or something like that. Some would kiss me while the other soldiers laughed. When going through towns and seeing French signs, I would ask Lornie their meaning. I didn't know it then, but I was on my way to learning French, which would prove to be very valuable later in the war. We saw many passenger and freight trains pulled off on sidetracks so that our special troop train could pass on through.

Our train stopped at a small place, Debert, Nova Scotia, near Truro. Trucks met us there to carry heavy stuff to our new camp as we started marching to the camp. This was a new camp with all the buildings constructed of unpainted wood. Its main purpose was a holding place for troops to wait while a troop carrying convoy to Europe was being assembled in Halifax Harbour. While we waited for a convoy, we trained and sometimes we would get a pass for a weekend. When I had a pass, I would wander around to see the sights. It was in Windsor that I met a very nice family, the Regans. Mr. Regan owned a department store. They had a large two-story home on a hill and they invited me to dinner. Their oldest son was older than I and next was their daughter, Maureen, who was about my age and a senior in high school at Mount St. Vincent in Halifax. The Regans also had a younger son and daughter.

There was a lively dinner conversation. They wanted to know all about Alabama and me. Alabama seemed to them to be a far off unknown place. Someone brought out a map for the benefit of the younger children and they were shown Montgomery in South Alabama. When you think about it, if you go from Windsor, Nova Scotia, to Montgomery, Alabama, and you reach New York, New York, you are only about halfway. When I told them about my family and my childhood, I mentioned that I started school at St. Mary's of Loretta, which seemed to please them because they were Irish Roman Catholics. Afterwards, when I got a weekend pass, I would go to see them. With a large family, they still had guest bedrooms and they invited me to spend the nights there. They had a number of maids from Ireland with their wonderful accents. The Regans' oldest son, Walter, was in college and Mr. Regan had given him a convertible. He and Maureen spent the weekends at home and we would go to dances and just run around. Walter would later serve as a member of the Canadian Parliament and the younger brother, Jerry would serve as the Premier of Nova Scotia.

One of the things soldiers and sailors hate the most is a thief. We had a thief in our barracks. During the nights when everyone was sleeping, he would steal watches, pocketknives and other personal items. My friend, Roy Palmer, setup an ambush one night. Just before lights out, he left his watch on a lavatory in the latrine. Then he lay down on his cot and pretended to sleep. Several hours later, he noticed someone going to the latrine and he followed. As soon as

Roy went into the latrine, he saw a soldier putting his watch in his pocket. Roy grabbed his hand and broke it, then led him to the guardhouse. The soldier was struggling and protesting all the way so Roy almost tore his arm off. The soldiers on guard duty locked up the thief. Early the next morning a sergeant came into our barracks and started looking through the thief's pack and found a bunch of stolen items. Most of the soldiers got their personal items back. We never did see the thief again.

When we went to chow, the Canadians would rush to get a seat close to the rhubarb. They loved rhubarb and I didn't care much for it, so I would get a seat close to the beef. One evening, Bruce Lewis and Lornie Roussain were drinking beer at the canteen. A corporal from a rifle regiment made some derogatory remarks about Alabama (that's me) and Lornie told him he was a liar. The corporal invited him outside, so everybody went outside, as this was the custom. It was not much of a fight. There was only one blow; Lornie knocked him out. I heard about this later. Roy and Lornie were about the strongest guys I have ever known. Lornie had worked in the woods of Northern Quebec and was built like a line backer.

One afternoon after we finished training and returned to our barracks, there was a letter addressed to me lying on my cot. In it was an engraved invitation from the Regan family. The invitation read:

"MR. AND MRS. WALTER REGAN OF WINDSOR, NOVA
SCOTIA, ARE PLEASED TO ANNOUNCE THE FORTH-
COMING HIGH SCHOOL GRADUATION FROM MOUNT
ST. VINCENT, HALIFAX, NOVA SCOTIA, OF OUR DAUGHTER,
MISS MAUREEN REGAN. WE REQUEST MR. DANIEL C.
HOUSTON OF LANIER HIGH SCHOOL, MONTGOMERY,
ALABAMA, TO SERVE AS OUR DAUGHTER'S ESCORT FOR HER
GRADUATION BALL AT THE ROYAL YORK HOTEL, HALIFAX,
NOVA SCOTIA, ON THE ------------ EVENING OF ------------------."

It was too late in the evening to ask for a pass. The mail was late. The graduation ball was the next evening. We had already received our training orders for the next day. I washed my clothes. I got out my kilt uniform and blancoed my gators, washed my socks, flashes and sporran. Using my buttonhook, I shined and shined all my brass buttons. Then I lay awake and worried all night. As soon as the pipers and drummers were finished with reveille the next morning, I was already in my battle dress and running to see my platoon sergeant. I showed him my invitation and requested permission to speak to our sergeant major. My platoon sergeant was rubbing his eyes awake and said, "Alabama, damn if you don't come up with strange things. You are a good soldier, the sergeant major likes you, but don't push it." Continuing running to company headquarters to see the sergeant major, some enlisted personnel and officers saw me and one of them said, "Alabama, what's up?" I showed them my invitation and they shook their heads in disbelief. After some conversation with the sergeant major in his office, he stepped into our company commander's adjoining office and showed my invitation to Major Duncan. I heard the major laughing and then he said, "What the hell, give Alabama a pass." The sergeant major came back, wrote out a pass, handed it to me, and laughing he said, "Alabama, have a good time." Later, I understood why they were laughing. How could a kid from Alabama and a Pte. (Private) soldier receive an invitation like that? Only high-ranking officers received invitations to graduation balls like this one. As it turned out, there were generals and admirals there as well as high-ranking civilian officials. Our brigade commander, a Brig. Gen., was there. The first time I saw him was when we were out in the field and having noon chow. He stopped by and ate with us. I thought he was from the Sally Ann (Salvation Army) because of the red band around his cap. All British Generals have red on their shoulders, lapels and caps.

Now I had a pass in my pocket and I ran to my barracks and dressed out in my kilt uniform. I still had patent leather black shoes from the U.S. Navy, so I wore those instead of hobnail boots. Knowing that I had to reach the hotel in Halifax before the time certain, I hurried to the gate at our camp. Catching a ride on a 1500 weight army lorry (truck) to Truro, I started hitchhiking to Halifax. In those days there was not much traffic. You could wait for an hour before a vehicle came by. The people were kind to their soldiers and they would stop and ask if they could help. It did take several rides to reach downtown Halifax. Knowing that the Regan family and other important people would be staying in the Royal York Hotel, I walked there and went into the lobby. I asked the clerk on duty for the room numbers of Mr. And Mrs. Regan of Windsor. I went upstairs to their rooms and told them I had arrived. Going back down in the elevator to the lobby, I looked around until time for the ball to start. The "Escorts" for the graduating young ladies assembled in one of the large rooms awaiting the arrival of the ladies. Many of the Escorts were young officers of the army, air force and navy. Some were civilians. Soon the young ladies arrived accompanied by the "Ladies in Charge". The young ladies were very beautiful, excited and dressed in their fabulous ball gowns. The graduates were to line up in alphabetical order, and then their escorts would stand beside them. Upon a signal, each couple would proceed down a flight of stairs while the announcer presented each graduate and her escort. After the stairs, we would pass by a receiving line formed by the guests. Next, the first dance would be a lead out starting in alphabetical order. Also, there were tables of food, punch and wine, an open bar, a "Gentlemen's Smoking Room" and a "Retirement Room for the Ladies".

We heard the orchestra start playing softly and we were on our way. The Brig. Gen. was in the receiving line and he recognized me. After shaking hands, he smiled and introduced Maureen and I and to his wife saying to her, "Dear, this soldier is in OUR Brigade." We danced and danced and every now and then we would stop awhile, have some food, punch, or a little wine, and talk with the guests. The orchestra would take a break while the gentlemen went to the smoking room and the ladies would retire to their room, to freshen up, gossip and relax. It was explained to me later that this Ball was one of the great annual social events in Nova Scotia. Mount St. Vincent was a private boarding school for girls and it must have cost their parents a large sum of money to pay for all of this. Some of the naval officers that I met, I would see again during the war.

As it got late, the older people retired and we young ones stayed up all night. At daybreak, Maureen and I went to walk. We walked along Halifax Harbour and watched ships loading and other ships unloading. An immense activity was taking place everywhere. We walked back to the hotel, kissed and said goodbye. I hitchhiked back to camp. We would never see each other again. Maureen became a nun before the war was over. However, her mother Rose M. Regan, and my mother Callie, wrote letters to each other for years before they passed on. During the war, my mother included the news about the Regan family in her letters to me.

Headquarters Debert, Nova Scotia

Late Spring, 1940

In a few days after I returned to camp from the ball, we received orders to be prepared to move out at a moment's notice. The exact date and time were top secret. We were beginning to feel the realities of war, "Loose Lips Sink Ships" and other phrases were being said. In the meanwhile, one of our soldiers and his girlfriend had discussed many times whether to marry before he left or wait until after the war. They finally decided to marry before he left. She boarded a train in British Columbia and was on her way to Nova Scotia while he made all of the arrangements with the army; change of beneficiary, allotments of pay (in the Canadian Army our insurance was paid by the army) and the arrangements for their marriage in Truro. As they started their marriage ceremony the order came to move out to Halifax. Two Royal Canadian Mounted Police (the R.C.M.P. also serve as the Military Police (M.P.) for the Canadian Army) appeared at the ceremony, allowed the completion of their marriage and then told the soldier he must return to camp immediately. He kissed his crying bride again and returned to camp with the M.P.'s. All of us were sad when we heard about this.

After dark, we loaded everything in lorries and in convoy headed for Halifax. We did not stop for anything until we reached the docks in Halifax and unloaded everything in the lorries to our assigned ships. This included the entire brigade consisting of the 1st Battalion Canadian Scottish, two rifle battalions and other supporting units. Our assigned ships were three large cruise ships, Peninsula and Oriental Liners (P. & O.) which had been stationed in Asia, then moved to the Atlantic and converted to troop ships. Each ship would carry one battalion plus some support units. These were large ships with swimming pools and the like. Below decks, bulkheads (walls) had been removed to create large open spaces for living quarters for soldiers. Wood tables and benches were installed and anchored to the decks. We stowed our weapons, packs and kit bags under the tables. There were hooks located overhead of the tables for hammocks. At night, we would unroll our hammocks, hang them up and go to sleep. In the mornings, we would take them down and roll them up. Private staterooms and baths had been taken out. There were large latrines with lavatories hung on the bulkheads and water closets made out of wood with holes cut through the wood. These wood seats would run from port to starboard so that every time the ship rolled, they would be flushed by seawater. On large rolls, seawater would splash out of the holes so the best place to have a bowel movement was amidships. After a day or so at sea, most of the men were seasick.

The ships' officers were British Merchant Marines and the crew was Hindi from India. Food was served twice a day and it was mostly large chunks of bread, salt mackerel and tea. I was one of the few that didn't get seasick; therefore, I could have all the food I wanted. As soon as we were onboard and settled down, we were issued life jackets and were instructed to wear them at all times or have them at our side to put on in seconds. At night we used them for pillows. We were given tags to tie on through a buttonhole in our battle tunics. The tags had our names, serial numbers, and lifeboat station numbers and locations. I later mailed mine home and my mother kept it for me.

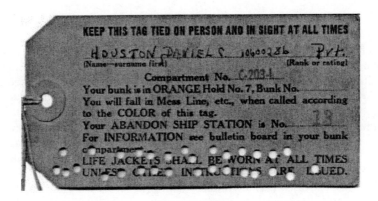

KEEP THIS TAG TIED ON PERSON AND IN SIGHT AT ALL TIMES

HOUSTON DANIEL C. 10600286 Pvt.
(Name—surname first)   [Rank or rating]

Compartment No. C-203-L
Your bunk is in ORANGE Hold No. 7, Bunk No.
You will fall in Mess Line, etc., when called according
to the COLOR of this tag.
Your ABANDON SHIP STATION is No. 79
For INFORMATION see bulletin board in your bunk
compartment.
LIFE JACKETS SHALL BE WORN AT ALL TIMES
UNLESS ORDERS IN THE SHIPS ARE ISSUED.

The Authors Tag.
The reverse served as a meal ticket and thus the punched holes.

We cleared Halifax Harbour the same night we boarded and at daylight the convoy began forming at sea. The second mate asked for some soldiers to volunteer for submarine watches and other duties. Several of us volunteered. This was a large convoy. Other than the troopships, there were freighters and oil tankers with destroyers as the escorts. The troopships were located in the center forward area behind the destroyers, which were in the lead, while other destroyers covered both port and starboard flanks. It is difficult to imagine the navigation skills required for all these ships to turn at the exact same time to run zigzag courses in the night, fog and rough seas. Every noon, the flagship would drop a large ball for all ships to reset their clocks and watches. We were running under wireless (radio) silence because the German submarine wolf packs could pick up any broadcast signal. The signalmen communicated between ships with their signal lights at night mounted on the bridge and the old fashioned way of signal flags when the visibility allowed.

We performed lifeboat drills and were shown all of the ship's signals. "The Smoking Lamp is Lit," means you can smoke and when it is out you cannot smoke. "General Quarters" meant we were under attack. Each lifeboat was under the command of a sergeant or corporal and we trained to launch lifeboats. Of course, we did not lower them overboard, but learned how to handle the rigging to lift and swing them overboard and then lower them after we were onboard. These ocean-liners did not have enough crewmembers to handle these and other duties.

Some of us had started standing submarine watch and manning the Lewis Machine Guns mounted fore and aft and port and starboard on the bridge deck. During this period of time, submarine detection devices were the rudimentary beginnings of the electronic systems of today. Therefore, the human eye was an important tool for submarine detection. We stood watches in the bow, stern and bridge. We searched for the wake of a submarine periscope. Submarines had to surface to periscope depth (the periscope above the water) in order to fire torpedoes. The officers were thankful for our help because the operation of a cruise liner is so much simpler than the operation of a troopship under the command of the navy in a war zone. During storms, we would have to leave the bow. It was like a runaway elevator ride. The bow would rise up, up, up and then drop, plunging the bow into the sea. In these conditions, the destroyers would disappear from view when they went down in the wave troughs. Those of us who were standing watches were given more freedom of the ship, going to the bridge and such. As an example, when I got hungry, which was most of the time, I would go to the galley and the Hindi cooks would give me things like a whole baked chicken and curry. It was too spicy, but I ate it. Since the Hindi cooks could not understand English, one of the junior officers assisted me by telling the cooks to lessen the hot spices. The cooks giggled.

When we were at sea for about a week, some of the Hindi crew, mostly the stokers and engineers below decks on one of the other troopships stopped working. They knew that if the ship were torpedoed, they wouldn't have a chance to get out. They were driven by fear and wanted to go home to the warm waters of the Indian Ocean. This was a great fear. If that troopship lost speed and couldn't keep up with the convoy, it would be a sitting duck for the submarines. The flagship (a destroyer) signaled the captain of the ship to use the soldiers onboard to man whatever necessary stations. The ship had from 1,500 to 2,000 soldiers with many talents onboard. Quickly, the soldiers started stoking the boilers with coal and operating the machinery under the direction of a junior officer. This continued for the remainder of the voyage.

Sometimes we could hear the explosions of depth charges in the distance as the destroyers raced about. Once I saw a destroyer cross our bow at flank (full speed) and it was so close I thought we would collide. Destroyers were called "Greyhounds of the Sea" because of their speed, in excess of 30 knots. The speed of a submarine and/or torpedo was about 20 knots. When a destroyer spotted a submarine on or near the surface, the destroyer would try to ram it at flank speed to rip the hull open. This would not damage a destroyer because of the armor plate at the bow and keel. The Royal Canadian Navy had started building corvettes for convoy duty to replace destroyers. These ships were smaller, lighter with less armor plate and smaller guns and were faster. The Royal Navy had issued standing orders to all convoy escort vessels to intercept and take the hit of a torpedo fired at a troop ship. We would later see the old four stack (smokestacks) of the U.S. Navy destroyers traded to the Royal Navy for convoy duty. This was by an agreement reached between President Franklin Roosevelt and Prime Minister Winston Churchill for the Lend-Lease Program.

Sleeping in hammocks was good with the gentle swaying of the ship. However, we were so close together that during storms some of the hammocks would swing opposite from the others and bang together. One night, just before I fell asleep, I started thinking about certain things. I had not reached Europe and had already been issued three military serial numbers. I wondered what my friends at Lanier High School were doing; football games on Friday nights, what did the coach say to the team? school dances on Saturday nights; my classmates were living in another world.

The convoy passed North of Ireland. In the distance, it was emerald green because the Gulf Stream gave it so much annual rainfall. Ireland is truly the "Emerald Isle." Sometime during the night, the convoy split up with the ships proceeding to different ports. Our ship headed up the River Clyde on a beautiful sunshiny morning. As we traveled along the Clyde Bank, our pipers and drummers stood at the bow and played the old songs of Scotland. Our ship was flying the "Union Jack" and then the Canadian Flag and the Flag of Scotland were raised. On both sides of the Clyde Bank we could hear the humming sounds of building ships, repairing and outfitting of ships. As we passed, the people would stop working and cheer while the ships all saluted with roaring blasts of their horns and whistles. Our ship docked at Glasgow, Scotland. All troops were ordered to pack up and prepare to disembark.

Late Spring 1940

After dark, we were ordered to disembark with full field packs and carry our own kit bags and rifles on our shoulders. Full field packs means all webbing with straps, Bren gun pouches, bayonets and canteens on the side, a respirator on the chest, a large pack on the back, a smaller pack on the side. For battle we would wear only the small pack (battle pack) on our backs. We were ordered to fall in formation as we left the ship and then we marched to board a waiting troop train. Lorries came to the ship and carried heavy equipment to the train. As the train headed south in the darkness we were given further orders for the duration of the war. NEVER talk about where you have been or where you are going. NEVER talk about your regiment or members thereof. All outgoing mail will be turned into your company H.Q. and shall be censored by an officer. You are now in a war zone and all applicable references to war zones in the Kings Rules & Regulations (K.R.&R.) shall be followed. Your letters will state what country you are in but not your exact location such as, "Somewhere in England." Your return mailing address shall be: State your name, rank, serial number, battalion, company and last: "Canadian Expeditionary Force," "London England." If you become separated from your unit while on leave or for any reason you will report to a safe place in London and they will direct you to your unit. The location of the safe H.Q. will be given to you later. Under no circumstances will you inquire about the location of your unit from any others. The British Railway System will give you free transportation. All troop movements (large ones) will be at night because the Luftwaffe (German Air Force) reconnaissance aircraft will spot the troop movements in daylight.

The train continued to rumble south. No one knew where we were going except the senior officers. From time to time the train would stop at a railway station. At the first stop some of us got off the train and went inside. That is how we discovered the Navy, Army, Air Force Institute (N.A.A.F.I.) ladies. They gave us a cup of hot tea and a crumpet. They were elderly (not all that old except to me at the age of sixteen) lady volunteers who helped all military personnel by patching uniforms, sewing on military patches, knitting and darning socks, cardigan wool sweaters and so forth. I started having trouble using the English pronunciation of towns where we stopped. One of the towns was Worcestershire. I was calling it "Wor-chester-shire" and then I realized it was pronounced like a sauce that we used on steak at home and it was called "Woos-ter-sher."

The next day the train stopped at a small town named Aldershot and we unloaded and marched to our new barracks. The barracks were two-story buildings with a wide street running between the two buildings. The buildings were drab looking and must have been very old. The British Army had used them for decades as a holding center for troops going overseas. We used the street as a parade ground. The large rooms were bare except for rows of steel cots. There was not a single cot that didn't need repair. The rusty metal springs were sagging and broken. There were spaces for our kitchen, mess hall, offices and officers quarters. We learned about food rationing the hard way. After we had eaten several meals in this new place, someone inspected the garbage cans and found a few whole pieces of bread and some other pieces of food. The entire battalion was ordered to fall in and as we stood at attention, the regimental sergeant major gave us a stern lecture. We would not have any bread the next day and further, "whatever food you put in your mess kit, you had better eat it or you will answer to me!" "You should be ashamed, civilians and military here and the military around the world are going hungry." He certainly made his point.

Regimental sergeant majors are the toughest men in the British Army, having worked their way up from private, they answer to no one except the Lt. Col. or Col. in command. They are warrant officers 1st Class, they wear a crown surrounded by a wreath on their sleeves and they are "Sirs." They are in command of company sergeant majors who are warrant officers 2nd Class and wear a wreath on their sleeves and they command all non-commissioned officers (N.C.O.) and enlisted personnel. While we were at this place we would march out to the woods and open spaces and have training exercises.

The main thing that I remember about Aldershot was the time when we were notified we would be "inspected" by the Princess Royal (the King's sister). We shined our boots and blancoed our gaiters and canvass webbing. The next morning we fell in formation at the appointed time. We stood at attention with our rifles at order arms. We waited and waited and waited. After two hours our officers became concerned so we practiced the "Royal Salute" which is different from a "General Salute." The "Royal Salute" is reserved for the King and royal family. Finally, word was received that the Princess Royal would arrive within minutes and there would not be a "Troop Inspection" but just a drive by. We were ordered to break ranks and half of us were to line up on each side of the sidewalk facing the street and each other. As the Princess Royal rode by in her Rolls Royce accompanied by a General we were to shout: "Hip-Hip-Hooray." When the Princess Royal did drive by we all shouted: "Hip-Hip-Boo....." This was completely spontaneous. No one had said a word and I thought that we would receive the wrath of the powers that be. We were however, dismissed without any officer or noncom saying a word. I suppose that they felt the same as we did. Canadians were strong individualistic self-sustaining people. This was natural for so few people living and working in the vast lands of Canada. The population of Canada at this time was about the same as the City of New York, (seven million).

Eating Chow in the Field

Early Summer 1940

After a short stay at Aldershot, we moved to a "Kings Park" in Southern England. What Americans call Federal and State Parks are called "Kings Parks" in England. They are much smaller and contain natural woods, open spaces, flora and fauna. When we made long marches we would sing some of the old songs such as: "It's a Long Way to Tipperary" and some new songs such as: "We'll Hang Our Washing on the Siegfried Line Mother Dear." We thought that we would be sent to France at any time. The 1st Canadian Infantry Brigade which included the 48th Highlanders (my previous unit) was somewhere in France. However, the news from every direction was bad. April came and the Nazis conquered Denmark and started their invasion of Norway. In May the Nazis conquered Belgium, the Netherlands and Luxembourg and started their invasion of France. The allies were driven back and during the last part of May and the first part of June the British Army, and whatever elements of the French Army that could, evacuated France at the port of Dunkerque (Dunkirk). In June, Italy declared war on France and France fell to the Nazis. It is amazing that all this happened in less than three months.

I wrote this brief description of history in order for the reader to more easily understand the happenings of the next several years after June 1940. As an afterthought, the 1st Canadian Infantry Brigade, which included the 48th Highlanders, (my former unit) were cut off by the German Panzers (tanks) and could not reach Dunkerque. They commandeered a French train and with the help of some French engineers and railway men drove the train backwards to Brest on the West Coast of France. Brest, on the Atlantic Ocean, had a large oceangoing fishing fleet. Many of the captains had been discussing whether to leave or not. They knew what the Germans would do to them. When the Canadians arrived there was no more doubt. The Canadians had kept up with events by wireless (radio) and told them that French General Charles de Gaulle had reached England and guaranteed them that they would have a safe-haven in England. The fishing trawlers were loaded with the Canadians and many captains and crews carried their families. The trawlers sailed to the Royal Navy Base, Portsmouth, England. All of this was told to me later by some of the soldiers I had served with previously in the 48th Highlanders.

Suddenly, there was the realization that England was in the range of German aircraft and the range was growing shorter each day. Also, if the German ground forces continued advancing they would quickly occupy the French coast on the English Channel. We moved to the south coast of England west of Dover and started defensive preparations. The defense activities were feverish. The following actions for defense had already been taken or were in the process of being completed. The civilians living on the south coast were evacuated, coastal artillery was placed on the high cliffs of Dover, observation stations were placed, miles of concertina wire was strung on the beaches, beaches were mined, concrete tank traps were constructed on the beaches. Barrels containing oil were buried or otherwise concealed upland with buried pipes running out underwater so that valves could be opened and when the oil ran onto the water it could be set afire to destroy German invaders. Concrete pillboxes were constructed inside existing structures, 90-millimeter Bofor's anti-aircraft guns were installed and camouflaged, and other preparations were made. My unit and other military units, together with some civilians were involved with these actions.

SUCK A ROCK 9: Somewhere in England

Here we are stringing wire.

The English have a way with words. Stencils were made and the following words were painted inside each concrete pillbox:

" IN CASE OF AN INVASION
ANY MAN LEAVING THIS POST
WILL BE SHOT "

The South Downs of England started with a ridge and then sloped downward for about two or three miles to the English Channel. Going north from the channel they extended for several miles as a series of ridges and slopes. One afternoon we stopped to make camp and eat when we were partway up the last ridge before the Channel. As I looked down the slope to the water, I thought this would be a perfect place to invade but also a perfect place to defend with modern weapons. Then I remembered from history class how England was last conquered. This must be the place where the Norman "William the Conqueror," invaded England and defeated Harold, the last of the Saxon Kings. Back in those days there were many kings in these Islands. Harold had pleaded with other kings to help him, but they ignored his pleas and suffered the consequences. I started talking to the other soldiers about this and one of them said: "Alabama, there you go again, you're crazy and don't know what you are talking about." We were sitting on the ground eating out of our mess kits and everyone in our company could hear our conversation. Suddenly, our Sergeant Major Campbell broke in and said: "Alabama is right and you guys don't know what you are talking about." Our lieutenants and captain had remained silent and I thought one of them would speak up. But then, our Company Commander, Major Duncan, started talking and gave all of us a lesson in history. This was a good thing. We had been too busy for any type of discussions. Major Duncan had a degree in Electrical Engineering from the University of Vancouver. He not only complimented me, but encouraged every soldier to learn everything that they could. The place that we were talking about turned out to be where the Battle of Hastings was fought in 1066 and where Harold and the Saxons lost. This was a special point in time for me, I was always the youngest but I was also the outsider, new kid on the block and that sort of thing. Afterwards, all the officers and enlisted men looked at me in a different way, I could see that in their eyes.

Our battalion had been working on the defense of the beaches. While we were still camped on the South Downs some British Engineers, officers and noncoms met with us. They had mapped out foxhole positions for us to dig and camouflage. It was important that German aircraft would not ever photograph these positions. We worked at night and as we dug the holes others would carry the soil away to hide. The engineers worked with us as we dug the infantry holes in zigzag positions. After we finished, the engineers brought us the camouflage nets. These nets were not temporary. They were made similar to Christmas decorations out of aluminum, painted to match the grass. About a year later we went back to see these foxholes. We had to use a map to find them and they were still in good shape.

SUCK A ROCK 10: Somewhere in England

Summer 1940

We moved from the South Downs, marching about 30 miles northward to another Kings Park. There we built our own camp using prefabricated steel buildings. The buildings were called Nissen huts; designed by a British engineer. They were similar to what I later saw in the United States called Quonset huts. We poured concrete slabs in rows and as the concrete setup we would go back to the first one and bolt the steel members and sheets together. As quickly as possible after erection, we camouflaged them with paint and dirt added. We erected different sizes for different purposes. When I became Major Duncan's assistant to run the wiring, I think some of the soldiers were envious. We would build many more Nissen huts during the next year and we would move many times in the next two years, so many times and places that I cannot recall all of them.

The Canadian soldiers became the experimenters with weapons, training and military tactics. Every soldier would be trained to be efficient in every infantry weapon; to drive military vehicles; to learn all procedures required to be the complete soldier. There was a schedule called "Tests of Elementary Training" (T.O.E.T.) listing the required tests to be completed. From time to time, we would add other tests to the list. Some of the tests were: Rifle, Thompson Sub-machine Gun, Light Machine Gun Bren, Anti-aircraft Bren, Pistol, Boyes Anti-Tank Rifle, Mortars 2", Sniping, Range Finding, Bayonet Fighting, Unarmed Combat, Grenade, Gas Test Drill, Map Reading, Physical Training, Driver Motor Cycle, Driver Internal Combustion, (includes Lorries, Bren Carrier, Tanks), Street Fighting, Fire Inoculation and 72-Hour Endurance Test.

The rifles we used were 303 caliber Lee-Enfield short, bolt action, clip-loaded. The same ammunition was used in Bren Guns. Compatibility of ammunition is critical. We received some Thompson Sub-Machine Guns covered in Cosmoline (grease) and packed in wooden crates from: "Thompson Sub-Machine Company, Chicago, Ill. U.S.A." We opened the crates, cleaned the protective coating of cosmoline off, read the instructions, took them apart and after reading about the drum (round) magazines, we loaded them and prepared to test fire. The 50 round 45 caliber drum magazines such as the gangsters used, required loading and then turning the spring tension (like an old alarm clock) to a specified number of turns depending on the model year of the magazine. Example, Models, 1929, 1930, 1931, etc. required different windings. We knew right off the bat; this would never work in combat. Also, the infantry could not carry this type of magazine. Nevertheless, we test fired them anyway. We needed a close-in weapon to equal or at least counter the German Machine Pistol. The Germans had designed and tested their weapons for years while the allied nations just talked. We, in the infantry, called the Machine Pistol the "Burp Gun." The rate of firing for a Burp Gun was 1,200 rounds per minute and it was accurate. Therefore, if you were hit by a "Burp Gun", in one burp you could have thirty rounds in you.

We continued to work with the Thompson's. After a number of us test fired, the results were the same. After firing two or three rounds, the muzzle would rise so much that we could not hold it on target. These weapons did not have any kind of strap on them. We tried putting on a strap, letting it hang down on the ground, stepping on it to keep the muzzle down, then firing. This was not a practical solution. The results of our tests were sent to the Thompson Submachine Gun Company. Their engineers designed and they manufactured box magazines, adjustable leather shoulder straps and "Cutts Compensators" mounted on the ends of the barrels. The compensators had slots on the topsides to allow some of the gas produced by the explosions of the cartridges to escape thereby reducing the muzzle rising. The 45-caliber ammunition was compatible with the pistols used by the British and also the Browning and Colt auto-load pistols used by the U. S. Army.

The Author with a Thompson Sub-Machinegun

The Bren Gun was a completely new design weapon to be used as a light machinegun, an automatic rifle and an anti-aircraft weapon. They were excellent and had different mounting systems such as mounting them in pairs, mounting on tanks, lorries, and Bren Gun Carriers.

The Boyes Anti-Tank Rifle was a new design weapon; five round bolt action, 55 caliber, shoulder fired with a swing down Bi-pod and an extra long barrel. It had more power than an elephant rifle or a Sharps 50 caliber buffalo rifle. The ammunition was steel jacketed armor piercing. Although it could not pierce a tank, it could pierce an armored car or half-track. The Boyes was carried by infantrymen and we used them to shoot into the firing slots of enemy pillboxes; causing great havoc inside, as the shells would ricochet off the walls in all directions. They were also good for things such as shooting into engine air intakes on tanks. It was also a very heavy weapon at 35 pounds.

The two-inch mortar was a new design that was carried and fired by only one infantryman. It was lighter than other mortars and the main difference was that it could be loaded and then aimed and fired by turning a knob which then drove the firing pin into the firing cap on the mortar shell. Other mortars required one soldier to aim while another soldier dropped in the shell, which would fire when it hit a fixed firing pin in the bottom.

Bayonet and unarmed combat training went together. In bayonet training, we used the "British Bayonet Drill" and the "German Bayonet Drill" for obvious reasons. Also, we trained against left-handed soldiers and vice-versa. The objective in unarmed combat is to kill the enemy as quickly as possible, using your hands, entrenching tool (shovel), knife, boots or whatever you might have. Hobnail boots are made with a solid steel toe plate, a solid steel heel plate and steel hob nails between and therefore, they are an excellent fighting tool; a short kick to the shinbones or elsewhere will bring a man down. A short drop kick (as in football) to the groin is a WOW! Many people thought we were trained in martial arts as they do in Asia, but we were not. We did not box or dance around. You must kill fast before the enemy kills you. We trained with one soldier using a bayonet in its scabbard and locked onto a rifle and the other soldier without a weapon but with his hands and arms tightly wrapped with cloth. You must block a bayonet thrust and then block the follow through with the rifle butt. After we became good at this, we would sometimes use naked bayonets.

The grenades used by the U.S. Army and the British Army were Mills Hand Grenades developed in World War I with a factory set timing of seven seconds. If you pulled out the cotter pin and held the lever down, then releasing the lever as you threw, the enemy could pick it up and throw it back. Seven seconds is a long, long time. There were two ways to counter this. One was to release the lever and wait several seconds before making the throw. We learned how to take a grenade apart and short fusing it as the other way. Different armies taught different ways to throw a grenade. The perfect throw is to get the distance and height required for the grenade to explode about seven feet above the ground and then the shrapnel will cover a larger area. The U. S. Army method to throw a grenade was to shot-put it. This was too difficult. The British method was to bring the arm all the way back and then with a stiff arm launch it. This was better. The "Alabama" method was to throw a long, high pass. This was natural and best. We completed these tests and others over and over again for the next two years.

Summer 1940

The summer of 1940 was a very busy time. Before, during, and after the French surrender in June, the heads of state and other government officials of nations in Europe that had been occupied by the Germans and Italians were making their way to London. They came by air, fishing trawlers, navy vessels and other ways. General de Gaulle and some of the French Army got out at Dunkirk. Field Marshall Petain, who had ordered the surrender of France, was made Head of State by the Germans. He was old and feeble and later was replaced by a Nazi who moved the seat of government to Vichy, France. All of the conquered nation's leaders setup provisional governments (governments in exile in London) and they were called Free French, Free Denmark, Free Poland, Free Norway and so forth. All of these country's overseas territories vowed to continue to fight.

For example, the Vichy French and Petainist were for the Nazis and were collaborators. The French people who continued to fight were the Free French, de Gaullest, Freedom Fighters, Underground or French Resistance. In Norway, the Germans installed a Norwegian Nazi leader, Major Vidkum Quisling, as the head of government and thusly Quisling became a hated word. The British and French had a sizable army and navy force fighting the Nazis in Norway, but were forced to leave as France was falling.

The British continued preparations to defend the United Kingdom. Concrete tank barriers were installed at choke points on roads; drums of oil were concealed where there were curves in the roads at cliffs so that when opened the oil would cover the road and tanks would skid off the cliff. Signs at roads and railway stations were removed. The Home Guards were formed by veterans of World War I. They were issued the long barrel Ross Rifles used in the Boer War and World War I. They patrolled their assigned areas, especially at night. If one of them told you to halt, I would strongly urge you to do so, they could shoot. The Air Raid Wardens were formed with arrest powers. They mainly checked on any exposed light and assisted the fire fighters. Barrage balloons were installed throughout the land. As the Luftwaffe intensified their bombing of London, children were sent to live with other families on farms and in small villages in the Midlands (with parental consent). Some of the bombed out people went to live at the underground railway stations. Food, petrol and other items were rationed by law. Women in large numbers were joining the auxiliaries of the Army, Navy, and Air Force. The massive bombing attacks on cities, by the Nazis, started in August 1940.

Meanwhile, the highest ranking military planners decided that a small, well trained special force was needed because it was no longer practical to send larger forces to the continent as was done when Norway was falling. A message was sent to all infantry regiments asking for volunteers who were young, in good health, strong and absolutely without dependents. I volunteered again.

SUCK A ROCK 12: Somewhere in Scotland

Summer & Fall 1940

The military has a reputation for being slow. Pay is slow, decisions are slow, changes are slow, orders are slow, etc. In this case, everything was fast, all red tape was cut, and paperwork was simple. Five days after I had volunteered for this unknown duty, I was told by my platoon sergeant to report to the C.S.M. (Company Sergeant Major).

When I walked into the C.S.M's office and started to say, "Sir, I have been ordered....." The C.S.M. wasted no time and said, "Alabama, you have two sets of orders, sit down and we must be certain that you understand them. First and foremost, the only thing you will say to any officer or enlisted soldier here is you have been granted two weeks leave which you applied for a while back." Then he continued explaining these orders to me. He started handing me papers. This is your leave slip, notice there is a date starting your leave and then there is no date ending your leave. You or your commanding officer may need to fill in this date or we will upon your return. Here are your passes on the railways. You will act and look like any soldier on leave. You will not need any dress uniform, wear your battle dress and carry your combat pack. I asked, "Sir, should I carry a weapon and ammo?" The C.S.M. replied, "That would be your normal leave pattern." So, I carried a Tommy gun and some ammo. The C.S.M. explained the second order. I was to report to a certain major, who would be my commanding officer, and someone would meet me at a railway station in a small village in the Highlands of Scotland. All of the railway stations and times were given to me.

When I went back to our hut, the soldiers started asking the usual questions because their minds have nothing better to do. I said, "My two week leave has been approved and I am getting ready." I boarded the train to London. At the station in London, I boarded the fastest train to Edinburgh, Scotland, "The Flying Scotsman." The only stops were at major cities. In Edinburgh, I boarded a train going north and got off at a small village in the Highlands. I noticed that some other soldiers from different regiments got off the train also. A sergeant and a driver with a lorry met the others and me. We handed him our orders and after a quick glance at them and a list he had, we got on the lorry and headed for camp. The camp was in a rugged place and looked new with Nissen huts of different sizes installed. We were guided to a Nissen hut; went in, each of us selected a cot, placed our packs and weapons on our cots and the sergeant told us that chow would be at 1700 hours and he left. We introduced ourselves and found the latrine, washed up, and went to the mess hall.

What impressed us the most was there were not many soldiers there. The next morning, the sergeant came by and informed us that we would be individually interviewed in alphabetical order during the day by the commanding officer, a captain, three first lieutenants and the sergeant major and in the meantime, report to the supply sergeant who would issue us certain items. We did as ordered. We noticed each soldier was being interviewed for a long time. One of the soldiers that arrived with me wore the patch of the Free French and platoon sergeant's stripes of three down. I had noticed that he spoke fairly good English with a slight French accent. We started talking and he wanted to know if I was from Quebec. He was reading my uniform also. So, I told him, "I am a stranger here like you." I explained that I was from Alabama and an American volunteer. He replied, "But you speak some French?" I explained how my friend from Quebec had been teaching me. Then he explained his background. "My family are farmers in Northern France and we are related to everyone in our region. I am not a regular army soldier, but I volunteered and we never had much chance of fighting because we were always moving backwards. I had the good luck to reach Dunkerque and escape with the others." I said, "My nickname is "Alabama" and yours will be "Pete" for Pierre." Pete started laughing and said, "O.K., then we must be brothers." Only a handful of people knew my age, I became seventeen years old in 1940. My guess was that Pete was about twenty-two. We were instant friends; we did not know how we would be as brothers later.

When it was my turn to be interviewed, the sergeant major said, "Private Houston come inside for your interview." I replied, "Yes, sir." I entered the large Nissen hut and saw the officers seated at a large table with stacks of files around them. I saluted, which they ignored. The major said, "Private Houston, this is your chair, sit down; we have some questions to ask." Each of them was looking through files lying in front of them. They wanted to know everything about me. Even to the extent of who my parents were and grandparents. I realized they were preparing a complete dossier on the others and me.

For the next two weeks, the training was intense. We learned to drive four-wheel military lorries (trucks), Bren gun carriers (all tracks—drive like a tank) and ride Norton Motorcycles. We were taught to operate wireless transmitters and receivers. We climbed a high wooden tower that had a deck projecting out at the proper height and above that a frame which held an open parachute. After an instructor showed us the proper method to buckle up to the parachute, we would jump.

The soldiers being trained were not only from different regiments, but also some were Freedom Fighters from France, Norway, the Netherlands, Belgium, Poland and other countries. We learned that one of the purposes of Commando training was to build a cadre of soldiers from different countries that would be a coordinated fighting force, especially in small groups. All uniforms, all equipment and all weapons would be British. All military commands would be in English.

Some of our additional training included firing of all infantry weapons. One of the exercises, called "Fire Inoculation," was to dig a hole deeper than our heads then four or five soldiers at a time with steel helmets on, would get in the hole. Then others would fire rifles, Bren guns and mortars over our heads. This test was to determine if any soldier would break under fire. Some did and they were dismissed from training and returned to their units. Another unusual test was to dig two deep one man holes about fifteen feet apart. One soldier would stand between the two holes and another soldier would throw him a grenade. When the grenade hit the ground, the soldier between the two holes would pick it up and toss it into one hole and jump in the other hole. Yes, we did have training casualties.

I had already been through a great deal of this training with the Canadians, which was a help to me. One morning after breakfast, we were assembled in the mess hall and the major spoke to us. As he called out our names to introduce us, each would stand, and he made remarks about each of us; including sometimes our regiments, and then commended each soldier. All of this was in good humor and we laughed a lot. For example, when I was introduced, the major said, "Private Houston is an American Volunteer. That is a bloody good show. But he is from Alabama where they sit in the shade and drink mint juleps. In my studies, I discovered that there was a General Andrew Jackson and a General Sam Houston that spent much time in Alabama. Maybe Sam Houston was a relative of Pvt. Houston, and I believe that Pvt. Houston will make a good soldier ……. some-day."

As the major continued the introductions, I was amazed at how the soldiers from Europe had reached this place. How can someone escape from Poland? The Norwegians continued to fight when all was lost. These were good men from everywhere. The staff at the camp continued construction on the obstacle courses, more firing ranges of different kinds and other improvements. A new class was coming in as we were leaving to return to our units. The major assured us that we would be back for more training.

Bren Gun Carrier

Fall 1940

When I arrived back to the Canadian Scottish, there was some mail waiting for me including two letters from my parents. The envelopes had been opened and taped back together and they had been stamped in large letters. One of the stamps read: "PASSED BY SPAIN SECURITY, MADRID SPAIN" and the other stamp read: "CENSORED BY THE GERMAN HIGH COMMAND, PARIS, FRANCE." I opened the envelopes. The letters had parts cut out and were mostly in shreds. I was ticked off. I wanted to kill the Nazis like right now.

In a previous letter, my mother had told me that they would be sending my letters by Airmail because it took so long by regular mail. In 1940, the only Airmail from America to Europe was via Pan American Clipper (seaplane) from New York to Lisbon, Portugal and then return via the same route. It also carried some passengers (expensive!) and was the only aircraft in the world that could cross any ocean. My mother also said she was keeping in touch with Mrs. Regan in Nova Scotia and Mrs. Lewis in Sault Ste. Marie (Bruce Lewis's mother).

I carried my letters to the sergeant major and then we went in to see Major Duncan. Some phone calls were made and the next day I was on my way to London to see a certain major at a certain address. The address was for an apartment in an expensive apartment building. When I knocked on the door, the major opened the door and without returning my salute invited me in. He quickly made it clear that all meetings there were informal regardless of rank. The major was wearing the uniform of the Royal Scots Regiment; which is identical to the Canadian Scottish, same tartan, except for the cap badge. He introduced me to a captain of the Scots Guard and to a civilian. We sat down at a large table and a sergeant brought in a tray of tea and crumpets, cigarettes and ashtrays. I placed my letters on the table and they each brought out notebooks, pencils and pens from their briefcases and immediately started working. After studying the letters, they started asking me everything about my family and me. When I was asked if my family had any relatives or close friends in Canada, I told them that my mother corresponded regularly with Mrs. Regan and Mrs. Lewis. They wanted to know more about them and when they learned that Mrs. Lewis was Bruce Lewis' mother, I could tell their brains were clicking. One of them said, "I suggest that Mrs. Lewis would be a reliable and cooperative contact with her oldest son being a volunteer and a friend of Alabama's and also a friend of Mrs. Houston."

These men were experts and fast. I thought they must be MI 5 (Military Intelligence) and later I knew it. It became obvious that no one would stop working until a plan was in place. Every now and then, one of them would leave to make a phone call or something, or the sergeant would come in and tell one of them a message was waiting. A message was received from Canada; Mrs. Lewis would be a loyal contact. I had arrived at this apartment about 10:00 hours. At noon a quick lunch was brought in and we could go to the bathroom.

It was apparent to me that these men were preparing a counter plan to the Nazi mail interception. I was glad that I had answered their questions truthfully because I had a feeling that they already knew some of the answers and were testing me. They gave me a pen, paper and envelopes and told me what to write to my parents. In the letter to my parents, I explained briefly what had happened to my mail. Then, I explained that they could write to me at anytime and say whatever they wanted to by placing my letter in an envelope addressed to me and then placing the envelope in another envelope and then mailing it to Mrs. Lewis. She would mail the letter to me from Canada. Also, officials in Canada had informed Mrs. Lewis about this.

The next batch of letters I was writing consisted of telling my parents to continue writing to me about every two or three weeks and send these letters via Air Mail the same as they did before. In each letter, write about family or whatever and then include in your letter the following words (at this place I wrote words given to me by the major). The words were things that MI 5 wanted the Nazis to believe (propaganda) and my mail would be checked to see what they would cut out. When I finished writing, the major said, "We will make certain that your mother will receive these letters and the only ones that know about this will be your parents and Mrs. Lewis." I thought about this, "Is my mother now a spy?" Then I thought, my parents are tough, although I am the youngest in the family; I had seen pictures of my father driving his 1912 Buick delivering the mail when Rural Free Delivery was established by the U.S. Postal Service. Women were not allowed to drive vehicles in those days. However, my mother, Callie, had her own horse and buggy and was the substitute mail carrier. She never got stuck in the mud and could use a bullwhip like a stagecoach driver.

After we finished working, the major said; "Alabama, we have had a bloody good show today, it is now time to clean up, dress up, go to the club and then dinner. You will spend the night here." I said, "Sir, I am not an officer." They laughed, the major said, "You will be tonight." The civilian stood up and said, "It has been nice to work with you and we will meet again." He shook my hand and said a strange thing; "Alabama, we need more good soldiers like you to win this bloody war." Anyway, the plan worked, as we would learn later.

After the civilian left, the major, the captain and I stayed at the table for a few minutes. The major asked the captain, "What rank do you think Alabama should have?" The captain replied; "Probably 1st Lt., because 2nd Lts. have no command." (In the British Army, a second lieutenant remains in training until they are promoted to first lieutenant and then they have enough ability to command a platoon.) We went into another room; the major opened a closet and selected a highland officer's tunic (worn with kilt uniforms), a Sam Brown belt, officer's sporran and officer's balmoral (worn by officers in lieu of a Glengarry). He opened some drawers and selected the proper insignia, two pips for the top of each shoulder (first lieutenant) and the other required items as an officer in the Canadian Scottish Regiment. I was wearing my kilt uniform and everything matched (Hunting Stewart Tartan). The major showed me a bedroom and bath and informed me that this would be my bedroom for tonight. Wow, this was a big place. I believe it was a mini-headquarters for MI 5 and other security agencies. Also, the major and others probably lived there.

We went to several officers' clubs that night and had a drink at each. I had the feeling that they were testing me to see how I handled myself and if I would get drunk. Also they wanted to see how other officers accepted me. The only unusual thing that happened was when I was introduced to an elderly Brig. Gen. at one of the bars. He said, "By Jove, they do promote them young these days, but I see you are Commando and they need young men." (I was wearing Commando patches, black background with white letters.)

We went to dinner at an expensive London restaurant. When we started eating, I noticed they were looking at me and one of them said, "Alabama, you are an American and yet you eat like a European." I replied, "Yes, Sir, I was shown that at Commando School." They laughed. Europeans spot Americans by the way they use their silverware when eating; also by other ways, such as body language. Then I was asked what had I noticed during the day. I replied, "Your apartment must have many rooms, including wireless equipment, for you to work so fast. The civilian walked with a slight limp and had some trouble with his arm. I believe he would be an excellent commanding officer." They both hesitated and then one of them said, "He is in the R.A.F., he is an ace and was shot down and severely wounded." After dinner, we returned to the apartment. The next morning, I returned to my unit.

About two weeks before Christmas my regiment, the 1st Battalion Canadian Scottish was camped near a small town in the South of England and I was given a pass. The Battle of Briton was in full force. For a teenaged Alabama boy, it was a wonder to walk about this town. I went into a department store and saw that the shelves and tables were mostly bare. Ladies were shopping trying to find something for their children. Then I saw a large table holding a pile of yo-yos. No one was looking at the yo-yos.

While I was growing up in Montgomery, there would be yo-yo contests and I was one of the best. I started playing with one, I was doing the "trapeze," "walk the dog," "around the world" etc. Suddenly, I was smothered by ladies rushing to get yo-yos. Some ladies started to leave with a yo-yo, however, the manager came and asked if I would show them how the yo-yo worked. Standing on the table, I demonstrated moves of the yo-yo, explaining how to make new and better strings by twisting sewing threads together and waxing them. Some ladies hugged and kissed me. Quickly all the yo-yos were sold. I have always wondered how the yo-yos got there. All the ships that reached the United Kingdom were supposed to carry only essential cargo, food, military supplies and the like. It was however, a great feeling to return to camp knowing that some children would have a yo-yo for Christmas.

Winter & Spring 1941

My unit kept on moving and training. Many things had happened and other things were happening. The Canadians were still the experimenters and innovators. Since the conquest of Europe by the Nazis and the Fascist, the British Army and others recognized they would have to change their M.S.&T. (Military Science and Tactics). The Western Allies had prepared for World War II the same as for World War I. France had constructed the massive Maginot Line opposite the German Ziefreid Line to use for trench warfare with fixed positions. However, the Germans had developed a complete mobile army to carry everything with them. They could attack fast, furious and change directions at any time. Their panzers (tanks), infantry, artillery, engineers, medics, fuel and all other supplies were mobile and moved together. They simply moved around the end of the Maginot Line in the Low Countries and usually out numbered the enemy because the Allies were scattered. Thus the Maginot Line, with many of the French soldiers, was captured from the rear.

The Canadians had started training with the new weapons to develop infantry squads as a complete fighting unit. In the past, there were infantry rifle squads in companies to form battalions and machineguns and mortars in separate companies to form battalions. The new squads consisted of at least one Bren gun, one Boyes anti-tank rifle, one 2" mortar, one Tommy gun and sometimes more. The remainder of the squad carried rifles. All soldiers carried ammunition for all of these weapons and were trained to use all weapons at anytime. When we were tired on long marches, we would pass the heavier weapons up and down the line. Using the new squad formations, we practiced taking enemy pillboxes with live ammunition. A different type of firing range had been built with concrete pillboxes of different shapes and sizes. All of our training was as real as possible. We would crawl toward a pillbox and while we were still out of German machinegun range, we would open fire with the long-range 55-caliber Boyes anti-tank rifle. If we could get at least one round in a firing slot, it would kill the machine gunner, maybe some others, and drive the rest of them crazy. At the same time, we would open fire with the 2" mortar with its open rifle sights and being able to see the target, it was very accurate. While this was going on, the Bren gunner would crawl close enough to be within firing range and start repetitious firing (automatic) and the remainder of the squad would be trying to get to one side and down under the German machineguns. At a given signal, the riflemen would complete the final assault by pitching grenades in the firing slots.

Training for street fighting took place on the south coast of England. People had evacuated their houses and other buildings at the time of Dunkirk. We surely did damage many buildings. Firing mortar rounds through the windows, pitching grenades through door openings and then shooting up rooms with Tommy guns. The government sent a man dressed in a black suit and Derby hat to follow after us and write down the damages in his notebook. He or another man also followed us when we maneuvered against other units through the countryside. Tanks did much damage when they went through rock fences and some small buildings. One time, we were in a small village when we saw two tanks from opposing sides ram together and since they were the same model tanks, neither one could push the other one back. The tracks kept grinding and spinning on the cobblestone street. Soon the cobblestones were breaking loose and the tracks were digging up the earth beneath them creating a large hole. The water main broke and water gushed up in the air. They stopped, backed out of the hole and went their own way. When we were marching or training and darkness came we simply laid down on the ground to sleep. When it was raining, my friend, Roy Palmer, and I would try to find a tree or bush to tie our ground sheets above us to keep some of the rain from hitting us. We often slept back-to-back trying to keep warm. I remember on a dark, cold, rainy night, I crawled into a sheep pen to get out of the rain and trying to get warm. The sheep did give off some heat. One night I slept in a hedgerow and when dawn came, I was awakened by a bird a few feet above my head going "cuckoo-cuckoo." I had thought that cuckoo birds were a myth, but this was a real one.

During maneuvers against other units and darkness came, we dug foxholes so as to form a battle line. The holes were dug in pairs so that everyone had a "Foxhole Buddy." The reason for this was because we took turns, two hours on and two hours off for guard duty, which we shared with our partner. There was a full-blooded Indian in our platoon from a tribe in Northern Canada. His name was Jim McCrae and he was an orphan. Jim told us how the government had sent him, when he was young, to some kind of school in the south. He tried to escape several times, but they caught him and each time they would tie him up and whip his back. He did have lash scars on his back. When he got older, he finally escaped and went back to his tribe in the north. The Indians hid him from the government until he went south and joined the army. Sometimes when we were in camp, Jim would get a letter from his girlfriend that he had met at the school. We called her "Minnie Ha Ha." He would lie on his bunk and read her letter over and over and giggle. During the nights we spent in foxholes, Jim would crawl to my hole. I could not see or hear him but I felt a presence. He would giggle and I would say, "Jim, some night somebody will kill you." He would say, "Alabama, how would you like your egg?" I would reply, "with another one." Jim would crawl away giggling. He did this many times. As you may imagine, we did have casualties. Some casualties happened during training and some from going on missions. I will write some more about Commando School and Missions later. When someone in our company was killed, volunteers would be asked to form a burial detail of six pallbearers, four to six soldiers for a firing squad, one piper, one drummer and one soldier to give the orders. The cooks would prepare sandwiches or something for our meals. The number of meals depended upon how far our camp was from the Canadian National Cemetery. We would travel in a lorry and arrive at the cemetery at a time certain. The people in charge made all burial arrangements so that we could start the funeral immediately on arrival. As we carried the casket to the grave, we used the command, "By the right, slow march." The drummer would beat the drum slowly as the piper played. The "slow march" is used only for special occasions and funerals.

The cemetery was established during World War I and was huge, with many shrubs and trees. As cemeteries go, this one was beautiful and well kept. I don't know why, but every time I was there, it rained a slow drizzle. The saddest funeral of all was when we buried one of our soldiers and found out that he was an orphan and there was no one to notify. We were silent all the way back to camp.

I do remember one time when our detail was traveling to the cemetery. We saw a nice green park and stopped there to eat our lunch and look at the gorgeous girls. It was a beautiful spring day and many people were there sunning. As we sat on the nice, soft green grass eating our lunch, some of the gorgeous girls came over to talk to us. I asked them what was the name of this place. One of them said, "Oh, this is Runnymede on Thames." I said, "I remember about King John and the Magna Charta." She replied, "Oh, there is a monument right over there," and pointed to it. The girls asked the usual questions. They could tell we were Canadians by reading our patches and the maple leaf on our lorry. They could also tell that I was an American Volunteer because I was wearing another patch with a khaki background with the letters in red, "U.S.A." By order of the King (me thinks it was the Queen) all American Volunteers in His Majesties Forces would be issued this patch.

Invariably, Europeans would say they had relatives in such and such a place in Canada, or in my case, the United States and ask do you know them? These girls asked where we were from. We told them, but like most Europeans, they did not understand how vast Canada and the United States are. One of the girls said she had relatives in Chicago; she named them and then asked if I knew them. My reply was, "How far is it from here to Inverness, Scotland?" She replied, "Oh, that is many miles away and I have never been there." I replied, "My home is in South Alabama, and if you will add many miles to that distance that is how far Chicago is from my home and I have never been to Chicago."

After we finished lunch, I walked over to the monument and read it. Sure enough, this was the spot where King John was forced to sign the Magna Charta by the barons in 1215 A.D. This document was the beginning of freedom and liberty for the Western World. We thanked the girls for talking to us, said goodbye and continued on to the cemetery.

Winter & Spring 1941

Before and during this time period, we continued to go to Commando School, (from time to time, in Scotland, Isle of Man in the Irish Sea and other places), for further training and we went on missions; sometimes called raids. Many people thought we were cloak and dagger spies. That was not our real purpose. What the Western Allies desperately needed was information and the way to obtain this information was from the resistance people and guerrilla fighters in the conquered nations. Likewise, these people desperately needed the support of the Allies.

You might think that we had enough training; but no. The Commando training and the Canadian training closely paralleled each other. We had a test called "72 Hour Endurance Test." We were issued a package of hard tack and a canteen of water. We marched for three days and three nights in the rain, fog, sleet, snow and sometimes sunshine, taking a ten-minute break each hour and maybe an hour or two at night. We did this at least every two months. It sure did help to suck a rock during these times.

I have a vivid "flashback" of some of the times during these marches. We had been marching day and night and as the sun rose on a beautiful clear day, we could see we were on a long, long road. Then I saw a two-story house with an open window upstairs and the curtains were gently swaying in the slight breeze. I thought, maybe someday I would have a house like that and sleep in a nice soft bed with sheets. On another seventy-two hour march, we were marching down a road in the late afternoon, in our usual battle formation with a good space between squads and the squads staggered on each side of the road. This was in case of a strafing attack by German fighter planes. The Germans started doing this in 1940, but after we developed the new squad formations, we could put up so much firepower we started hitting them, they quit. We could see ahead of us our soldiers passing a pub (a public house, a place to drink, sing songs accompanied by a piano, and throw darts). People were running in and out of the pub bringing mugs of beer and handing them to our soldiers as they marched past. Only a few soldiers could get them because of our formation. This was my squad's lucky day. We were on the pub side of the road and just as we reached the pub, the order to take a break came down the line. We sat down on the sidewalk and talked with the people as we guzzled our beer. The other "flashback" happened as we were marching along and the nails holding the steel plate on the heel of my right boot came loose. When my right boot came down, it would do a double click. The other soldiers were going crazy. They started screaming at me, "Alabama, cut it out." We were tired, our legs and feet were numb, but I couldn't stop. I broke formation, went to the sergeant major and got permission to double time ahead and take over the position of number one scout.

Another training exercise was a forty-mile march in one day. Our normal marching pace was three miles per hour with a ten-minute break. Therefore, within fourteen hours, we would make the forty miles. We ate breakfast early and started out at 0400 hours (4:00 A.M.) We stopped for an hour to eat and rest. Our cooks would go ahead of us in lorries, setup a field kitchen and prepare the food before we arrived. We would finish the march about 1900 hours (7:00 P.M.).

Our training was not over. We went to a secluded lake, unloaded rubber boats from our lorries and practiced different methods of getting off and on ships and submarines. This was not an easy thing to do. The Royal Navy sent some expert chiefs to work with us. The soldiers that could not swim well were seriously handicapped because we would overturn from time to time and this was in calm water. Those of us who could swim pulled them out and let them rest. We made camp and practiced every day until we found the best procedure. We could not wear life jackets (too bulky) with our other equipment. Since we would use submarines to get in and out of Europe in small groups, we concentrated on using submarines.

The procedure we settled on was to carry four-man and/or two-man rubber boats, not inflated, aboard the submarine. We would not carry our respirators, gas capes, bayonets, or steel helmets. We would carry our combat packs (light), canteens and Tommy guns wrapped in gas capes to keep them dry. When our submarine reached our destination at night, it would surface. With the sailors help, we would take the rubber boats and other equipment topside. We would inflate the boat using a cartridge (CO2) similar to the way lifejackets (called "Mae West") worn by aviators were inflated. We carried several extra cartridges. When the boat was secured alongside, we would get in wearing our packs and the sailors would hand us our weapons and other equipment that we were to deliver. We always hoped for high tide so that we would not have to walk across mud flats.

The officers at Commando School would select teams for different missions and then we trained for our particular mission. Nothing was ever a coincidence. Everything was done for a particular reason. Usually there would be an officer in command; a captain or at least a first lieutenant, a noncommissioned officer, a sergeant or corporal, a Freedom Fighter from the country where we were going, who knew the language and people; and a private (Tommy) like me.

My first commando mission was to France. The other team members were a captain, a corporal and guess who; my friend, Sergeant Pete of the Free French Army whose family were farmers in the North of France. We carried lots of good French money from the Bank of England, a wireless transmitter and receiver, two small wireless receivers so that our French friends could listen to BBC, London and a bunch of British Army maps. Later on, we also carried Sten Guns, which were lighter copies of the Bren Gun that could be folded up. There were other items such as satchel charges and grenades. We also carried instructions for the wireless, certain codes for different groups and the like. What we were really doing was to help setup communications and assistance for the Allies and the resistance people.

The operation went smoothly. We got out of the submarine, in the darkness, inflated and loaded our boat and rowed ashore. We deflated and hid the boat, strapped on the packs containing the wireless equipment. Pete led us about nine miles to a farmhouse. He had told us not to worry, that we were going to his relatives' home. Pete slipped into the darkened house and returned in a few minutes to signal us to come in. We left our hiding place and slipped in one at a time. Pete introduced us, (not real names) of course. We delivered the equipment and instructions so they could hide them. They showed us a hiding place. We hid and got some food out of our packs and ate. We went to sleep and slept until dark of the next day. We left after dark and met the submarine at a designated time and place.

Later on during these types of missions someone that we could identify would meet us. This was always dangerous because some of the people started working with the Nazis and would turn in those who were suspected of being in the resistance. The Gestapo tortured thousands of resistance people to death.

Those who completed Commando School were issued Commando patches. However, we did not wear them very long. One of the soldiers, wearing his patches, took his girlfriend to a pub one night in Wales where she lived. He was English. There were a number of coalminers in the pub and one of them started making nasty remarks about the soldier and his girlfriend. Coalminers are strong men. The more the man drank, the more belligerent he became and obviously was trying to start a fight. The soldier and his girlfriend remained silent and then left. The coal miner and some others followed them into the street. The miner took a full swing at the soldier. The soldier blocked the blow and did what he was trained to do, he attacked and broke the miner's neck, killing him. A constable came and since the miner was dead, he arrested the soldier. A well-known barrister defended the soldier and at trial, the judgment was that the soldier had acted in self-defense and although the defense was more than necessary, it was caused by his training. We stopped wearing patches, it wasn't worth it and besides we knew who we were and why tell the enemy or anyone else.

Not everyone was selected to go on small missions. I knew why I was selected. I was young, strong, a first class runner (I had enjoyed running all my life), a good swimmer, an excellent shot, a good map-reader, spoke some French and had no relatives in Europe that might affect my judgment, and last but by no means least, I never got seasick. It was a terrible thing for most soldiers to have to go ashore under fire while vomiting; trying to run and return fire all at the same time. Also, if a soldier stepped into a hole over his head while in the water, he would go straight down, loaded with equipment and ammunition. His only chance would be if he could hold his breath long enough to remove his packs, webbing, helmet and so forth, and swim up. A group of British doctors and researchers worked a long time trying to develop a medication to prevent seasickness.

We continued to go on missions from time to time. On one of the missions to Northern France, we had made our delivery. We found out that some of our friends had been betrayed. We had delivered new codes and were returning during the night to the coast, when one of the resistance men scouting ahead for us spotted a Gestapo Agent observing a building across the street from him. Normally, we would simply have gone around him, but it was necessary to cross a railway track at this point and he would see us. There was a full moon, he was standing in the shadow of a building and every few minutes he would light a cigarette. My commanding officer gave me the nod and I crawled in a circle to get back of him. When I was in position, I waited for him to light another cigarette, knowing he would use both hands. Just as soon as he started lighting, I rushed in back of him, with my left hand under his chin, I pulled his head back and in the same moment, drove my knife in his throat and leaving it in started sawing it. He tried to grab my hands and twist loose, but it was too late. He made gurgling sounds and blood was spurting out of his throat. I held him up until he stopped moving and then eased him down. Within seconds, the resistance men were there. I took off my large khaki scarf and wiped the blood off my hands and sleeves and handed it to them to dispose of. I wiped my knife off inside the agent's coat and put it back in the scabbard on my leg. Things happened fast. More resistance men appeared. We saw them stripping the agent, picking up the cigarette butts, cleaning up the blood and I heard someone say a farm wagon was on the way. We could not wait any longer, so we continued to the coast.

Sometimes, people will ask when was your first kill in close range. Others want to know, but are embarrassed to ask. I know that I had made some kills at the range of a rifle in Norway when we were there in company strength. While all of Europe was going down, the Norwegians continued to fight as long as they could. This was my first kill in close range. It was necessary.

Whenever we returned to the United Kingdom from a mission, there would be a debriefing team there to meet us. They wanted to question us as soon as possible. They gave us food and water on the submarine. They gave us a rum ration while they questioned us. We were always dirty, exhausted and needed sleep. They wanted to know what we had seen, heard, smelled, felt, everything. Afterwards, we were given leave. Sometimes, we would shower and change to our clean battle dress and sometimes we would go to the nearest pub, if one was open, and drink to unwind. We had two battle dresses; one to work in and the other clean one for dress-wear.

We later learned what happened to the body of the Gestapo Agent while on another mission. The resistance people burned his clothes, a small piece at a time, in their kitchen stoves. The Germans would have killed many people if they had found his body. They carried the body, hidden in a farm wagon, to a farm several miles away; and during the night placed the body in the hog pen. The next morning, there was nothing left. There was a man called "The Produce Man." He was a French veteran of World War I, and hated the Boche with a fervor, but he learned to conceal it. Before the war, he had a truck and would go around to the farms and buy produce, chickens, eggs, pigs and the like and carry them to the markets in the towns to sell. After the Germans occupied France, they allowed the Produce Man to continue working; except he carried the food to the German camps for the officers. They paid him for the food and gave him petrol and oil for his truck. The Produce Man was always welcome because he brought them the best, such as butter and eggs. Remember, in those days, there was not any refrigeration. All the sentries recognized him and would wave him on in at their camps. He was an excellent courier, moving freely around the whole district. So it came to pass, he carried the hogs that ate the Gestapo Agent to the German officers' mess for them to eat.

The German officers hired local women to wash their clothes. They went in and out of the German camps freely. They picked up their dirty clothes, took them home, washed and ironed them and took them back and got some more to wash. They learned the officer's names, took photographs, counted tanks, half-tracks, artillery pieces and so forth. The British bought up the things made in France and the other occupied countries from shops in London and elsewhere. These were items that we delivered such as knives, bed sheets and clothing with secret hiding places built in, watches, clocks, French pistols with ammo and cameras with film. The cameras were special made, not James Bond type of course, but they were small and accurate. Sometimes the Germans left papers in their clothes, which would be photographed by the washwomen. The resistance people were constantly risking their lives for the Allied cause. All of the exposed film ended up back in England.

British scientists had developed a system to locate aircraft and ships by using radio waves. They called it "Radio Location." Radio Location Stations were built and manned by trained technicians at strategic locations. This system would later be named "Radar." The Germans were working on the same system and I heard that a spy had gotten some of the technology from the British. However, the British kept ahead of the German scientists. The Germans built Radio Location Stations in France and other countries.

We knew when and where the German stations were located by communications from the resistance people. They were able to tell us everything we needed to know; how to get there; the terrain; locations of guards and when they changed. We formed combat missions to go in, kill the guards, place satchel charges and get out. We set the timer on the charges so that they would blow up the station when we were several miles away. They continued to build them and we continued to blow them up. The Germans tried to blow ours up, but were not successful because they did not have resistance people in England.

SUCK A ROCK 15: Somewhere in Great Britain

When R.A.F. night fighter pilots were asked how did they know who to shoot down, they said, "We eat a lot of carrots." The scientists had also developed an "Identification Friend or Foe System." All the R.A.F. aircraft constantly broadcast a signal and if a light did not come on in the cockpit of the other R.A.F. aircraft, then the pilot knew that the aircraft he was after was the enemy.

Spring & Summer 1941

It is difficult for me to place everything in chronological order because many things happened during nearly the same timeframe. My accent had changed and my memory of America was fading. My mentor, the major in London, had told me that I could now pass as a Canadian. "Not ready to be a Limey and all that", he said.

In the times I am writing about, the army had a thing called leave policy. Those in high places knew that this would be a long war. Everyone was given leave and those that I remember were; weekend leave: 3-day leave, 7-day leave, and 2-week (fortnight) leave. Each company had a schedule and you would take leave according to the schedule. You could swap leave with someone else but you were required to take leave. As I became older more things became clear to me. Every combat unit sent in reports so that they could be posted on the giant maps in the War Room, London. This was where Prime Minister Winston Churchill and high-ranking officers were most of the time. The numbers of available troops were approximate with an allowance for those who were wounded or sick in hospitals and those on leave. All of this was done so that the generals would know the locations and how many troops were available at any given time. If a soldier was in the guardhouse they would take him out if it was his turn for leave. When he returned he would go back to the guardhouse to complete his extra duty sentence.

I do not remember all of my leaves. When I was asked where I was going, I would usually say all the way to the North of Scotland. I did go to Southern England; the Midlands, Northern England, Wales, Scotland and most of the time to London because all railways went through London and soldiers had free passes on the British Railway System. I met many nice families at pubs and sometimes they would invite me to dinner and sometimes to spend the night. Man was I dumb; these nice people were giving me their best food. No telling how many Ration Coupons they would use up. These nice people did appreciate soldiers. So, I started a crusade. When I returned to camp, I would tell my officers and anybody who would listen that this was not fair. Then many other soldiers with the same experience started talking and saying we should be issued Ration Coupons when we went on leave. These should be special coupons that could not be bought or sold, they could only be given to families that gave food to a soldier and if not used, turned in when the soldier returned from leave. Finally, someone in government heard our plea and did make the change.

In 1940 or early 1941 the Eagle Club was established in London to serve American Volunteers in His Majesties Forces. I joined when I was on leave and still have my membership card. When I was on leave during these years, I would stop by the Club. They gave us free cigarettes, passes to shows similar to Broadway, movies and the like. I first saw the movie "Gone With The Wind" at a flick in London with a free ticket. It was at the Eagle Club that I met other Americans including the volunteer pilots in the R.A.F. There were three fighter squadrons with American Pilots. They sometimes called themselves the "Texas Air Force" or the "Confederate Air Force." The pilots were sergeants the same as Luftwaffe pilots. Whenever anyone was at the Club and had been wounded and was wearing a cast on their leg or arm, we all signed it.

The Eagle Club made arrangements with the BBC (British Broadcasting Corporation) to broadcast a program for the Club to the American Volunteer's homes in America. We gave our home addresses to the Club Officials and our families were notified by mail as to the time and frequency modulation by the British Embassy in Washington. My mother saved the letter and I still have it. At the time of the party many of us members were there. Some high government officials were there. Prime Minister Winston Churchill arrived a short time before the actual broadcast and gave a short speech thanking us. The band played good old American songs, I remember they played "Ma, I Miss Your Apple Pie" during the broadcast. I am sure that many of the mothers cried. The announcer introduced each of us, named our hometowns and then we would speak a few words to our families. We couldn't say much because of censorship, we were just somewhere in England. I learned years later that the Montgomery Advertiser printed a story about this.

The Queen came to the Eagle Club sometimes to pour tea. She is still one of the world's most gracious ladies. She always made it a point to talk to each one of us and she had a sharp memory. The first time she poured tea for me at the Eagle Club, her eyes sparked and she said: "Alabama, are you still doing well? I have heard good things about you." She always reminded me of my mother and I replied, "Yes, Your Majesty." This requires some explanation.

Soon after we arrived in the United Kingdom the King and Queen started "Inspecting the troops." We paraded around the drill field and passed in review. Then as we stood in formation at attention the King and Queen, with some generals, walked passed the lines of soldiers. The Queen did all the talking. Every now and then the Queen stopped in front of a soldier. Usually she would ask their names and where was their home. She stopped in front of me and asked my name and where are you from? I replied, " Daniel C. Houston from Montgomery, Alabama, Your Majesty." She said, " Oh, you are an American Volunteer," and turned to our Lt. Colonel commanding our battalion and said, "Colonel, would you arrange for this young man and 4 or 5 others to come to Windsor Castle on Sunday (the date) at a certain time?" The colonel replied, "Most certainly, your Majesty." The Queen said, "Thank you, you have good looking soldiers and many of them are tall and you must be proud of them," as she moved on down the line.

At the appointed time we arrived at Windsor Castle and soldiers from one of the guard regiments opened the gates and directed us to a place to park our lorry. Soldiers were stationed at strategic locations around the castle grounds and at each station there was a bombproof shelter made entirely of steel. One of the King's assistants, a civilian, came out and guided us inside to what looked like a small informal dining room. We passed other rooms and a huge library. One of the great traditions in England is teatime. That is why they have so many "Tea Shoppes." There were five of us and we were seated at a table. On the sideboards were trays of different kinds of crumpets and of course also the teapot, cups and saucers and silverware. The King, Queen, Princess Elizabeth and Princess Margaret came in while we stood at attention. Then we were all seated again except the Queen and she started pouring tea while the servants served us the trays of crumpets. Elizabeth was a year or two younger than I and Margaret was younger than Elizabeth.

The Queen started the conversation and wanted to know what it was like where we lived. Of course, Elizabeth and Margaret had private tutors but it appeared that the Queen wanted them to have first hand knowledge of people and geography of the world. The other four soldiers were from British Columbia and told them about the Rocky Mountains, the salmon runs, logging, mining, panning for gold, Hudson Bay Company, trapping for furs and how the Japanese Current in the Pacific kept the coast warmer than one might expect. I told them about the south and misconceptions, how the accents were different. One of the things they didn't know was how far west the State of Florida extended and not only did California grow citrus fruit but Florida also. The girls were very interested and asked me lots of questions. Sometimes the King smiled and made short comments. The Royal Family seemed to enjoy the conversation.

After the tea was over, we thanked the King and Queen, said goodbye and they wished us good luck. The same civilian assistant guided the other four soldiers on a tour of the castle and grounds. Elizabeth and Margaret wanted to show me their horses because I had told them about how my cousin Joe and I had ridden horses to his one room schoolhouse in Covington County, Alabama. So the Princesses guided me on the grand tour. By the way, the reason the Queen knew my nickname was because the other soldiers called me "Alabama" when we were explaining the great distance from Montgomery to the headquarters of the Canadian Scottish at Victoria on Vancouver Island, British Columbia. Another by the way, before we left camp to go to Windsor Castle, we received a stern lecture from the regimental sergeant major about manners and the other four soldiers were carefully selected. The Queen wanted privates, which is what we were.

Horseracing and many other things were canceled during the war. There were not any racehorses at Windsor Castle. There was a small stable with about six parade horses and a trainer. All of the "Royals" were trained riders almost from birth. These beautiful horses were there to continue the training of the Princesses.

After we looked at the horses, we went round and about looking inside and outside of the Castle. The coronation coaches were in a garage type building. We went in. They had diamonds and other precious stones imbedded in them including the wheels. I felt one of the wheels and said; "Now if I could just get this wheel off, take it somewhere and sell it, I would be rich." The Princesses laughed. We were walking on a stone walkway when they stopped, pointed down and one of them said; " King John is buried down there, and he was hung on that beam over there," pointing to a large beam over the walkway and spanning between the two buildings. The tomb of King George and a white marble statue of an angel were in the chapel. They said that at a certain time the statue would glow as if it were alive. When the tour was over, I thanked them, said goodbye and headed over to our lorry to return to camp. I wrote my parents a letter about this trip and learned several years later that the Montgomery Advertiser published some of it.

In our Nissen hut camps, there were some huts for latrines with showers and lavatories. There was never any hot water even on the coldest of days. Anyone going on leave would carefully plan their strategy to have a cold shave and shower. There was no good way. Most of us would strip naked, run to the latrine, shiver all the way, do everything as fast as possible, and then run back. We washed our clothes the same way except we would wear our long underwear or something. In the huts where we bunked, there was a small one eye wood or coal-burning stove. To dry our "wash" we ran ropes over our heads and hung the wet clothes to dry. I was blessed because I did not have to shave until I got older. When some of them asked: "Alabama, why don't you have to shave?" I would reply, "Because I am part Indian," (most of the soldiers did not know how young I was). One of the places that I went to many times while on leave was a large dance hall and showplace in London. I think the name of it was Covent Gardens. During the early days of the Battle of Britain when we carried packs and weapons on leave, we would go in and stack our weapons and packs against the walls. There was a large sign at the entrance, which read: "PLEASE DO NOT GO ON THE DANCE FLOOR WITH YOUR HOB-NAIL BOOTS ON." We would take off our boots and dance in our socks if we did not have dress shoes. There were long bars running down two walls of the huge room where you could purchase all kinds of beverages. The stage for the bands was the revolving type so that one band would go off while playing and the other band would come on while playing. This is how they would take their breaks. The girls always outnumbered the soldiers about 4 or 5 to one. The girls would stand in the center of the dance floor and they would "break-in" whenever they wished as the dancers gradually circled the dance floor.

One evening when I was there they were having a raffle for charity. People bought tickets and later in the evening they would have a drawing. I was wearing my kilt uniform and my "U.S.A." patches. After a while the band stopped playing and then there was a loud drum roll. An announcer said: "Ladies and Gentlemen it is time for the drawing, there is an American Volunteer here and we ask that he draw the winning ticket." Everyone started applauding including myself. As the applauding stopped, everyone was looking at me. I was embarrassed; my only excuse was that I had drunk some beer and whiskey. I went up on the stage and the announcer said: "Where are you from?" I replied: "Alabama." The band started playing "Stars Fell on Alabama," after playing a few lines the band stopped. I reached in the box and pulled out a ticket and handed it to the announcer who read the number into the microphone. Everyone looked at his or her ticket. Finally, a young lady held up her hand holding the ticket. She came up on stage and handed the ticket to the announcer who looked at it and said: "Ladies and Gentlemen we have a winner," as he handed her a package wrapped with bright ribbons. She unwrapped the package and held up the prize. It was an onion, a big nice onion! I know this sounds crazy or maybe a joke, but it was neither, when you realize all the shortages of food and other items in England at that time, an onion was hard to find. Razor blades were not thrown away when they were dull; they were taken to places that would re-sharpen them. After more applause, I asked the announcer to please play all of the song and asked the young lady: "Will you please have this dance with me?" She replied: "I would be delighted." She was very good looking. Holding hands, we went on the dance floor and danced as the band played on. No one broke in and when the song was over we went over to the bar, got two beers, and sat down at a table and talked. There were many good bands in England during this time playing the same songs and style music of Glenn Miller, Dorsey Brothers and other great bands in America.

In my letters home, I always asked my mother to please send me a Whitman's Sampler (box of different kinds of chocolate candy). So, about every month or two, I would receive a parcel containing a Whitman's Sampler. I would let each soldier in my hut select the piece of their choice. They never did know how I knew every piece. There was a diagram in the cover of the box showing every piece in both layers. I took the remainder with me on leave to give away. I usually gave it to families that I met, especially those with young children.

Sometimes I went to the Midlands on leave. There were many small towns and villages that had factories located near them. Many of these factories produced war materials and the workers were young women sent there from all over the United Kingdom. Women were not drafted. However, young women of certain ages that were not in one of the women's auxiliary units of the military and had no children or other dependents were sent to work in these factories. There were thousands of them. Whenever I went to a pub, I met bunches of them.

If I had enough money, I would sometimes spend the night at a small hotel or in a pub that had rooms to let. The employees would show me my room and always say, "I will knock you up in the morning, please leave your boots outside the door." They had no clocks in the rooms and when I got up in the mornings, my boots would be shined.

At a N.A.A.F.I. sponsored dance in Edinburg, I met a young lady who was a chief petty officer in the 'WRENS' (Women's Royal Naval Service). Her name was Sam (Samantha) Bailey and her home was Newcastle on Tyne, also she was stationed at the Naval Base there. Sam was on leave and had attended her friend's wedding. Her friend had married an officer who shipped out with his unit that morning headed for Egypt. The friend's name has been forgotten, but she was an interesting person. She was the daughter of a British diplomat, stationed in Tokyo, and had a Japanese mother. She had been sent to England for her education. Months before Japan entered World War II, she was trained by MI 5. She wore a flat automatic pistol on her thigh. None of this would have been revealed to us, except we were military. A group of us spent the night at the friend's apartment in Edinburg.

Sam invited me to visit her home, so we caught the train headed south to Newcastle. I met her parents and spent several days there. Sam got us two tickets to the theater and we went to see "Peter Pan." All of the actors were girls and this was "traditional" type theater, which I enjoyed. In London the shows were, "musical" type, with mostly nearly naked girls. Later we went to Sam's office at the Naval Base and I was introduced around. She worked in the office of the Harbour Master and they were extremely busy day and night scheduling all kinds of ships entering and leaving port. My leave was expiring, so we said goodbye and promised to write each other. I headed south to camp. We did write several times, but we never did get our leaves scheduled at the same time. The way we moved and lived, it was difficult just to write letters and impossible to have any long-term relationships.

The Germans tried to force the United Kingdom to surrender by massive night bombing of the large cities. If I were in London on leave and had no place to spend the night, I would go down to one of the underground railway stations and sleep on the concrete. Concrete makes your body stiff; the ground is better. Families whose homes had been bombed lived down there; women, children and old men. Each family had their own spot. They would leave their belongings there in the daytime and go to work or to some of the parks. I always wished I had something to give the children. Later on, when the Allies bombed German cities, such as Dresden, people who had not been made to suffer by the Nazis as the people of London had, said we should not have bombed German cities.

Summer & Fall 1941

In July, we started preparations for a large-scale raid. We trained in company size formations to land somewhere. Most of the soldiers were Canadians with some support troops, such as Royal Engineer sappers. There were a hundred or so Free Norway fighters who had been trained at Commando School. This caused us to silently speculate that we were going into some place in Norway. With this many, we would not use rubber boats.

As I recall, one night in August, we boarded a Royal Navy destroyer and headed out to sea. The next day, the ships formed a convoy heading north. They were all fast ships, destroyers and corvettes. Then we knew we were going to Norway because we were issued some Norwegian money.

After we were well out to sea, our commanding officers briefed us using maps. We were not going to Norway, but instead some Norwegian Islands, named Spitzbergen, a long way north of Norway at the top of the world. We were told where each group would land after the Germans were hit first by the big guns on the destroyers. After the Nazis occupied Norway, they occupied these islands and forced the Norwegians to work for them. I think there were some coalmines there, but I didn't see them. One of the things I noticed, as we sped north, was the change in the air. There was more oxygen in the air from all the ice caps and it was stinging my lungs until I got used to it.

Of course, I volunteered to work with the sailors, and I had been on this destroyer (H.M.S. Malcolm) before. As the convoy approached the islands, the ships slowed down and formed a battle line during the night so that they would be in position to start the bombardment at daylight.

At daylight, everything started to shake, rattle and roll as the Malcolm fired salvo after salvo into the German defensive positions. As the ships closed in, the Germans started retreating. All those who controlled the guns were ordered not to hit the docks. The ships went in alongside the docks one at a time. As the soldiers climbed down the cargo nets hanging over sides and reached the docks, that ship would back off so that another ship could come in. The Norwegian soldiers went in first to find the people. While all this was happening, other ships gave covering fire with smaller guns.

When my group reached a dock, we immediately formed our squad formations and went after the Germans in our pre-planned direction. As the soldiers reached shore, the ships ceased firing. We killed most of the Germans. Some tried to hide in the high ground, but the Norwegian soldiers had found the civilians in hiding and they would point out where the Germans were. My guess is that about eighty Germans surrendered. When the civilians came out, we all stood in shock. They had been used as slave labor with little food or anything else. The women had been raped over and over again. If you can imagine how now hardened Canadian soldiers felt, that is just the beginning. There was a Norwegian girl about fifteen years old kneeling down and crying. She had been raped repeatedly. The girl identified a German lieutenant that had surrendered. Norwegian soldiers dragged him over in front of the girl. They then stripped his clothes off, while he was pleading for mercy, they cut off his genitals and ordered the girl to look up. A rifle was placed at the lieutenant's head and the girl was told to pull the trigger. She did.

The Norwegians did not want to take any prisoners, and neither did we. Some senior officers arrived and told everyone that we were not murderers like the Nazis.

We prepared to leave. Some of the Norwegian people returned to England with us and some stayed behind. The sailors were busy unloading supplies: non perishable food, medical supplies; wireless transmitters and receivers, weapons (including some 90 MM. Bofors), diesel engines with spare parts for their fishing trawlers; drums filled with petrol, diesel fuel, oil and grease, and the like. Also, the people could now use the German equipment. We arrived back in the United Kingdom in September.

To understand how the Free Norway soldiers felt requires knowledge of how the Nazis treated the Norwegian people. When the Nazi's invaded Norway, they killed many innocent people and after they consolidated their conquest, they tortured others to death. The Norwegians are great soldiers and sailors.

One of the great secrets of the war (in my opinion, the greatest of "What Ifs") was the building by the Germans of a "Heavy Water Plant" on a Norwegian river. This meant that German scientists were working on a hydrogen bomb. Heavy water is hydrogen with a specific gravity of 1. A Heavy Water Plant extracts hydrogen from water, which consists of two parts hydrogen to one part of oxygen.

The Allies worked on producing an atomic bomb later in the war by using uranium 25. I think they got the uranium from Port Radium on Great Bear Lake in Northern Canada. As we know, the Allies were successful in producing the first Atomic Bombs. It was not until the "Cold War" with the Soviet Union that the United States built a Heavy Water Plant on the Savannah River.

The point of all of this is "What If" the Germans had produced Hydrogen Bombs first? Remember, the Germans were the first to produce rockets with warheads and jet aircraft. It was the Norwegians who slowed down and finally stopped the Nazis from developing the bomb and paid the price with their own lives.

Norwegian soldiers hid in the mountains while the German Army launched massive searches for them. They almost died of starvation during the bad weather of the winters because the British could not make airdrops to them. They finally got into the Heavy Water Plant and set satchel charges. The explosion damaged the plant, but did not destroy it. It was shut down for a while for repairs and then placed back in operation. Meanwhile, the Germans tortured to death any of the soldiers or resistance people they could capture.

The Germans decided to move the heavy water they had produced to Germany. The large container was loaded on a Norwegian ferry. Satchel charges were hidden onboard and when the ferry reached deep water, it was blown up, killing the Norwegian captain, crew and passengers. This was an awesome sacrifice.

One time we were building a small camp of Nissen huts. There were some houses nearby and as we worked, some small children, boys and girls about five years old, would watch. Each day they would come closer. One day a boy said to me, "Mister, have you ever seen a banana?" I replied, "Yes, I have, they grow in warm countries further south than where I live." His mother came out and apologized saying, "We have told the children they could watch, but not to bother you." Other mothers came out and I said, "Mam, they are no bother." All of us talked. The only thing we had to give the children was chewing gum. They did not know what to do with it, so we showed them. It made them happy. I wished that I had a box of Whitman's Sampler chocolate. The mothers told us that their husbands were in the 8th Army in the desert and that the children did not remember them. The sadness of war!

Many people have asked me if the King's Rules and Regulations (K. R. and R.) for their military were more strict and demanding than the United States military. I found it to be just the opposite. I have never met an officer or noncommissioned officer who was not well trained, honest, absolutely fair and reasonable. Under the regulations, their first duty was to take care of the needs of the soldiers first. All officers and enlisted men ate together when we were in the field. The privates always ate first. Whenever we stood in line for anything, privates went first.

An example of how careful they were to be fair and just was when I was being court-martialed for being AWOL (absent without leave). I met a girl named Farrow at a dance in Edinburg. Farrow was from the Hebrides Islands west of Scotland and invited me to visit her home. I told her I would really enjoy that because I had wanted to see the islands. Farrow gave me instructions on how to reach her home on the Isle of Lewis. I wrote down the instructions. Go by train to a port on the northwest coast of Scotland, then by ferry to the island. The only problem was, it would take at least two weeks' leave and probably more, but I would try.

Back at camp, I found out when I could get my two weeks' leave and wrote Farrow a letter telling her the dates. When I left camp, I told my friends where I was going and I would probably be over-leave when I returned. We always did that. I traveled as fast as I could, and when I left the ferry at the island, I was told there was a message for me at the office. The message said for me to telephone her at a certain number, which I did. Farrow and her father picked me up in a lorry to take me to their home. I met her family and many other nice people.

All of the older boys and young men were gone, most of them to the Royal Navy. They raised sheep and some vegetables on the island, but the main industry was fishing. They laughed when they told me that the salt mackerel that I ate on ships came from there. They had large sheds where they cleaned fish and packed them in salt in wooden barrels. Her father was in the fishing business so he was allowed petrol for his lorry, which was needed to haul different items. I think he was the manager of one of the fish companies. Farrow had two brothers who were gone to the Navy.

We went to a dance and I met many other girls. Since there were no other young men, I danced with all of them that I could. Some of the girls danced with each other or their fathers. Everyone had some Scots whiskey, which was distilled on the island. I had difficulty understanding many of them because they spoke the old Celtic language of the Gaul's. They said they liked to hear my Alabama language. We sipped our whisky and sang the old Highland songs with the piano and bagpipes playing. Some of the songs I knew and some I didn't.

It was time to leave; this was always a sad time. These were strong, hard working, isolated people, the kind of people that always took care of themselves and their neighbors. I looked in my pack and got out the things that I had brought for them. I gave them cigarettes, chewing gum, a box of Whitman's Sampler, and a Thorens cigarette lighter that I had bought in London for the father and some ration coupons. Farrow and I hugged and kissed, bid farewell and I promised I would return if ever I could. I never could return.

When I returned to camp, I was four days overdue (AWOL). I reported to the Duty Sergeant and he carefully noted the time in his daily report. He said, "Alabama, consider yourself under open arrest until further notice." The next day I marched to the Company H.Q. with one of my friends in front of me and one in back of me. They did not carry weapons; they each wore their web belts with bayonets attached to show they were on duty. We went in to H.Q. and saluted the major who was seated at his desk. The sergeant that was on duty when I returned had prepared the charges and specifications for my court-martial was also present. The sergeant major ordered me to remove my cap, which I did. No one could be court-martialed while wearing the cap badge of their regiment. The sergeant major read aloud the charges and specifications and then asked me if they were correct. They were correct except I noticed that he read my serial number starting with a "K." So, I replied, "My serial number starts with a "B, Sir." The major said, "sergeant major check the record." The sergeant major went to the files, returned to the major's desk and said, "The serial number starts with a "B, Sir." The major said, "Alabama the charges are dismissed." I tried to comment that I was guilty because I didn't want the sergeant to get in trouble, he was a nice guy. The sergeant major was already saying, "Detail dismissed," so we did an about face and left. Evidently, what happened was the sergeant assumed my serial number started with a "K" because all those who enlisted in British Columbia were issued a serial number starting with a "K." My serial number was issued in Ontario.

Sometimes we had church parade on Sundays when we were not moving or doing other things. Those who were Roman Catholic or Jewish were automatically excused. No one had to go, but if you didn't, you would likely be assigned duty while the others went. One Sunday, we assembled and listened to a sermon by a Church of England padre. It seems that the point of the sermon was that we were all going to die and go to hell. The older soldiers were incensed and complained to the officers saying they did not want to hear any more sky pilots. Church Parade was discontinued.

When we were in camps, we would go to the mess hall to eat. The Duty Officer and the Duty Sergeant were required to eat with us. One morning, the breakfast was awful. The word was passed to not eat it and to wait for the Duty Officer to arrive. When he arrived, the older soldiers complained. The Duty Officer sat down and started to eat. After a few bites, he stood and said, "It is awful." He went into the kitchen and ordered the cooks to prepare another breakfast. We waited until it was ready and then we ate.

When Canada was holding national and local elections, I don't remember the date, a voting officer and his assistants came to our battalion in a specially equipped lorry. Company after company was ordered to fall in and form a voting line. I stepped out of line in order to speak to my sergeant major. I said, "Sir, I am not registered to vote and I have no home in Canada," (I was also underage, which he knew). He said, "Alabama, are you a soldier?" I replied, "Yes, Sir." He replied, "Then you vote." I voted for Prime Minister Mackenzie King because he was the only one I had ever heard of.

We were given Canadian cigarettes and chewing gum. My friend, Roy Palmer, was about the only soldier I knew that did not smoke. Roy gave me his cigarettes and I gave him my chewing gum. On long hard marches, I had shown him how I sucked on a rock. He said he used chewing gum the same way. One time our battalion received some wooden kegs of Canadian beer. We had a beer bust that night. We gathered together, all officers and men, in the mess hall. Someone had setup a boxing ring so that anyone who wanted to box, wrestle, or whatever, could do so. We drank a lot of beer. The regimental sergeant major was a big, strong man and he was also a fencing champion. He gave us a lesson and I couldn't understand how a man that size could move his feet so fast, as fast or faster than a ballet dancer. He had all the necessary equipment for fencing and he quickly disarmed everyone that tried him. Then he would demonstrate what they did wrong. It must have been near Christmas because the pipers played some Christmas songs on the bagpipes.

I didn't know they could play songs such as "Jingle Bells." Thinking about drinking beer, sometimes when we knew we would be moving on lorries the next morning, the older soldiers would send someone into the nearest village to buy a bunch of lemon extract. They mixed the lemon extract with water in the fire buckets. When someone said it was a good mix, they drank it from the fire buckets.

Fall 1941

Most people say they remember where they were on Sunday, December 7, 1941; the day the Japanese attacked Pearl Harbor. I don't know where I was that day. I do remember where I heard about it. We were on a mission and two or three days after Pearl Harbor we returned, tired and dirty, to camp. It had turned dark and was raining when several of us decided to go over to the canteen and have a beer. The canteen was in a small hut and only had a few items such as toothpaste, shaving items, soap and the like. It was only open at certain times and we were allowed to buy only one bottle of Canadian beer. There was a small wireless on a high shelf and BBC news was on. The news was about the attack on Pearl Harbor and reactions around the world. The British Embassy in Hong Kong had been overrun. There was no word from the Ambassador or the Governor of Hong Kong and the others. Prime Minister Winston Churchill and President Franklin D. Roosevelt had issued joint orders to all British and United States military forces to join together to fight the Axis powers. One of the soldiers turned to me and said, "Well, Alabama, the Americans are finally in it, what do you think?" I replied, "I don't know, but it was bound to happen."

The B.B.C. (British Broadcasting Corporation) played a vital role in the war. They not only broadcast Greenwich Mean Time (the world standard) as they had always done, but also coded messages to resistance fighters and Allied Military Forces all over the world. They had experts on their staff from the countries in Europe and helped establish escape routes to Spain for downed aircrews and others. Spain was a neutral country and the British Embassy there could help Allied Personnel return to England. The B.B.C. had a young girl named Petula Clark who would sing and talk to military units. Every now and then she would read messages prepared by officials which were codes; such as, the moon is blue or green or whatever. For example, if she sang "Stars Fell on Alabama" that was for me and depending on what was said before or after would be the message. This was important when there was a betrayal of the resistance people. The officials would add in other things that meant nothing so that the Axis people would spend time trying to decode them.

Lord Ha Ha and Axis Sally (traitors) broadcast the Axis propaganda from Berlin. They were having a great time saying now that the Axis powers had joined together the Allies were retreating on all fronts. They said, "The United States Navy's Pacific fleet had been largely destroyed and the Japanese now controlled the Pacific Ocean". I don't think that Tokyo Rose (traitor) started broadcasting from Tokyo until sometime later.

My tonsils had been giving me trouble from time to time so the doctors arranged for me to go to a military hospital at Thursley, Surrey, to have them removed. It seemed to be not much more pain than having a tooth filled when they were removed on Christmas Eve, December 24, 1941. The next day, being Christmas, the nurses bought kegs of draft beer for the ambulatory patients. There were some patients there who had been wounded and they were in bad shape. The nurses made funny hats out of paper for us to wear at our party. When it was time to drink beer, the nurses decided that I couldn't have any because it was too soon after my tonsils were removed. I argued about it, but to no avail. That evening, just at dark, I walked out of the hospital at the ambulance entrance and went down the street to a pub. My uniform and other clothes were stored somewhere in a closet. I had on pajamas with my great coat over them. We kept our great coats because it was cold. The pub was crowded and the people were having a great time singing and drinking. When they saw me, they knew I was an American volunteer because of my patches and they guessed I was from the hospital. When they saw my pajama pants below the bottom of my great coat, they pointed at them and howled with laughter. Someone said, "You Yanks will do anything." I said, "I beg your pardon, but I am not a Yankee, I am from Alabama." I had no money or anything else, but no matter, they were buying me beer and whiskey faster than I could drink it. I celebrated with them until the pub closed, returned to my ward and silently went to bed. Afterward, my tonsils never did bother me again. I still have some pictures taken at this hospital because I had mailed them to my mother and she kept them and others.

After I was dismissed from the hospital, a few days later, I went to the Canadian Scottish Company at the Holding Center. The Holding Center was a camp where replacement soldiers were sent before going to their assigned units. Also, officers and enlisted men were sent there for a short while when released from hospitals. Each regiment had their own company represented there. It was similar to the United States Army Replacement Depots (Repo Depot).

There was a very interesting soldier in our company there. He was being sent back to Canada because he had become 50 years old. His name was Harry Bartholomew and he was from the Peace River District in Alberta. When anyone in the Canadian Army became 50 years old, he was returned to Canada and discharged. Our battalion padre was sent back when he became 50 years old. Harry didn't like this rule. He said he could still kill a mountain sheep or goat a longer distance than anyone and he didn't wear glasses. Harry was born in England and shipped out as a cabin boy when he was twelve. He left his ship in Vancouver while still young and went to northern Canada and learned how to trap for furs. He had spent two years trapping on Victoria Island. He traveled mostly by canoe, but when he went into the mountains and setup trap-lines he would take sled dogs and pack horses to carry everything. It was necessary to build a cabin, build shelters one day's journey apart in a circle that returned to the cabin before the winter snows. When snowfall came and the horses could no longer graze, he killed them and smoke cured the meat to feed the dogs.

Harry told me many things about the wilderness (bush country they called it), trapping, cabin fever and how to survive. He was hired as a guide for the Government Survey Party to map the Great Slave Lake. He said there was big money in furs for anyone that knew how to do it. One time, after selling his furs, he had over $20,000.00 in cash in his pocket. He decided he would go to England for a visit and boarded the train headed for Halifax. The farthest he got was Montreal. The money was spent on women and drink; so he returned to the northwest. Harry asked me to come to see him at Peace River when I returned from the war and he would teach me how to trap. When I asked him for his address, he laughed and said, "Just ask for me, everybody knows me."

Winter & Spring 1942

After I returned to my unit from the Holding Center, a Private Mackenzie and I were instructed to report to the Canadian Military Headquarters in London for an interview. No one seemed to know much about this; all we knew was that it was some kind of interview for an appointment. We reported to headquarters as ordered. A sergeant there told us that Mackenzie would be interviewed at a certain time, and I would be interviewed at another time. We had a couple of hours so we wandered around and returned at the appointed time.

When it was my turn, the sergeant guided me to a large room with a large table in the center. There were about ten high-ranking officers seated at the table. After I was seated, a colonel in the Royal Canadian Mounted Police (R.C.M.P) started explaining what it was all about. He said, "The R.C.M.P. Academy in Ottawa needed cadets and all the good young men like you are over here in the army. We have been going over your records and at this point it appears that you are qualified. The qualifications for a cadet are: minimum six feet tall, good physical condition, between certain ages (I had now turned 18) and pass a written test." Different ones asked me questions and I was told that no decision was needed at this time. After the interview, the officers thanked me for coming and wished me good luck. A sergeant then guided me to another room setup as a classroom with desks. Another sergeant handed me papers and asked me to be seated and complete the test.

There were a number of things that I already knew about the R.C.M.P. They served as Military Police for the Canadian Military Forces; they served in Canada the same as the United States FBI, the U. S. Marshals and others all rolled into one force. While the Provinces of Canada had their own police forces, the R.C.M.P. was the only police in the vast Northwest Territories. The R.C.M.P. had the same organizational structure as the army; same ranks, pay and promotions. Upon graduation, after four years at the academy, the cadets were assigned as privates to different duties and locations. They moved up in rank according to their abilities. The R.C.M.P. Academy was similar to the United States Military Academies except in addition to regular college and military subjects, law enforcement subjects were added. After I finished the test, I turned it in and returned to camp. The test was the usual college entrance exam covering algebra, geometry, English, history, geography and some elementary navigation.

At camp, everyone wanted to know what the interview was about. Mackenzie and I explained it. Some of my friends started saying, "Alabama, you'll not like it, you'll be sent to the Arctic for two years at a time," and stuff like that.

Some of the sergeants in our battalion had applied to attend Officers' Training School in Canada. O.T.S. was not like the Officers' Candidate School (O.C.S.) at Fort Benning, Georgia, which was a 90-day school. (Graduates were called "90-day wonders"). O.C.S. graduates were commissioned second lieutenants and were sent straight to the infantry as replacements. O.T.S. was a two-year school and graduates were second lieutenants who were sent to various staffs for further training because they could not command troops until they made first lieutenant.

The sergeants were taking correspondence courses to help them pass the O.T.S. tests in different subjects. The sergeants were eager to talk with me about the R.C.M.P. test. After talking for a while, they wanted me to help them study for the O.T.S. tests, so I agreed. During evenings or weekends, or anytime we were not on duty, I went to the noncommissioned officers' quarters. The sergeants scrounged up a large table and chairs and setup one of their rooms for study and tests. By the way, our sergeant majors and officers encouraged this sort of activity and actually helped. They changed or swapped duty schedules so that none of us would miss a study period and later the test taking. In lieu of a chalkboard, we pinned maps to the wall with the backsides out. For example, if the study material had algebraic equations to solve, I would write them on the back of the maps to go through the method to solve them. Everyone wanted our sergeants to pass. Sometimes we would work through the evening meal but somebody would bring us something to eat. We had been together through so much and for so long we became more like family. Everywhere I went someone would say, "Alabama, how is the study going?"

One of our majors had agreed to be the administrator and monitor for the tests. Canadian headquarters sent the tests to the major and he would give each test to the sergeants. Of course, I could not be present during the testing. The major sent the tests back to headquarters for grading. This process continued for some time.

About a month after I had the interview and test for the R.C.M.P. Academy, my company commander, Major Duncan, received a message that I had met all qualifications for the R.C.M.P. Academy. Mackenzie's company commander received the same message. The message also contained instructions and forms to fill out. There was an acceptance form for me to sign; another form was for the lieutenant colonel commanding our battalion to release me. Other forms were for my transfer and the like. The regimental sergeant major called me into his office. After discussions with my sergeants and officers, I decided to decline. This would have been my career as an R.C.M.P. and I would not get to go home except about once a year. Private Mackenzie accepted the transfer.

Sometime during the spring of 1942, a bulletin was sent to all military units. The bulletin stated that all Americans in His Majesty's Forces could transfer to the United States Military Forces if they so desired. Those who decided to transfer must sign the proper papers for their commanding officers to send in. Again, after discussion, I decided to sign the papers. My major said, "Alabama, we would like for you to stay, but the United States is your country and with your training, you would be a big help to them. You should receive many promotions. The only reason you have not been promoted here is your age." My friend, Roy Palmer, also signed the papers. He was born in the State of Washington, but spent about all his life in Canada where the rest of his family was born.

There were many things happening during the winter and spring of 1942. The 34th Infantry Division landed in Ireland in January 1942. They were the Minnesota-Iowa National Guard and were the first National Guard Division to be federalized in 1941; also they were the first division, including regular army divisions, to go overseas. We were seeing more and more American soldiers.

One day I was instructed to report to the major's office. Major Duncan said, "Alabama, you have been selected to be the instructor for some United States Marines to go through Commando School." I tried to protest, but I couldn't win. I said, "Sir, I have no rank," The major told me not to worry, all arrangements had been made; report to the school at a certain time and date.

When I arrived at the Commando School, I reported to the commanding officer. The major that I knew when the school started was now a full colonel. The other staff members had also been promoted. The colonel welcomed me and explained what I should do. There was an order from on high to train a squad of United States Marines so they could return to the United States or the Pacific Theater to train others. The colonel said, "In two days, twelve marine sergeants will arrive and a hut will be assigned to them. Before they arrive, other arrangements will be made. Someone will sew the rank of staff sergeant on your battle dress so that you will outrank them. You are hereby promoted to the rank of provisional (temporary) staff sergeant." A staff sergeant is the highest non-commissioned officer in the British Army and wears three stripes with a gold crown above them. There were others in the office. The colonel then introduced me to a captain and a company sergeant major who would be my commanders. They would handle any problems, and I would turn in my daily reports to the sergeant major. The colonel continued, "You will bunk with the N.C.O.'s and in the interest of time, the marines will not go through some of the training exercises, but will concentrate on the training they need the most. The captain has prepared a schedule for you and it may be changed as needed. Good luck."

I found my bunk in the staff N.C.O. quarters, unloaded my pack and other gear. I then went to the captain's office to meet with him and the sergeant major. We studied the schedule and also determined what equipment would be needed. The supply sergeant was called in and we went over equipment needed for each day. There were many details we worked out during the next two days.

When the United States Marines arrived, we were ready. It was obvious they did not need physical training and that the United States Marine Corps did not want to be embarrassed by any failures. The Marines were in top physical and mental shape; obviously having been hand picked, the youngest was about twenty-two. I did not wear my U.S.A. patches and I had lost my accent, so they didn't know I was an American teenager.

These were some humorous times. Whenever we moved somewhere, we always marched in formation as all soldiers do. Each day, I picked one of the sergeants to give the commands, which were United States Military Drill. There was no point in teaching them British Drill. After several days, I started giving the drill commands. Not only were the marines surprised, but also the British, Canadian and other soldiers were surprised and started watching us. Seeing this, just for fun, I gave close order drill commands with all the turns and so forth. Strangely enough, no one asked how I knew and I didn't say anything until days later when the training was finished.

The marines were easy to train. For one thing, they were eager to learn. The United States Marines were already fighting the Japanese in the Pacific Islands. We showed them how quickly we produced paratroopers and the firepower of our new squad formations. They were particularly interested in how to prepare for invasions. We taught them how to get scouts or pathfinders ashore prior to invading by using rubber boats off submarines and the importance of getting wireless (radio) equipment ashore for communications. We did not know at this time that the marines would soon get to observe a large-scale raid into France. After the training was finished, I told them how I knew United States Drill and we said the usual good-byes. I packed up, took off the provisional staff sergeant insignia and returned to camp in Southern England.

In May 1942 Major Duncan received a message requesting that I report to the major's office in London. Upon arrival at the major's office, the major and captain explained to me that some great things were happening. General Eisenhower had been selected to be the Allied Supreme Commander of the European, African and Middle East Theater of Operations. At last there would be a complete and final chain of command. General Eisenhower had formed his staff with representatives from all branches of service and from all the Allied Nations. Tomorrow evening there will be an informal get together dinner for the General and his staff at a major hotel. Before the dinner, mid-level officers in the information business will meet in private rooms to establish the protocol for processing intelligence information. We have been working with the

French Surite and others. President Roosevelt has formed a higher-level intelligence organization named "Office of Strategic Services" (OSS).

"We want you to go with us as a Canadian 1st Lt. and as my assistant. Our real concern is the Axis powers could have an agent in one of these groups. No one will pay much attention to a Canadian 1st Lt. Just wander around, have a drink with different ones and go to the bathroom when others go. It's amazing what some senior officers will say in the hearing of a 1st Lt."

While the meetings were going on, I did just that. After the meetings were finished, I was in the bathroom and a French officer came in and went into a stall. Going into an adjoining stall, I peeped under the stall and saw the officer looking at a small device (maybe a camera or recorder?). He placed the device in his pocket and left.

When General Eisenhower and his staff arrived, they formed a reception line and we all went past and shook hands and introduced ourselves. Then we, the major, the captain and I went to dinner at an officer's club. I told them about the French officer and described his insignia to them. The incident may have been harmless, and I never knew what happened afterward.

Summer 1942

In the summer of 1942, our training became intense. We did long endurance marches and cross-country runs to get into top physical shape. We noticed that many units seemed to intensify their training as if something large was about to happen. The last of July, I went back to Commando School to train with three others for a mission. The other three were a British first lieutenant, a Free French sergeant, and a Royal Air Force fighter pilot. Most of the training was to get the fighter pilot in good physical condition, show him how to shoot and how to get on and off a submarine.

Sometime in August, we were briefed for our mission. The mission appeared to be easy enough. We were to go to a place in France at night in a submarine; go ashore and meet a farmer with a horse and wagon. He would conceal us in the wagon and take us several miles inland near a Luftwaffe aerodrome. We would leave the farmer, work our way to the flight line in the darkness and take out any guards if necessary. Then we were to help the fighter pilot, who had been trained to fly German fighter aircraft, start the engine on an ME-109 (Messerschmitt) and as he was taking off, we three were to double time away from the aerodrome. The pilot would fly the aircraft to England while we were going to a predetermined hiding place to spend the rest of the night and the daylight hours of the next day. Then, after dark, we were to meet the farmer again to return to the coast and meet the submarine.

Under the principle of "Need to Know," we were not told everything, but we understood that the Germans were using some kind of fuel additive in the ME-109 that allowed them to out run anything when they were in a tight spot. We studied maps and up to date air-photos and then memorized our route. When all preparations had been made and just before we left England, we were told that there would be a large raid at Dieppe starting at daylight on August 19, 1942. Our mission was to arrive at the aerodrome and leave the aerodrome before daylight. The aerodrome was located to the south of Dieppe. We proceeded as planned. We left the farmer and headed toward the aerodrome about three miles away. We noticed that it was getting dawn, so we hurried. The air photos showed a gully or a wide deep ditch running parallel alongside the runway starting about the middle of the runway and ending about 100 yards from the flight line. Evidently, the Germans had constructed the gully to drain the runway. We planned to use the gully to approach the flight line. A fast conference was held. We were in the open countryside and if we turned back, we would surely be seen at daylight. The only hope we had was to try to reach the gully before daylight and after the pilot took off, shoot our way to a vehicle to use for our escape.

The lieutenant told me to get to the gully as fast as I could, and they would follow as fast as they could. I dropped my combat pack and everything else except my Tommy gun and two extra clips of ammo in my pocket. I sprinted and reached the gully. Looking back, I saw the sun rising and the others running toward the gully. All of the alarms went off because the raid had started at Dieppe. I prayed they would not be seen. A German, in a twenty-foot high tower near the entrance road to the aerodrome, started firing a machinegun at them. All three went down. The machine-gunner continued to hit them to make certain they were dead.

With the alarms sounding, the ground crews started getting all the aircraft ready for takeoff. My only chance was to get to an aircraft and fly it. Leaving the end of the gully, I sprinted toward the flight line. While I was in the open, I sensed the machine-gunner firing at me and something stung my left arm, but as soon as I reached some buildings, he couldn't see me. As I raced, I saw an aircraft with the engine running and the pilot going toward it. In the confusion, maybe I could make it. Two of the unarmed ground crewmen got in my way as they ran to start aircraft. I shot them. As I reached the aircraft with the engine running, a ground crewman was pulling the wheel chocks and the pilot was starting to climb into the cockpit. I shot the crewman and stuck my Tommy gun to the back of the pilot's head and fired. Blood and brains flew everywhere in the cockpit and on me. With my left hand I snatched the pilot back and he fell to the macadam. Climbing into the cockpit, I dropped my Tommy gun and as soon as I could, I grabbed the stick, found the throttle and with my feet found the rudder pedals and throttled up. Going straight out to the runway and then to turn for take off, I almost lost it; I was going too fast and I did not have the feel for the brakes yet to use them to turn. Anyway, I did get lined up with the runway and I had turned so that I could use the longest part of the runway. Not knowing the wind direction, this was all I could do. These seconds seemed like hours. However, the raid on Dieppe and the necessity for all pilots to scramble created enough confusion so that most of the Germans did not know what had happened and they did not fire at me.

Lining up on the runway, I went full throttle. The ME-109 had great speed and power, which I could feel pressing my back against the seat. However, I barely cleared trees and buildings as I pulled up because I didn't use the entire runway. Adrenaline was still flowing as I raced over trees and such at full throttle, but I knew that I had to throttle back and think. I climbed some and started easing back on the throttle. Where to head? To the north was the fighting at Dieppe; to the east and south was nothing but Germans. My only chance was to head west staying over France for a while. Next I had to close the canopy and get the landing gear up. Of course all the instruments and controls were in German. It was cold, but I was sweating. Finally, I found the landing gear control and raised it. Then I could throttle back some more because with the gear down it acted like a brake. The instruments were metric, but I could read the vital ones; such as the compass, tachometer and altimeter. After I calmed down some, I started thinking more clearly.

When I was growing up in Montgomery, I would ride my bicycle out to the Municipal Airport and hang around; sweep the floors, clean up oil and grease for the private pilots who owned aircraft. I didn't have enough money to take lessons, but one of the pilots who gave flying lessons and took people up for rides, let me take off and land his Piper Cub on two occasions when he was checking his engine out after working on it. He showed me the basics of flying, such as stalling out for a landing.

The R.A.F. pilot who was with us must have had a wireless frequency to call for fighter escorts to take him to England. If I crossed the coast of England, I would be shot down. So I turned on the wireless and started listening. Noticing some blood in my left sleeve, I took my khaki handkerchief out of my pocket and tied it around my arm by using one hand and my teeth because I was afraid to turn loose of the stick. Not knowing how to trim the aircraft, it was doing a lot of swaying.

Meanwhile, my course was about southwest to stay over France and when I saw Brest on the Atlantic Ocean, I started a gradual circle to the north so as to miss Land's End at the southwest tip of England. I happened to know there was a radiolocation station there. I increased my altitude to 3,000 meters, which would be about 9,000 feet. Continually turning the dial on the wireless, sometimes I heard English, but I wasn't sure. Many Germans could speak perfect English. After passing around Land's End, I headed north towards St. George's Channel. I thought this is getting bad, real bad. I could head to Ireland, which was a neutral country, and jump except I didn't have a parachute, or I could find a level field and maybe land.

By now, I figured out that the Bristol Channel was due east of me. Suddenly, I heard what had to be R.A.F. pilots talking to each other and to a woman in a control tower at an aerodrome. The woman had to be a WRAF (Women in the Royal Air Force). Pushing the button on the microphone, I said, "This is Alabama, I'm flying an Iron Cross out of Dieppe. I need help." There was a long, static filled silence. Finally, the woman said, "Alabama, repeat your message." I replied, "Wilco, this is Alabama, I'm flying an ME-109. I am not a pilot. TELL EVERYONE NOT TO SHOOT. I need the Texas Air Force to escort me, over." The woman said, "Roger, do not change your frequency, what is your position, over." I replied, "Roger, I'm headed due east toward the Bristol Channel, at about 9,000 feet." The woman said, "Roger, Alabama, help is on the way, keep transmitting, keep talking, over." I replied, "Wilco, tell the guys at the Eagle Club I need their help, I'm tired." I continued to hold the microphone button on and started singing, "It's a Long Way to Tipperary." "Way Down Upon the Suwannee River," "Stars Fell on Alabama," "Yellow Rose of Texas," "Shall We Gather at the River," etc.

When I saw a Spitfire pull up on my port side, I stopped transmitting. Then another one pulled up on my starboard side and another one came down and got in front of me. A pilot said, "Let's go home, Alabama." I replied, "Roger, that." Following the lead pilot, we started going down as we approached an aerodrome. I transmitted, "I need someone to show me how to land. I'm hit, this cockpit is a bloody mess, and I'm trying to fasten the seat belt." I had forgotten to do that. A pilot said, "Alabama, we will get you down. On final approach, we will guide you over the runway and then we will go around, there will be one of us in front of you and one alongside, listen for instructions." I replied, "Wilco." As we went around the pilot said, "Gradually throttle up as you put your landing gear down." I did that. Then the pilot said, "We are lined up to land, I am in front of you, watch what I do. When I throttle all the way back, you do that and gradually pull the stick back to your belly, hold the rudder pedals in the center." I did that. I hit hard, really hard, the first bounce would have put me through the canopy, except I had fastened my seat belt. It was too high when I stalled it. There were more bounces while I held the stick back in my belly as hard as I could. When it settled down, I let it roll. It rolled almost to the end of the runway and stopped. With the engine still running, I unbuckled the seat belt, opened the canopy and started climbing out. Suddenly, people and vehicles surrounded me. Some of them picked me up and laid me down on a stretcher. I'm sure I looked and smelled horrible.

The stretcher was placed in an ambulance, the ambulance headed for the infirmary. My fatigue was so great that everything started to blur as the doctors and nurses started working on me. They cut my clothes off, stopped the bleeding in my left arm, washed my body all over, gave me some shots, x-rayed my arm and then I was asleep.

It took a while for me to wake up. I could hear some voices and when they saw me move, they started giving me water, tea and food. I couldn't remember when I last had water and food; it seemed like a month ago. They told me there was a deep gash in my arm and the bullet must have grazed the bone causing a hairline fracture. They had sewn up the gash and put a cast on my arm, which I had not noticed. As I continued to drink water and eat, I heard someone say, "The air vice-marshal is here."

My hospital type bed was rolled into another larger room that had tables and chairs in it. My thought was, this is for a debriefing. Officers of the air force and army came in and many were high ranking. An army brigadier general handled the introductions. The air vice-marshal was second in command of the R.A.F. They were all seated and told me to continue drinking water while I was being propped up on the bed. The brigadier general must have been in command of commando operations because he did most of the talking. He pulled papers and maps out of his briefcase that turned out to be the entire plan for our mission. The brigadier looked at me and said, "Do you prefer to be called "Alabama" or "Private Houston?" I replied, "It doesn't matter, Sir, but many people know my nick-name and do not know my real name." The brigadier said, "Alabama will be it then. You seem to have many pilot friends and what you did was a bloody great thing. What we want you to do is tell us what happened in your own words, starting at the beginning."

So I started telling them everything I could remember. In the first place, the plan was an excellent plan; the only problem was the timing. I told them in detail how everything went according to the plan. In my opinion, the only miscalculation was the time it took traveling with the farmer because after we left the farmer and realized we were behind schedule, we started double-timing about half the time. When I started talking, the brigadier had another officer pin the maps on the wall and trace our route with his swagger stick as I talked. I told them that if we had had one more hour of darkness, the mission would have been completed as planned and that the other three were only about fifty yards from the gully when they were shot. Some more maps were pinned on the wall and I described my flight to England. An officer did some calculations and said to me, "Alabama, You made a long flight. Weren't you concerned about the petrol (gas) supply?" I replied, "Yes, Sir, but I knew I wasn't going back, so I just might make it. That was just one of my worries, if I had eaten anything, I probably would have lost it." They laughed.

Tea and crumpets were brought in, so we took a break. I noticed that many British Red Caps (Military Police) were round and about. All of this must have been under heavy security. Someone asked about the ME-109 and we were told that it was in a hanger and the engineers were working on it. I said, "Did anyone wash it out?" They laughed again. Some of the officers said they would like to see it.

The meeting was started again and they asked me a number of questions. One of them was, should the others and I have been present at the pilot's briefing so that we would have known the wireless frequency? My reply was, "Sir, I already knew too much to be captured, I would have used the pill anyway." The pill was a small cyanide tablet which when bitten or swallowed caused instant death. The alternative was to be captured, tortured for information and slowly dying. The Germans never considered commandos to be prisoners of war. The officers thought I was correct even under the "Doctrine of Need to Know." The meeting came to an end. An air force officer made arrangements to take some of them to see the aircraft. All of them came by me and shook my hand. My bed was rolled back to my room and I slept some more.

I was given a new battle dress with the proper patches sewn on, suspenders, underwear, socks, shirts and the like. I spent two more days at the aerodrome and the WRAF lady came by to see me, as did some pilots who signed my arm cast. Of course, I received a lot of kidding about my "perfect 3-point landing," "how many times did you land that airplane?" and so forth. I returned to my unit and stayed there about four days. I received some pay and a pass with instructions to go to a certain hospital at a certain time to remove my arm cast.

During this time, I was learning the details of the Dieppe Raid. The 2nd Canadian Infantry Division was the main force and in 8 hours of fighting on shore had many soldiers killed or wounded. This was awesome considering how small the Canadian Army was. They only had 3 infantry divisions, the 1st, 2nd, and 3rd and this loss was great. The Royal Navy was offshore providing fire support and the R.A.F. was providing air cover and close-in support. One of the London newspapers headlines read: "YANKS LAND IN EUROPE." The article went on to explain that some United States Marines were onboard one of the ships as observers. There were many Allied observers on the ships because this was the prelude to the Allied invasion of Normandy on D-Day. I talked with some friends in the Cameron Highlanders who were there. They told me how tough it was to get out. One Canadian soldier had a Boyes Anti-Tank Rifle and he stayed behind firing at the German machine gunners so the others could get out. He kept firing until they got him.

I went on leave and when I arrived at the Eagle Club I received more kidding by the pilots who were there. They told me that I was now a member of the "Texas Air Force." At the hospital my arm cast was removed and the stitches in my arm were pulled out. After x-rays the doctors said that everything was healed

After returning to camp I received a message from my friend, the major in the apartment in London. After arrival there I noticed that the major was now a lieutenant Colonel and the captain was now a major. They explained why they wanted to see me. Every so often they had dinner meetings at an officers' club with their Allied counterparts. (meaning intelligence officers). They wanted me to go with them to a dinner meeting and some American and Free French would be there. The Free French especially wanted to talk with me about the mission. The colonel told me that I could speak freely with them about all the details. When we were getting ready to go, the colonel put two pips (1st lieutenant) on each shoulder of my battle dress. As the war went on and on all officers and enlisted personnel stopped wearing dress uniforms and started wearing the battle dress all the time. All battle dresses were identical so all I needed to do, other than wearing the pips, was to wear an officer's balmoral in lieu of my tam-o'shanter.

At the Officers' club we went into a private room setup with a table and chairs for dinner and a small bar setup to serve ourselves. There were four American officers and three Free French officers there besides us. After introductions we poured our drinks and sat down to talk. The American Officers were from the United States OSS (Office of Strategic Services). As I started telling them about the mission I could understand the concern of the Free French. Had any of their resistance people been compromised? The Free French sergeant was the only French connection the Germans would know about. I reassured them that there could not be any connection made to the farmer and the French Sergeant. The lieutenant and the pilot were all good soldiers and died while doing their duty. After we finished all questions about the mission, the others started discussions about other intelligence business. Why was I allowed to hear these things? The answer is simple. They knew that all commandos take a special oath of silence and to violate that oath is treason.

After we returned to the apartment, we talked some. The colonel told me there was some talk about me getting a medal, perhaps the Victoria Cross. I told them about the Canadian Soldier that stayed behind to help the others get out and was killed. That is real bravery. In my opinion, the Victoria Cross is the highest honor any soldier in the world could receive. Not many are awarded and most of them are posthumous. I said, "Why not award the Canadian Soldier who died, the Victoria Cross? And besides that, I have already signed the papers to transfer to the United States Army."

They seemed to be saddened because I would be leaving but they said that they understood. They asked me how long I had been gone from Alabama. I told them and then they asked: "How old are you now Alabama?" I replied, "I'm nineteen now, sir." Then, the colonel told me that they had planned to award me a field commission as a 1st Lt. but had waited until I was old enough. They told me that they wanted me to do "odd" jobs for them. They wished me well and we went to bed.

Summer & Fall 1942

Immediately, after returning to camp, I received orders to report to an officer at a British Depot located at Thursley, Surrey, England, to transfer to the United States Army. My friend, Roy Palmer, was not there. He had already left to transfer to the United States Army. Evidently, those who had signed up for transfer were called up in small groups. I told Bruce and Lornie and others goodbye, good luck. I turned in my weapons, ammo, packs and such, to the supply sergeant. I kept my knife, some personal items in a kit bag and my clean battle dress to wear. My kilt uniform was in a kit bag at some friend's house where I had started leaving it. I stopped by and picked it up on my way to Thursley.

The British Depot at Thursley was a busy place. Those of us who were to transfer to the U.S. Army were placed in a barracks together. This was a mixed group from different units. Some of the sergeant pilots that I had met at the Eagle Club were there. While walking around in the evening, I accidentally ran into one of my sergeants who was there to return to Officers Training School in Canada. He insisted that I go with him to the non-commissioned officers' quarters to see the others. My other sergeants who studied together with us were there plus sergeants from other units. They setup a bar and the first thing they did was hand me a drink. The second thing my sergeants did was to introduce me, "Alabama," to the others. My sergeants bragged so much about me until I was embarrassed. Anyway, we had a good time telling old stories.

The next day, we were given a written exam, then a physical exam. We entered a long barracks type building, stripped down, formed a line and were examined by British doctors of different specialties. We were X-rayed and then given all the required military shots from A to Z. At the center of this building was a door. When we stepped through this door, the American doctors did the same things. We protested having to take the same shots again, but the doctors said they were required to give shots and record them for anyone enlisting in the U.S. Army. The British doctors said that they were required to give shots and record them for anyone being discharged from their army. We were caught up in professional jealously because each doctor did not want to miss anything that his counterpart might find. They did find that one soldier had tuberculosis and he didn't know it.

Everyone had been saying we would be transferred. However, we were not really being transferred, we were being discharged from His Majesty's Forces and then enlisting in the United States Forces. The United States Army had sent a recruiting officer, a captain, and staff to the British Depot. When we had finished all of the requirements, we went into a room to be sworn into the United States Army.

The Captain said, "You will receive your discharges from His Majesty's Forces and your final pay immediately after you are sworn in." The captain continued, "Something important for you to know, in the past groups there were some people who were already in the U. S. Army that were sworn in; that is illegal and they are now in trouble. If any of you are already in the U. S. Army, tell me now and I can handle it without any problem." Soldiers started speaking up. One named Farr said, "Sir, I was in the army in Panama." One named Pitts said, "Sir, I was in the army in the Philippines." One named Eddie Aftewitz said, "Sir, I was in the army in China" (he told me later that he had deserted with his company commander's wife). One named Kosmic said, "Sir, I was in the U.S. Marines in China." Then I said, "Sir, I am in the U.S. Navy." The captain said, "All of you step aside," and he swore in the others. Then he told those who were already in the army to wait and he would interview them and take care of the details. Then he told Kosmic and me to go see the Naval Attaché at the United States Embassy, Grovenor Square, London, to get our discharges.

I went to my barracks, showered, packed a small bag, put on my kilt uniform and went to the U.S. Embassy. Kosmic told me, "To hell with it, I don't want to serve in the army. Since I can't go back to the marines, I'll stay where I am." When I walked into the huge foyer of the Embassy, the marines on guard duty started saluting me. I returned the salutes with the British salute; knowing all the time that they could not read British insignia. I spotted a sergeant sitting at a desk at the bottom of a grand stairway. When I walked over to him, he stood up, saluted and said, "May I help you, Sir?" I said, "Yes, I am here to see the Naval Attaché." He said, "Just a moment, Sir," as he picked up the phone and made a call. After the call, he said, "The Naval Attaché is in and he will see you, Sir." The sergeant gave me directions to his office. I went up the stairs and found the correct door. When I went in a yeoman first class escorted me to an inner office of a navy commander. The commander was seated at a huge desk loaded with papers. I saluted. The commander looked up and said, "What may I do for you?" I said, "Sir, I would like to get a discharge from the navy." He replied, "Navy, what navy?" I replied, "Sir, the United States Navy." He told me that the only thing he could do would be to send a dispatch to Washington and ask for instructions. He told me to sit down and he called the yeoman in. He said, "State all of the details and the yeoman will prepare a dispatch." I stated all the details; including my serial number and the things that had happened in Norfolk. The reason I needed a discharge was I could not be sworn into the U.S. Army without it. He appeared to sympathize with me and told me to return in a few days to see what instructions would come from Washington. I thanked him and returned to the depot. In a few days, I returned to the commander's office at the embassy. The commander said, "I'm sorry, Washington is busy with other matters, but all we need is a simple answer and I will keep trying."

Of course, Washington was loaded with military officers who attended great parties to increase their rank. To understand this, my case was minor and who cares? Therefore, my conclusion was I needed some help. Naval Attaché's throughout the world are in the intelligence business. This commander must have heard something about me because he tried to help. Anyway, all I could do was to see my friend, the major (who was now a colonel) in the apartment in London. Without an appointment, I went there and the staff sergeant whom I knew let me in. He was now a sergeant major. He told me the colonel was out. "He'll be back in two or three hours and if you will wait, I am sure he will want to talk with you." When the colonel arrived, I told him about my problem and he said, "Damn, they must love paperwork. Alabama, go back to see the commander three days from now. I'll tell them it is needed for the war effort or something." I thanked him and returned to Thursley.

In three days, I was back in the commander's office. He said, "Alabama, we have received instructions to give you a dishonorable discharge. I don't agree with it, but it will not matter when you serve honorably with the U.S. Army, it will be the same as if it were cancelled." Somebody up high must have talked to somebody. How did he know my nickname was "Alabama"? The yeoman filled out the discharge and the commander signed it and gave it to me. He and the yeoman wished me luck. I thanked them and returned to the British Depot.

I went to the recruiting captain's office and showed him my U.S. Navy discharge and he said, "Another group has arrived and you can join them. You will have to repeat the procedure as you did before." That meant I would have to take the written exam, the physical exams and the shots over again; which I did. After I was sworn in with the others, on September 3, 1942, the captain gave us the necessary tickets, papers and so forth to proceed to Liverpool by train and then by ship to Belfast, Ireland, where trucks would meet us and carry us to the replacement depot. We were all given a new serial number. I thought, I am still a teenager and this is my fourth serial number. Later, I found out our serial number series was lower than the regular army and we were considered to be regular army because we had enlisted. We didn't ever have a draft board. There were not many of us, about 300 that had enlisted in England. Army clerks prided themselves because they knew all the draftee serial numbers as well as the regular army serial numbers. We would have trouble from now on with the clerks because they had never heard of our series of service numbers. We all went to the British paymaster and received our discharges and final pay. This was my third military discharge.

We arrived in Belfast with the only event worth noting was that on the ship everyone became seasick except me. I kept on eating with the chairs and tables sliding across the deck. The trucks met us at the dock in Belfast and carried us to the replacement depot at Ballymena, Ireland. We checked in and were told we were free to look around until the next morning. I went to a dance that evening sponsored by the N.A.A.F.I., still wearing my kilt uniform. As I met different girls, they would ask me, "Are you Protestant or Catholic?" I replied, "Which are you?" Then I would be whatever they were. Sometimes people would ask me, "How do people of different religions get along so well in America?" I told them, "We don't think about it much. The United States is a republic with a constitution that requires freedom of religion and a complete separation of church and state. Religion is a matter of personal choice."

Fall 1942

The next morning after breakfast at the replacement depot (Repo-Depot), we were informed that we would be interviewed one at a time and this would take a long time as there were about thirty in our group. In the meanwhile, the rest of us were issued uniforms and other equipment by the supply sergeants. When it was my turn to be interviewed, they asked about my training and so forth. There were many high-ranking officers there, including a brigadier general. They wanted to assign me to the commanding general's defense platoon. I had heard that Roy Palmer had been assigned to the defense platoon. Since I didn't want to be around generals I declined. I requested to go to the rangers or airborne, but they said it was not possible to do this overseas. So I was assigned to an infantry line company in the 34th Infantry Division. The 34th was the Minnesota-Iowa National Guard and was the first National Guard Division to be federalized in 1941 for World War II. They also were the first division to go overseas, having arrived in Ireland in January, 1942, after Pearl Harbor in December, 1941.

That evening I went to the same dance that I had gone to the night before. This time I was wearing my new Class A United States Army uniform. When I met the same girls, they were dumb-founded, so I had to explain how I changed armies.

The next day, the interviews continued and we did close order drill for a couple of hours, led by drill sergeants who were changed every thirty minutes, while the officers watched. They did their best to make one or more of us goof. Finally, they told the officers, "These guys know drill better than we do." Some of us were assigned to different line companies and some went to other places. There was one guy that had been a sergeant in the Royal Army and was in command of a radio location station. Also, he had served as a captain in the U.S. Army during the Mexican border troubles. He was given a field commission as a captain and was sent immediately to the United States. Another one had been to West Point for three years and was a sergeant in the Royal Artillery. He was given a field commission as a captain and was assigned to the division artillery.

After packing my kilt uniform, battle dress, and other items in a canvas kit bag, I carried it to the postal clerk to mail it to my parents. I told the clerk that if all of it didn't get there, I would find him and hurt him bad. He assured me it would get there. Although it was not necessary (we got free postage) I gave him some money anyway. I kept my Tam-o-Shanter and all of my papers. My Tam-o-Shanter and papers were carried inside my shirt wrapped in a gas cape which I had cut up to use because it was waterproof. Later, I heard that when the postman delivered the kit bag to my home, the neighbors thought I was dead and the government was sending my belongings home.

We were transported by U.S. Army 6x6 trucks to our different assignments. My battalion with its four line companies, plus a headquarters company, was in a camp of Nissen huts in the boondocks about twenty miles from Enniskillen. Enniskillen is close to the Southern Ireland border and located on the River Shannon which goes to the Atlantic Ocean at Donegal Bay. I reported to the 34th Infantry Division (Red Bull Division or as the Germans later called us the "Skull Division"), United States Army. I was directed to my platoon, squad, and a GI (Government Issue) folding cot in one of the Nissen huts.

It's always the same old story; new kid on the block. A new soldier in an old outfit. It takes a while to fit in and for some, they never do. Because this was a National Guard Division, the companies were filled with friends, cousins, and brothers, from the same small towns. I didn't speak much, but when I did, they could not figure out where I was from because my accent had changed. Some thought that I was from New England. Soon there was payday. The Canadian and British Army had paid us every two weeks and if you missed one or had an emergency, you could get some pay from any Canadian or British paymaster in the world. The Canadian pay was $40.30 per month for a private. However, for those overseas, one half of their pay was deposited in an interest earning account in the Bank of Canada, so that soldiers would not come home broke. If a soldier was married, their wives and children received an allotment until the children were twenty-one and the wife received an allotment for life if the soldier was killed. This allotment was discontinued if the soldier survived and was discharged. Because I was an American volunteer, my one-half pay was deposited in the Chase National Bank of New York.

When the U.S. paymaster arrived and setup his table at our company, everyone got in line for pay. The process takes hours and if anyone was absent for any reason, his name would be "red lined" and he would have to wait until the next month for pay. Payments were made in alphabetical order with one exception. I was the exception. My name was called first because I was regular army. This caused more resentment, there were mumbles and gripes all along the line. I got paid and went about my own business. That night, there was poker playing and dice shooting in the huts. I heard three soldiers in our hut talking about how they were going to get the hillbilly into a poker game and take all his pay. Soldiers would talk in front of me because they did not know I was from Alabama. The hillbilly was a replacement obviously from the southern hills. These soldiers thought he was dumb because of the way he talked. Sometimes he did sound like he only had one oar in the water. I watched them play and the hillbilly acted like he didn't know much about the game. Every now and then they would explain it to him. With all three of them playing against him, he started winning and winning until he got all of their pay. They never did understand how smart he was. They blamed it on dumb luck.

One of the colonels that was present at my interview at the Repo-Depot came to see me. He was on the staff of the general in command of the division, as the division training officer. He wanted me to help train my battalion. We talked at length. For example, the U.S. Army had purchased gas capes from the British, and no one knew how to wear or tie them. We were in the office of the lieutenant colonel commanding our battalion, and he and other officers were present. The division colonel told the lieutenant colonel to setup a training schedule so that I could give instructions on certain subjects and in particular new weapons and new tactics. The next morning, the entire battalion assembled together. The division colonel spoke and then introduced me.

I had brought with me everything that we wore in the field, including my rifle and pack. Taking a gas cape, I demonstrated how it strapped on under the pack and then rolled it so that it was on my back and above my pack. Pulling the string that kept it rolled up, I was completely covered in two seconds from my boots to the hood flipped over my steel helmet. My rifle was slung over my shoulder upside down under the cape. But first, I had placed my respirator mask over my face before pulling the string. (Americans called it a "gas mask," but it wasn't.) I went through the procedure several times. Then I told them that the British had stopped wearing gas capes (they made good raincoats) and respirators because there was an unwritten agreement that neither side would use war gas. I talked about many things such as new weapons, new squad formations, no more heavy weapons companies or platoons because they couldn't move fast enough, no more trench warfare, the concept of armored infantry, how we had trained with tanks and how the British 8th Army and the German Afrika Korps were using armored infantry in the desert. Some of the officers asked questions about my training; which I answered. Some of them seemed to think I was lying when I told them about the seventy-two hour endurance tests, marching forty miles in a day, and the like. When I finished, the division colonel said, "Thank you, sergeant, all of you soldiers who came to us from the British can be a great help to us." I replied, "I am glad to help, Sir, but I am not a sergeant, I am a private." The division colonel turned to the lieutenant colonel and said, "This man should be a sergeant, make him a sergeant." The lieutenant colonel said, "Sir, all of our ranks are filled." The colonel replied, "I don't give a blankety-blank, I said make him a sergeant." The lieutenant colonel replied, "Yes, Sir." I was made a sergeant, but I never did sew on the stripes.

An order from on high was sent to all units in the 34th Infantry Division. All personnel who had enlisted in the U.S. Army from the British were to report to the United States Consulate in Belfast to get their American citizenship back. We were given a 6x6 truck. We did not need a driver; others and I had a British internal combustion engine license. We headed for Belfast. When we stopped on the way to take a leak, some of them stepped off the right of way and sank up to their knees in a black peat bog. There are many peat bogs in Ireland where it rains nearly every day. Arriving at the U.S. Consulate in Belfast, we started our processing. It was explained that we had to renounce our allegiance to all foreign royalties, potentates, and the like. We had to give them our names, parents' names, places and dates of birth, and whatever. We were told that it would take a good while to write everything up and therefore, come back tomorrow. Also, you may stay at the military police barracks and eat there. We had parked our truck there with the M.P. vehicles. The M.P.'s had a special cafeteria style large dining room. The food was very good and it appeared to be open at all hours. Many other American officials ate there. While I was talking with some of the M.P.s, we would ask each other where we were from. When I told them I was from Montgomery, Alabama, one of them said, "Our first sergeant is from Montgomery." I went to see him. He was from Highland Park in Montgomery where I was born and lived. He was older than I, but I remembered his name and knew his younger brother and he knew my older brothers. He also knew about me going to Canada.

The next morning, we returned to the Consulate. We were photographed and finger printed. Assembled together, a consulate official led us in the swearing in ceremony, as we held up our right hands, we repeated the oath the same as immigrants do to become United States citizens. We were given a citizenship paper and an identification fold up type card from the Adjutant General's Office, United States, complete with photograph, fingerprints and the United States Consulate's embossed seal, to use as a passport.

Having completed our business at the consulate, it was time to return to camp. However, since we might not have another chance, we all decided to stay over our leave time and see the town. Someone said that the U.S. Army overseas considers anyone AWOL over seventy-two hours to be a deserter. Therefore, we agreed to meet back at the truck in time to drive back to camp before seventy-two hours would be up. I went to several large dance halls and wandered around the city. When we arrived back at camp, we were notified that we would be court-martialed by our respective captains. When I was standing before my captain to be court-martialed the next day, he seemed to be more interested in the British court-martial procedure than anything else. Of course, my rank was reduced to private and the rest of the sentence was to march to a small village and back each night for one week, starting at 12:00 midnight (2400 hours). The sentence was predetermined because it did not matter what company we were in, the sentence was the same for all of us. The older soldiers who had enlisted with me almost drove the officers nuts by addressing them in the third person singular, which was the old army style and still legal.

We fell in formation at the battalion headquarters each night at midnight where we were met by M.P.s in a jeep. They were heavily armed, including a machinegun mounted on the jeep. The jeep was driven slowly back of us as we marched. It usually took four hours to march to the village and back using the U.S. Army cadence. We sang British Army songs such as "Bless them all, the long and the short and the tall; bless the corporals and their blanked sons, bless all the sergeants and W. O. ones -----" (Vulgarity has been deleted by using "Bless," etc.) Sometimes, when we felt like it, we would use the Highland cadence and speed up. We made up another song, "You Have To Be From Minnesota To Get Along In The Orderly Room." We heard a rumor that they really wanted to teach us a lesson. Another rumor was our medical doctors complained that our sentence was too harsh. One day during the week of our punishment, we had to do a twenty-mile march. Everyone was watching us to see if any of us would fall out. The lieutenant colonel was riding in his jeep and continued to ride up and down the line, stopping by each of us and saying, "Are you all right?" Each of us replied, "YES, SIR!" They still did not understand the extent of our previous Canadian and British Army training. A twenty-mile march was a big deal for the U.S. Army. Many of the soldiers would soak their feet when we returned to our huts. The Canadians and British did not believe in soaking of the feet because it made them softer.

All of these things continued to build resentment between us newcomers and the old ones. There were only about twenty of us who had enlisted at the British Depot in this battalion. Our older former regular army soldiers started calling the National Guard "Saturday Night Soldiers." The regular army soldiers did not like National Guard soldiers. During the close order drills, different soldiers would give the commands for practice. Whenever one of us gave the commands, we did better than the officers or sergeants.

Some Saturday nights some trucks would go to Enneskillen, and I would go when I could because there was a café there that served steak and eggs. I had not eaten that for years. One time I was eating something in our mess hall that was good but I could not, for the life of me, remember the name of it. I went into the kitchen and asked the cooks what it was. They showed me a can. It turned out to be sweet potatoes, which was one of our most important foods when I was growing up. I thought, Lord, I have been gone from Alabama too long.

One day I was scheduled to instruct the men in the use of the Mills hand grenade, bayonet-drill, unarmed combat and the like. We gathered together on our drill field, which was a grassy meadow. The officers and enlisted men sat down around me. The British grenade was the standard Government Issue (GI) for the U.S. Army during World War I and afterwards. The supply sergeant placed a wooden case of grenades in front of me. I demonstrated the three methods used to throw them without pulling the cotter pin because these were live. I had twelve men at a time to line up and throw them using all three methods. When everyone had taken their turns, they agreed that my method was the best. Then I demonstrated how to take them apart to short fuse them. Some of them were getting nervous and moving back.

Next we practiced bayonet drill and I asked some of the sergeants to help me demonstrate. With the bayonets attached to the rifles, I had them put the scabbards on to prevent accidental cuts. While they used the U.S. Army drill, I used the German Army drill against them to demonstrate what they needed to do to counter the German drill.

With the scabbards still on the bayonets, I wrapped my arms up with towels to demonstrate unarmed combat against the bayonet. We did most of this in slow motion because they were not trained enough to speed it up. I was hoping they would learn something useful. There was not enough time for complete training. I explained things that I had learned. A first lieutenant said, "I don't believe you. Do you mean to say you can take me while I am holding a rifle with a naked bayonet?" I replied, "Yes, Sir, but we don't practice that without extensive training because someone would get hurt." I was praying that he would drop it. He picked up a rifle and removed the scabbard and said, "I still don't believe you. Are you yellow or just afraid"? I replied, "Very well, Sir, just remember you are insisting and I don't want to hurt you." He said, "Everybody move back. I'm going to take this blow-hard." He moved the rifle from port arms to the bayonet thrust position. I'm sure he thought I would move backwards because that is the natural thing to do. Instead, I moved at full speed into him. Because he was right handed, I slapped the bayonet with my right hand making the bayonet and rifle go to my left and his right. This was to prevent him from following through to hit me with the rifle butt. My moves were like a football player throwing a high block, knocking the opponent back and down. As soon as I slapped the bayonet with my right hand, I grabbed the rifle with my left hand, pushing it further sideways and at the same time hitting him in the nose with the palm of my right hand and sticking my spread out fingers into his eyes. He was falling down backwards and had to let go of the rifle to use his hands to protect his eyes. When he hit the ground on his back, I swung the rifle and bayonet around and stood there with the bayonet against his throat. His nose was bleeding and he had his hands over his eyes. I had tried to poke his eyes just enough to make him turn the rifle loose. I stood over him for a few seconds, laid the rifle down and walked away. No one said a word. No one would look me in the eyes.

Fall 1942

We received orders to prepare to move. We stopped training, cleaned and checked weapons and did all the odds and ends to move. Our "ninety-day wonder" second lieutenant commanding our platoon came around asking us if we needed anything; parts for our weapons, etc. A soldier was sitting on his bunk cleaning his BAR and said, "Yes, Sir, I need a bayonet stud for my BAR" The second lieutenant went to the company supply sergeant and asked for one. The sergeant told him that he was out of them, but to try battalion supply. The second lieutenant hastened to battalion supply where the sergeant there told him he was out, but to try regimental supply. Our captain noticed the second lieutenant walking fast and asked him what he was doing. The second lieutenant told him. The captain said, "Lieutenant, those guys are pulling your leg. A Browning Automatic Rifle does not have a bayonet stud." Embarrassed, the ninety-day wonder disappeared. I thought, "Oh, Lord, this is our leadership and the soldiers are still playing boy-scout tricks. They have no concept of battle."

I was in our hut when a soldier sitting on his cot started unloading a GI Browning 45 caliber automatic pistol to clean it. He was working the receiver fast, back and forth, to unload the clip and it fired. The bullet hit the soldier on the next cot; blowing his stomach apart. Some of these pistols had been in U.S. armories since World War I and if the seer is worn down, this can happen. The soldier made two gross errors. First, he should have removed the ammo clip and checked the chamber to see if it was loaded. Second, the pistol should have been pointed straight at the floor or straight at the ceiling.

Next, another hard to believe thing happened. Our captain went to our lieutenant colonel and told him that he did not have the heart to order soldiers into battle to be killed! He was transferred to the regimental trucking company to be its commanding officer! After this, our officers and sergeants changed so often, it was hard for me to keep up with who was in command.

When it was time for us to leave, we were ordered to leave our extra clothes in the Company Street. The Company Street was mostly a mud-hole when it rained. My extra boots and some of my clothes were brand new, having never been worn. I thought, what a waste. About 18,000 men in a division were dropping clothes in the mud. I left mine in the hut.

We were transported by truck convoy to a port and boarded a ship which crossed the North Channel of the Irish Sea during the night. We disembarked at a small port in Scotland and pitched our pup tents. I noticed a small village up high in the hills about a mile away. Just after dark that evening, I went up there and found a small fish and chips place. I bought some and promptly ate them. To me, fish and chips were one of the best meals in the United Kingdom. One time I asked somebody why were they so good. They replied, "It's all in the grease, they save it and use it over and over again." I don't know if they were kidding me or not.

Next, I went into the local pub and ordered a beer. The civilians and a few British soldiers were singing and throwing darts, as usual. So I started singing the Highland songs with them. Gradually, they stopped singing and started staring at me. Then I realized I was wearing a United States Army uniform, which they had never seen. I explained and removed my tam o'shanter from inside my shirt and put it on. When I did that, they bought me a beer and we sang some more.

The next day, we repacked and marched to a railway station. A troop train carried us to the Midlands. We left the train in a small town and stayed in some buildings there for a few days.

SUCK A ROCK 23: Somewhere in Ireland, Scotland, England
& North Africa

Then, we boarded another troop train in the night and arrived at the shipping docks in Liverpool at daylight. We waited and waited on the docks all day. There were many rumors going around about where we were going. That night, we boarded ships and before daylight, the ships formed a convoy in the Irish Sea. I happened to be on a destroyer that I had been on before. I am not certain, but if my memory is correct, it was the H.M.S. Malcolm (His Majesty's Ship). Anyway, I volunteered to work with the crew again. That way, I got better food and didn't have to stay with seasick soldiers. As I have written before, the British sailors called me "Lofty." I had to remember to keep left on ladders and passageways. It soon came known to me that we were going somewhere in Africa.

The voyage was uneventful, except several times in the Atlantic Ocean off of France, Spain, and Portugal, battle stations were sounded. The destroyers protecting the flanks of the convoy fired depth charges as they made full speed runs. All of the ships in the convoy were British, and in addition to the war ships, there were many freighters carrying supplies to the British 8th Army and some American supplies. We heard, on a BBC broadcast, of Lieutenant General Bernard Montgomery's great victory at El-Alamein. This was the first major allied victory in the Europe-Africa-Mid-East Theater of Operations and was the turning point of the war. Field Marshall Alexander had been in command of operations in Africa and the Middle East until Lieutenant General Montgomery was promoted to Field Marshall after El-Alamein.

Arriving at Gibraltar, some of the freighters docked to unload supplies. Other ships anchored in the harbour, which was the usual procedure for convoys going to and from the Middle East. While at Gibraltar, all of the Americans were ordered to stay below decks. Someone said that Gibraltar was the most spied upon place in the world; being one of the major crossroads for ships. Also, neutral Spain was close by. One of the sailors loaned me a British Navy uniform. In addition to wearing my U.S. dog tags, I was still wearing my Canadian dog tags. Because I had valid identification, the captain allowed me to go ashore with some of the crew. There was a town with many houses where military families lived in peacetime. We looked around and went to some pubs. Through the decades, the British had carved out a fortress deep into the rocks. Huge coastal artillery batteries could fire in any direction and since these guns were larger than those on any battleships, they could sink an entire fleet of ships before they ever got within firing range.

We returned to our ship and were soon headed east in the Mediterranean Sea. One of the strange things that I did not know was that mirages can be seen on the sea as well as on the desert, we all saw them on this voyage. Just before making landfall, all hands were given a final briefing, both sailors and soldiers. Our ship and some others would land at Algiers. Other ships would land at Oran and Casablanca. We were not in the only convoy. Some convoys were coming in from the United States. There were no Germans or Italians at these ports. The ports were under the command of the Vichy French, but the understanding was neither side would fire. The harbours at Algiers and Oran were the state-of-the-art type, having been designed and built by the same French engineers that worked on the Suez and Panama Canals.

One night, as we steamed toward Algiers, some ships went down. Whether they were hit by torpedoes or had collided, I never did know. We saw a flash of light in the distance. We learned later that some of our equipment and supplies were lost. My writing has been mostly about what the Allies were doing. However, it is necessary to understand some of the things that the Nazis and Fascist were doing in the Mediterranean. They had gunboats similar to our PT boats. They had submarines and ships of war. The entire Italian Navy was in the Mediterranean and they had air superiority. The island of Malta was the most bombed place on earth. Of course, the British had some naval forces, including aircraft carriers with marine spitfires. British convoys had to run the "gauntlet" of attacks, especially near Sicily and Malta south of Sicily.

When we reached the entrance to the harbor at Algiers, in November, it was discovered that the Vichy French had placed a "boom" across the entrance. The "boom" consisted of a very heavy chain running across the channel and supported by floats. The destroyers formed a line and one after another rammed the chain to break it. When our destroyer rammed the chain, the Vichy French fired one round from one of the coastal artillery guns at it. The shell hit our destroyer on the starboard side just at the water line. The explosion made a hole about twelve feet in diameter allowing some flooding. The sailors quickly performed damage control and had hoses in place with pumps running before there was any serious flooding. The captain ordered the helmsman to steer a course down the coast to find a suitable beach to get the soldiers ashore because his first duty was always to save the troops.

The American soldiers were nervous and milling about, going from one deck to another and then another. The captain ordered me to find the lieutenant colonel in command of the soldiers and bring him to the bridge because he didn't want to use the speaker system to call him. This would have created more confusion. I found the lieutenant colonel and led him to the bridge. The captain was very stern with the lieutenant colonel because he was not commanding the soldiers, as he should have been. The captain said, "You get on the speaker and tell your men that everyone is safe. We are going to land on the beach. Then you order all officers and men to form up by squad, platoon and company on the open deck. You will be put on the beach in an orderly fashion, not as a mob." The captain handed the mike to the lieutenant colonel, who repeated the captain's orders. After that, the captain told the lieutenant colonel to stay on the bridge and wait for further orders.

A fairly level beach was spotted. Then I observed one of the greatest examples of professional seamanship that I could imagine. The captain did not head the ship straight in to ground it. As the depth was being called out and the bottom contours noted, the captain had the ship proceed very slowly at an angle to the shoreline. As the hull slowly went aground, all engines were stopped and the ship slowly listed to the port side making the starboard side, where the damage was, lift up so the damage could be repaired. Immediately, some of the crew started welding frames and steel plate to repair the hole. Other crewmembers started getting the boats ready to launch on the port side.

All of the soldiers were issued a "Class D" ration, which was a dense chocolate malt bar. You couldn't really bite it, but you could nibble on it. The soldiers were instructed to leave their barracks bags, heavy machineguns (water-cooled) and mortars onboard. We were wearing patches of the U.S. flag on each arm as well as our division patch, on our field jackets. We had larger U.S. flags on the backs of our jackets. The reason for this was the people and other Allied soldiers where we were going, had never seen a U.S. soldier. Also, the U.S. Army had recently changed from the British type round steel helmet to one that looked more like the German helmet. There were some other changes made after we left Ireland. We now had camouflage netting on our helmets and olive drab wool neck protectors, which we tied to our helmet liners.

The sailors launched the boats and carried squad after squad to the beach where they got out and waded ashore in shallow water. Some of us could have swam ashore, but the captain said equipment would be lost because we were still in deep water, due to the draft of the destroyer. All of this took about two hours and I was still on the bridge when the captain and all hands gradually relaxed. Everyone had been at battle stations for many hours. I jokingly said, "Sir, I do believe that I read in the KR&R, that a rum ration will be given to all hands at certain times and at the discretion of the commanding officer at anytime after long and hazardous duty." The captain said, "Lofty, you are bloody well right and I hope we are never in this situation again." The captain gave the order to the chief boatswains mate to sound off the cancellation of "battle stations." Then he ordered the chief to sound off the rum ration; those still on duty to receive theirs later. The stewards came up to the bridge bringing the bottles of rum and mugs. They poured each mug full and passed them out. As we sipped our rum and watched the boats carrying the soldiers ashore, I saw the captain, the executive officer and the others smile for the first time. I had told some of them about being at the helm of the U.S.S. Wasp and other things. I then found out that they knew other things about me. They knew that I was called "Alabama." They never miss or assume anything. I had pulled duty at the helm and any other thing that I could do to help the crew. Standing watches 8 hours on duty and 8 hours off everyday forever is not easy to do, especially if you do not have a full crew. Anyway, it was sad for me to leave such a good crew. The captain said, "I have received a wireless from the admiral. A sea-going tug and a destroyer will soon be here in case we need any help." We all said goodbye and the lieutenant colonel and I boarded the last boat going ashore.

On the beach, there was still some confusion regarding what to do next. I had an advantage. I have stated before how much I like maps. It is times like these that maps save lives. When I was standing watches on the destroyer bridge, the exec. (Executive officer, second in command) and other officers allowed me to study the charts and British Army maps for inland areas. Watching the navigator plot our courses during the voyage was a pleasure for me. The navigator showed me the exact spot where we went ashore. This was about twenty miles west of Algiers toward a small place named Cherchell. What we had to do was cross the mountains along the coast and head to the south, in order to reach a road on the other side. The road ran west to Algiers and east to Oran. I told the lieutenant colonel all of this, and that I spoke enough French to get by. It would take at least two days to reach the other Americans at Algiers because we would have to climb across the high ground. The lieutenant colonel said, "Houston, I want you to be our forward scout and I'll lead the men behind you." I replied, "Yes, Sir, I may have to backtrack now and then to find a place to cross. If I do, just stop so the men can rest." I knew that it would take a while for those men who were seasick to recover.

We traveled some that day and while it was still daylight, I found a place to stop for the night. I had read that in the desert there is not much twilight time. When I saw some of them start eating their "C" rations and drinking their water, I shouted, "Everybody listen up, save all the food and water you can. There will not be anymore until we reach Algiers, which will take at least two days." One of them said, "Sarge, you didn't eat anything, what are you gonna do?" I replied, "I'm sucking on a rock and in the morning, every one of you should find a nice rock and suck on it all day if you want to stay alive. Now, get all the sleep you can and keep your rifles loaded and by your side, but don't shoot any ghosts." I took my rock out of my mouth and showed it to them. Finding a good hiding place in the rocks, I went to sleep as if I were alone.

The next morning the lieutenant colonel seemed to have more confidence. He called the officers together and ordered them to assume more command over their units. He continued to talk to them about the stragglers we had yesterday and said, "It had better not happen again, either you officers or your sergeants will be in the rear of your units to help your men. If any soldier gets lost in this wild place, he will die. You will control what your men eat or drink or they will never make it."

By the way, this was not the same lieutenant colonel that we originally had in Ireland. The one in Ireland was much older and wore a hearing aid. My opinion is that the older Lt. Col. would not have been able to travel through these mountains. We moved all that day, stopping each hour for a ten-minute break. The only encouragement was when we started going down hill. I was about a quarter of a mile ahead of them and thought I could see the road in the distance, but since it was getting late, I stopped and waited for them to reach me and stop for the night. I didn't say anything about the road because it might be a false hope.

The next day we made better time going downhill, and when everyone knew the road was in sight, the pace increased. Reaching the road, we headed east towards Algiers. That night, I told them my guess was that it was still about fifteen miles to Algiers, but save some food and water for tomorrow. The next afternoon we reached some American soldiers who had made a pup tent camp outside of the city. They gave us some "C" rations and water. We pitched our pup tents and went to sleep.

Fall 1942

In the morning we found out where some other units were camped. The unit that we had joined had a few trucks and jeeps which they were using to go back and forth to the harbor docks to pick up equipment and supplies being brought there by Liberty Ships (freighters) from the United States. Other troops were also arriving from time to time. One day I went to the docks in one of the trucks and watched a Liberty Ship coming in to dock. Keep in mind that the captains of these ships were not used to docking them. Usually, a pilot captain would meet them at the sea-buoy and after going onboard, take command to bring the ship in. Then, tugs would maneuver them to the dock. There were no pilots or tugs. The captains had to dock their own ships. This one approached the dock as slowly as possible. Sailors on the ship started heaving lines to sailors on the dock, who were missing the catch. Sailors on the ship started cursing sailors on the dock for missing. Sailors on the dock started cursing sailors on the ship for bad throws. All the while, the ship kept slowly moving with all that tonnage the inertia must have been terrific. When the ship hit the concrete dock, there was a loud noise as the concrete started cracking and you could see the steel hull flex inward and then back outward as it bounced. The sailors on the dock ran. When the ship was finally moored, we loaded all of the supplies we were able to carry on our trucks and jeeps and returned to camp.

We stayed at this camp for a while, getting more weapons, ammunition, clothes, etc, and getting all the units sorted out and organized. Someone said that the 34th Infantry Division Headquarters had arrived and was camped down the road a few miles. This was an opportunity to see Roy Palmer. There was an Arab nearby with a donkey. He didn't speak much French, but he knew French money and he understood that I wanted to buy his donkey. He probably didn't understand that I would turn it loose when I got back. Anyway, I kept peeling off French francs until he agreed to sell. I slung my rifle across my shoulders and pulled out my bayonet to use as a stick. The way Arabs ride is to sit over the donkey's hind legs and while tapping him lightly with a small stick say, "Burro-Burro-Amshay-Amshay" and then the donkey will trot right along. As I traveled down the road, the Americans would point at me and start laughing. When I reached the headquarters, I rode around through the lines of tents until I saw Roy. I dismounted and said, "Hello, Roy." Roy looked up and sang out, "Coll-yer, by golly I heard you were dead. People have been saying that you went down with your ship." Roy was one of the few people in the army that knew my family called me "Collier." I said, "It must have been somebody else." We had not seen each other since before we enlisted in the U.S. Army back in England. We visited for a while and went to chow together. The next time we would see each other would be in Opelika, Alabama, after the war.

All of us were paid before leaving England in U.S. dollars. The U.S. Treasury seal on all the bills was in blue instead of green. It was called invasion money. We were told that the government wanted to keep track of it. While we were still camped near Algiers, we had a payday. We were paid 75 French francs per dollar. Keep in mind that the civilians in Africa had been cut off from information in Europe for several years. They still thought that one franc equaled one dollar. A bottle of champagne in Algiers only cost five francs. This made the American soldiers' rich. They went into the city and bought all kinds of stuff, taking carriage rides around the city and otherwise showing off. Of course, our next pay would be cut down.

Finally, it was time to move. All battalions were to be dispersed to the boondocks. My battalion boarded a French National Railways troop train and headed east. The American Legion was established in Paris after World War I and one of its groups is called the 40 & 8 (Forty & Eight). This group is named after the funny looking railway cars used to transport troops. These railway cars were the same ones used to transport soldiers in World War I and each car carried forty men or eight horses. The train stopped at small stations often. Arabs would push their carts alongside the train, selling us oranges, tangerines and dates. I ate all three with gusto. It had been years since I had oranges or tangerines. They were all good, especially when compared to "C" rations, which were a small can of beans or hash. Each of the dates had a worm in it, but you could eat around the worm.

We left the train at Sidi bel Abbis, marched west and made a pup tent camp toward Tlemcen. Sidi bel Abbis was the Headquarters of the French Foreign Legion before the war. After France was occupied by the Nazis and the Vichy French government was formed, the Legion moved to French West Africa to escape Vichy control. There were a number of brothels in Sidi bel Abbis because they had been serving the legionnaires. After we made camp, we were told that we had been through an area that had an outbreak of bubonic plague; so don't eat any local food. Of course, we ignored that. If we were hungry enough, we would eat anything. The U.S. Army Medical Corps sent teams to all the camps and gave everyone shots. We were issued a large bottle of Atabrine which was used to prevent malaria. Quinine was not available during the war. The Japanese had cut off the supply. We took the Atabrine tablets for a while, but stopped when nausea, vomiting and yellow colored urine occurred. Another item we were given was giant size salt tablets to prevent dehydration. When we swallowed one of these, we would try to throw it up. Since we rarely had enough food and water, it was hard to vomit. The tablets were too strong. I did steal salt at every opportunity. If I didn't have anything to put it in, I would put it in one of my pockets and nibble on it, dirt and all.

My papers, wrapped in a gas cape, were still carried inside my shirt. I thought, this is crazy, they will certainly be lost when we start fighting. I went to the postal clerk and got some labels to address the package. Then I opened up the gas cape and took the papers out and carried everything to my new second lieutenant (90-day wonder) for him to censor everything as required. I told the second lieutenant that I would come back when he was through with everything and rewrap the package for mailing. The papers were: Certificate of Completion of Training in the United States Citizens Military Training Corps (CMTC), Fort McCelland, Alabama; United States Navy Certificate of Appointment to Recruit Chief Petty officer; United States Navy Discharge; Argyll and Sutherland Highlanders; Discharge; Canadian Army T.O.E.T. (Test of Elementary Training listing all the weapons I was trained on); Canadian Scottish Regiment Discharge; Membership Card, American Eagle Club, London, England; American Red Cross Cigarette Card and others. The only things I kept was my Canadian dog tags and my tam o'shanter, which I kept inside my shirt. The second lieutenant must have gotten excited or something, because he carried my papers to our captain to show them to him and then they showed them to the lieutenant colonel, our battalion commander. When I returned to the second lieutenant's tent he said, "Private Houston, I want you to be my platoon sergeant. I have discussed this with our captain and lieutenant colonel and they said it was my duty to select my sergeant and they would approve the promotion of whomever I select." I explained to the second lieutenant that I did not want the stripes, but I would serve as the acting sergeant because no one else in the outfit had ever been in combat. This seemed to satisfy him. I took my package to the postal clerk and mailed it. Then I stopped by another clerk's office and signed up for GI insurance, which I had never done.

Soon thereafter, I was sitting on a rock by my tent cleaning my rifle, when a bunch of sergeants from other companies (about 10, I think) paid me a visit. Their spokesman started shaking his finger at me and ranting and raving about how long and hard they had worked to become sergeants, and they would not allow me, a newcomer, to become one without working for it. He went on and on, saying they would get me if I accepted the promotion. I had listened quietly and continued to reassemble my rifle and load it. Finally, I responded. I told them it was none of their business and anyway they were not qualified to be sergeants. Then I said, "I remember when some of you who were on the same ship with me were crapping in your pants before and during the crossing of the mountains." This infuriated the spokesman even more. His face got red, his eyes were flashing and while he was saying, "We'll get you." I shot his earlobe off. His face and eyes changed in disbelief. I said, "Keep on loud mouth and the next round will be between your eyes. If any of you want to get me, now's the time, I am ready to kill any or all of you cowards and add you to my list of kills." The sergeants moved away and would not make eye contact with any of the officers or soldiers. By then, a huge crowd of officers and soldiers had gathered around. Some of my soldiers who had seen and heard the confrontation from the beginning were explaining what had happened to the officers and men who had not witnessed all of it.

I crawled into my pup tent and lay there for a while. My blood was boiling. I felt like tracking each one of them down and killing them. I knew they were incompetent and so did they. They were playing the same games they had played in Ireland and the United States, and still did not realize the horrors they would have to face. There wasn't any foxhole buddy for me in this outfit. I carried both tent halves, tent pegs and the other rope to pitch my own pup tent. I was accepted as the acting sergeant by my own platoon, which was all that mattered anyway.

Noticing some cooking fires at night on a hill nearby, I figured that there must be a small Arab village there. As soon as it was dark, I headed up the hill to the village. There was a full moon, which was very bright in the clear sky. When the Arab men saw me, they gathered around and greeted me, (I think). I greeted them in English and French. Later, I learned how to greet in Arabic. I gave them some strike anywhere kitchen matches (the old fashioned long kind) as a gift. They seemed to appreciate that. They passed them around for everyone to see. They were nodding their heads and saying something. This would seem to be a small gift, but matches could not be bought in Europe or Africa at this time because of the war. The women were busy cooking in ancient ovens that looked like anthills, probably made of some type firebricks. The men were interested in everything, my canteen, my bayonet, my uniform and my rifle. I let them look at my M1 rifle, which they passed around (in anticipation of this, I had removed the clip). They showed me their long, old bolt-action French rifles. I started pointing to different things and saying their names in English and French, such as the moon. Then, they would say the names in Arabic and I would try to pronounce them in Arabic. They laughed, but I kept trying until I got it right, more or less. I did learn an important sentence. Give me water. It sounded like, "at tin ne maa." I later learned that Arabs have different accents depending upon where you are, just like in English and other languages. When the meal was ready, I ate with them. There was some type of bread and couscous, which had some of everything in it. The meat is usually sheep, goat or fish, and it is the number one dish for Arabs. After eating, we said goodbye the best we could and I headed back to our camp. On the way, I smelled and sensed something in the bushes; I raised my rifle to fire and came face to face with a hyena. The hyena ran away screaming.

Winter 1942-43

The order came for us to move. We loaded onto uncovered 6x6 trucks with 50 caliber machineguns mounted over the cabs. The trucks had fold down wood benches on each side. We placed our gear in the middle and sat on the bench seats. We had no idea we would live on these trucks for two weeks or more. Our camp was located in western Algeria almost to the border of Morocco. As we proceeded east, other battalions would join the convoy, including supporting troops, such as combat engineers, tanks, artillery, signal corps and medical corps, until the entire 34th Infantry Division was in the convoy. The convoy was so long that when we crossed mountains or plains, we could not see the beginning or end.

As the convoy passed through small towns or villages, the people would come out and wave their flags, which they had kept hidden for so long. Sometimes they would hold up bottles of wine and soldiers would lean over and try to grab them. The only successful way was for some soldiers to sit on the legs of the snatcher so he could lean way out and down. The convoy traveled day and night, stopping only long enough to refuel, eat, and go to the bathroom. One of life's miseries is trying to go to the bathroom over the tailgate of a bouncing 6x6 truck. It is the same as trying to go off the fantail of a PT boat. Sometimes we were hot, sometimes cold; sometimes there was rain, snow, sleet or hail. It was dangerous traveling at night in the mountains with only hooded headlights to see by. A few trucks and tanks slid off cliffs on curves in the dirt roads. Still, the convoy did not stop. The drivers were tired, and they would change drivers every now and then when they could.

One evening just before dark, the convoy stopped for the night on a high plateau. It was raining and the ground was all muddy. Some of the men tried sleeping in the back of the open trucks and some crawled under the trucks and lay down in the mud. There was a fairly large farmhouse with barn type buildings in the back of it on a small hill near us. By instinct I walked up to the farmhouse, which had to be owned by a French family. It was a feeling that I had from previously meeting French Resistance people. In the pouring rain, I knocked on the door. A male voice asked who was there (in French). I replied, "Je suie un soldat Americane, et un amie." The door was opened and I explained (in my broken French) what was happening. They had seen the convoy but were afraid to come out. The lady of the house came into the room and after some more conversation invited me to eat with them.

It must be difficult for you, the reader, to understand what all these people had been through. This was either December 1942, or January 1943, and I didn't know what happened for Christmas. It turned out to be a blessing for this family when I knocked on their door. They had been isolated for years. All they knew was Boshe propaganda. I told them how the Englanders had defeated the Africa Korps, how the Free French, under the command of General de Gaule, was now in North Africa, how the French Resistance people were still fighting in France and how the French General Le Clerc had brought the Free French soldiers, together with the Legion and Senegalese soldiers back from French West Africa. After I said that, the lady became real excited. Their children were listening and eating with us. The children were two boys and two girls. The oldest was about 14. The lady said, "Our oldest son escaped to join the Free French Army in French West Africa, do you think he will be back?" I said, "Yes, he should be with all the young men that escaped the Vichy French."

After dinner, we kept talking and sipping wine. They had relatives and friends in France. The last they heard was when the man of the house was told by his brother in France to get his oldest son out. I told them we together with the Free French, British and others were on our way to destroy the Germans and Italians in Africa. This was a large plantation located on the same latitude as between Charleston, SC and Savannah, GA. However, it was at high altitude and water was supplied by rains in the mountains. All the servants and farm labor had fled due to the war and they had no petrol for their tractors. They told me that they grew olives, mandarins, oranges, barley, wheat and kept sheep and milk-goats. They had constructed an aqueduct to bring water down off the mountains to a reservoir that they had built. They insisted that I sleep in their oldest son's room; I did that. This was the first real sleep for me in a long, long time. I could have slept for a week with the rain on the roof, but I knew I had to be back before the convoy moved. Before daylight, I got up and started dressing. Then I realized that the French family was all up. They had washed my clothes, had a hot tub of water ready for me to bathe in and breakfast was almost ready. I couldn't even remember when I had last had a bath or washed my clothes. After breakfast, I thanked them, they thanked me, and we said farewell. I would have paid all the money in my pockets for a box of Whitman's Sampler to give to those children.

The convoy moved on, but the destination was unknown because we would circle (a large, many mile circle) and sometimes backtrack. I knew this by looking at the sun and stars. Finally, the convoy started getting smaller as battalion after battalion unloaded and started marching. No one knew where we were except full colonels and generals. Without maps, we did not know where we were. When our battalion left the trucks, we were ordered to follow the road going east to a village where Free French had dug in to form a line of battle. The Free French soldiers were great big tall men from Senegal in French West Africa. Man, they liked to dig. They had first dug foxholes, and then they dug trenches to connect them. The Senegalese soldiers were paid a bonus when they went on patrol and brought back a German or Italian ear. Someone finally became wise. How do you tell the difference in German, Italian, British or American, etc. ears? The rule was changed; they had to bring back dog tags.

There were not many signs at the villages and some did not have signs at all. We finally learned some things. We were at Faid Pass. We were dug in forming a battle line south of the road and facing east toward elements of Field Marshall Rommel's Afrika Korps. This road ran east to Sfax on the coast of the Mediterranean Sea and west to Sbeitla and then to Kasserine Pass. My guess was the Germans and Italians were being supplied through the port at Sfax. The Allies had just finished forming a battle line from east of Gafsa at the south end, then running north through Faid Pass, west of Kairouan to Goubellat, then west of Mateur to the Mediterranean, west of Bizerta. The United States Army had formed the II Corps, consisting of our 34th Infantry Division (National Guard), the 1st Infantry Division (Regular Army), the 3rd Infantry Division (Regular Army), the 9th Infantry Division (Regular Army), the 1st Armored Division (Regular Army), the 2nd Armored Division (Regular Army) and supporting troops of all kinds. The II (U.S.) Corps was at the southern end of the battle line. The XIX French Corps was in the middle and the V British Corps was at the north end. The British 8th Army was still following Rommel. Of course, there were many gaps in this line.

Our position was within range of the German mortars. Every now and then, they would fire a mortar round just to harass us. We would be sitting around eating (we were dug in just below a ridge) and when a round was fired, the men would spill their food while jumping into their foxholes. I was trying to teach them to listen to the sound of the shell; if you knew what to listen for, you could tell they were firing over our heads at our company headquarters down the hill. I would have sworn that the Germans had an artillery spotter somewhere that could see everything. In the late evenings just before dark, a weapons carrier would bring up our food, water and the like. The German mortar men started consistently blowing it up with one round at a certain spot. At that rate, we were running out of weapons carriers, so they started coming up at night.

The Senegalese were only with us for a few days, then they had to pull out to join the other Free French to the north of us. We were sorry to see them go because they were good fighters. They did leave us with a present though, white lice, which stayed in our long underwear until March. The lice didn't bother us unless we got warm and then they would start crawling. We suffered in the cold winds in the months that followed. A French first lieutenant with the Senegalese wanted me to go on patrol with some of his best men to get the feel of the terrain between our line and the German line. I went with them twice. The second time, we went around and through the German line. We saw and heard a great deal of activity. After the Senegalese left us, I continued to go on patrol alone. It was difficult to get any of our soldiers to go on patrol because of fear and lack of training. I did not blame them, because fear combined with inexperience meant certain death with just one mistake. I had talked a few into going with me earlier so that maybe they would learn, but eventually I gave up on it.

The Germans started setting up a machinegun at night in no man's land to ambush patrols. Sometimes, we heard them firing. One night they killed all of the soldiers patrolling from the company that Eddie Aftewitz was in. Eddie was one of the soldiers who enlisted with me in England. He had been an artilleryman in China and with the British Army. He was angry and started getting ready one afternoon to go out that night to get the machinegun. He had four volunteers getting ready to go with him. When I found out about it, I went over to that company and tried to talk Eddie out of it. I told him, "They have setup an ambush and you'll never see them until they fire." They went anyway. We heard the machinegun firing. They never came back. I searched for them by approaching the approximate location of the gun by circling to their rear, but never found anything.

One night on patrol, I managed to crawl into what had to be a German supply dump. There were all kinds of supplies there. My main interest was the neatly stacked rows of artillery shells. They were in long rows with space between for trucks and tanks to drive through and load up. There was enough starlight to see all this, but there were also some deep shadows where I stayed and waited. Two sentries came by and I figured they were roving pickets, meaning they walked around with other pickets to cover the supply dump. I started timing them and thinking about how to blow up the artillery shells which would create a secondary explosion of other supplies. What was needed was a couple of "sappers" from the Royal Engineers with satchel charges. The "sappers" are experts in demolition. I thought the weather would be the same tomorrow night and I would try to get a couple of combat engineers with satchel charges. It took the pickets over twenty minutes to return, which would be plenty of time to set the charges.

The first thing the next morning, I went down the hill to our company headquarters and talked to our new captain. I forgot to tell you that the first sergeant that we had in Ireland that we called "Little Jesus," had, upon arrival at this place, dug his foxhole, got in it, went bonkers and wouldn't get out. The medics came and carried him away, so I didn't have to go though a first sergeant to speak to the captain. I explained to the captain several times what was needed and he seemed undecided about how to get it done. Finally, I got him off the hook by getting his permission to speak to the lieutenant colonel at battalion headquarters. He loaned me his jeep, and I took off at high speed down the road to battalion headquarters. Thinking about it while I was driving, this lieutenant colonel was the same new one that was on the ship and crossed the mountains with me and seemed to get better as time went by. At the very least, he would know that I knew what I was doing and I never would shoot the bull. My thoughts were right. When I started talking to him, he called his staff in. He ordered his second in command, a major, to call division headquarters so he could talk to them. The signal corps had strung miles of telephone wire to division headquarters and the major got a full colonel on the general's staff on the line. The lieutenant colonel explained to the staff colonel what was needed and the staff colonel told him they would send some combat engineers to my company headquarters that afternoon. I thanked the lieutenant colonel and he said, "No, Alabama, we thank you."

I scrounged up some food and water. The further back you go; the better the food. Also, I got to hear what the scuttlebutt was among the division and battalion officers. It turned out to be the same colonel at division headquarters that wanted me to be an instructor in Ireland. My lieutenant colonel told me that the staff colonel knew me and called me "Alabama." Also, he knew my nickname on the destroyer we were on. All of these things probably helped get an immediate, positive, response. The scuttlebutt was that the general commanding the II Corps, U.S. Army had built a bunker about twenty miles back of any other headquarters and was hard to reach or communicate with.

On my way back to my company headquarters, I stopped twice to find some good sucking rocks. Upon arrival, I explained to the captain what the plan was and he seemed to be pleased. Being tired, I lay down outside the captain's tent and went to sleep. That afternoon, a first lieutenant and a staff sergeant arrived in a jeep and they had two satchel charges with them. Explaining that the Germans had everything under observation from the company headquarters to the battle line up the hill, I suggested they leave the jeep back of the headquarters tent and we would casually walk up to the line. I noticed that both of them had removed all insignia and I asked to look at their dog tags. They hadn't properly taped their dog tags up as I had done because they clinged, clanged, and pinged. We bummed medical tape from the medics for this purpose. The U.S. military dog tags were made of metal and the chain on them was metal. It has always been a wonder to me, trying to understand who designs dog tags and other things for the military. As I have explained before, British dog tags are made of plastic and you wear them on a leather lace. Later, soldiers in Vietnam stuck their dog tags in their boots to keep them from rattling. That is the reason why many were buried without a dog tag on their necks. The lieutenant was wearing an enlisted man's uniform instead of an officer's uniform. All of the good officers (that is, line officers) did this.

We went up the hill, sat down on the edge of a trench and I carefully outlined the plan. I drew our route with approximate distances in the dirt. Each one of them would carry and place a satchel charge under two of the artillery stacks after we waited for the sentries to pass. I would cover them while they did this.

We slept a while, and then just before dark, we ate a can of C Ration beans, which was the main and only dish for combat infantrymen. After dark, we crawled out of the trench, over the ridge and about one hundred yards further before standing up. You should never stand up on a ridge or high ground because your silhouette can be seen. When we arrived at the dump and the lieutenant and sergeant saw the stacks of shells, they were astonished. While waiting for the sentries to walk by, the lieutenant put his mouth to my ear and whispered, "Oh, Lord, Oh, Lord, and I only halfway believed you." The charges were set and we left. This is how I came to be at this terrible place at this time, as I promised to explain at the end of Chapter 1.

February 1943

Several days passed after we had blown up the German dump. It must have been close to mid-February when one morning we received our Christmas mail and parcels. I received several letters from my parents and I hoped they had received my letter and papers so they would know where I was. I also received a parcel and blessings of blessings; it was a box of Whitman's Sampler Chocolates.

That afternoon, I woke up and there was an eerie silence. I usually had to sleep in the daytime because I would patrol at night. Everything was too quiet. I asked the others what was going on and they said they didn't know. One of them said, "Sarge, I saw a soldier carrying our ninety-day wonder lieutenant's sleeping bag down the hill." Looking around, I did not see any officers or sergeants and our company headquarters had disappeared. I crawled up to the ridge and saw German tanks and infantry forming up for an attack. There was a lump in my throat and anger was filling my brain. The officers had to know about this, but did not tell the soldiers. This was pure and simple desertion in the face of the enemy. The officers and sergeants had left in their jeeps, weapons carriers and trucks and since there was no transportation for the soldiers, we were abandoned. I started screaming at the soldiers, "PACK UP, AND GET OUT." I ordered some soldiers to go tell the others.

We had received a bunch of cigarettes that morning and knowing that we could not carry everything, I booby-trapped some of my cartons in the sides of foxholes using grenades. I wanted to teach the other soldiers how to rig booby-traps, but there was not enough time. One soldier had seen my box of Whitman's Sampler Chocolates and wanted to buy some. I noticed he was wearing two canteens of water. I said. "Money is no good here, but I'll trade you six pieces of chocolates, your pick, for your extra canteen." He replied, "O.K., Sarge." After he made his picks of chocolates, he unhooked his extra canteen, gave it to me and I hooked it on my web belt.

When we reached the road, it was getting late and rumors were flying. Someone kept saying, "Trucks will pick us up twenty miles down this road." I was screaming, "YOU CAN'T OUTRUN TANKS, DROP EVERYTHING YOU CAN'T CARRY, STARTING WITH THOSE SILLY GAS MASKS (respirators), GO WITH ME TO THE MOUNTAINS, WHERE TANKS CAN'T FOLLOW." Other soldiers from other companies had joined us. There must have been about three hundred soldiers milling around and none of them seemed to hear or didn't want to understand me. When the firing started, there was chaos. The babble of the soldiers grew more intense. We could clearly hear the Germans moving in on our former battle line. Our weapons platoons were firing their old machineguns and mortars. It was easy to determine which weapons were firing (that is for me). The U.S. Army machineguns were firing about five hundred rounds per minute and sounded like they would hang up and stop any second. The German machineguns were firing at twelve hundred rounds per minute. Then I could hear the German tanks advancing and minutes later our weapons platoons ceased firing because they were dead. This is another "flashback" that I have. It is just another bad dream. The doctors at the Veterans Administration Hospital in Biloxi, Mississippi, told me years later that I would loose my voice because of my screaming at soldiers under fire.

It is difficult to describe what was happening. In the twilight, these soldiers were going psycho. It seemed that there was only one thing that I could do. I placed my Whitman's Sampler inside my shirt and started double-timing to the north while there was enough light to get me away from the road. After about one mile, the high ground started and I lay down in the rocks for a while to rest and plan what I should do. I could hear the German artillery firing. The soldiers were being killed, wounded or captured. My heart was sad. I decided to sleep some and then travel when the moonlight came.

My thinking was to stay north of the road while moving west, but always keep on or near the high ground where the tanks could not travel. That night and the next day, I made some good progress. When night came, I rested some. When the moon shone, I continued to move. Then the next day, I saw something burning. It is amazing how a tank can burn for hours. It is not the armor plate; it is the wiring, fuel and ammunition. When I scouted around, it became clear that this was one of those running fights between scout tanks. As I recall, there were two German tanks destroyed and one British tank destroyed, plus another British tank that had the track and wheels blown off on one side, but it did not burn. The Bren guns and ammunition had been removed. The field piece (artillery) had been disabled. Keeping up my search inside the tank, I found a 55-Cal Boyes anti-tank rifle, mostly concealed, between the deck and bulkhead. It was in operating condition but not loaded. Then I spotted a box of shells. I loaded the rifle with five rounds (total capacity) and put another five rounds in my pocket. The box of shells was far too heavy to carry. There was an open tin of Compo (Composition Rations) which I had ignored. Looking inside the tin, I found an unopened package of hardtack and a can of treacle pudding. I thought, someone up there must be helping me. There would be a long way to go before I would find any allied soldiers. I had started out with very little food and only two canteens of water. I rationed myself with my Whitman's Sampler chocolates by taking my rock out of my mouth and sucking on a chocolate very slowly every now and then.

Carrying my M-1 rifle slung over my shoulders and the 35lb. Boyes rifle laying on my shoulder as I had done so many times before, my course was still about west. Early the next morning, I heard noises. Putting my ear to the ground, the sound was made by tanks and I headed south towards them. Staying on high ground in the rocks. I crawled around until I found a good spot to observe. What a sight! Down below in the valley was the road going from Faid Pass to the west. The Germans were making a camp. The tanks were forming up in lines. Half-tracks pulling 88mm artillery pieces with crews and supplies were lining up. Everything was there; personnel and supply trucks, fuel trucks, water trucks, Volkswagens for officers and motorcycles with sidecars for Scouts. They were eating, refueling, doing maintenance, making repairs, going to the bathroom and the like. Some soldiers brought out folding chairs and tables, placed them together, with maps on them for the officers. My mind was whirling. My position was out of ordinary rifle range, but as I have written before, the Boyes rifle, with its long barrel and 55-caliber steel jacket armor piercing shells, was more powerful than buffalo or elephant rifles. Simply put, I had hit targets at this distance before on level ground and another advantage was that I was now on high ground. There would never be an opportunity like this again. On the other hand, when anyone fires on German soldiers, they are well-trained and return fire in seconds, without waiting for any orders.

Decision time. If I fired, their 88mm rifles (screaming meemies) would swing around and fire in seconds and they would send infantry to hunt me down. My preparations were started. A position was needed to fire from the rocks so that the barrel of the rifle would rest on rocks instead of putting the bi-pod down. The combat pack, carrying a blanket and two shelter halves, went down a ravine. Steel helmet, empty canteen, extra Boyes rifle shells and whatever else was heavy were tossed down a ravine. An escape route was planned. The Ml rifle was placed back of the rocks so that it could be picked up while running. The high ground sloped down to a valley to the north. The valley was at least three miles wide and maybe five miles long. That would be a long run with Germans following. If there were only two or three rounds fired, it would take longer for the Germans to spot this position. This would be a long war; the only way I could get home was to kill the enemy. I took my tam o'shanter out of my shirt and put it on. The only things left in my shirt were some Whitman's Sampler chocolates and my stinking pair of extra socks.

Placing the Boyes rifle with the barrel resting between rocks, there was a complete field of fire, some of the officers were seated at the tables and some were standing. Assuming the ones seated were senior, five of them would be the targets. Lining up the five targets with the open sights aimed at their midsections, the barrel was moved from left to right to each target while mentally working the bolt smoothly to reload. Everything was ready. Pumping air in my lungs then holding a deep breath, I commenced firing. The first three officers were lifted up and slammed down by the impact. The fourth went sideways and someone standing moved in front of the fifth, so the shell hit him and the impact lifted him up off his feet. Immediately crawling back to my M-1 rifle, the bolt of the Boyes was tossed down a ravine and the rifle went down another. All the while I was counting down; 1,001; 1,002; 1,003; 1,004; then the first 88-mm shell hit the rocks where I had been. Often, the Germans would fire into rocks at us because they knew that if the shrapnel didn't kill us, the slivers of rocks would. A whole barrage of shells started hitting.

My legs were automatically moving fast to get clear of the shell bursts. It was imperative to be far enough across the valley before a patrol behind me could cross the high ground and with the high ground, be in rifle range. Reaching the valley, my body and my mind, went into double time of the long distance runner. Looking back, now and then, I saw a patrol after me. With a substantial lead, a rest break could be taken from time to time. The objective was to make the soldiers in the patrol run fast so that they would become exhausted. They would surely already be breathing hard because with their generals screaming at them, they had to run fast up the high ground, then cross it, and go down into the valley. I knew that it was unlikely that they were in the same physical condition that I was in. The patrol had ten soldiers in it and they must be killed while in the valley because they would have the advantage in the high ground.

When there was about two miles to the high ground across the valley, by instinct, the wounded rabbit trick was used. By staggering around and falling down, they knew they had me. They kept on sprinting to get within their rifle range to shoot me. I was resting each time. The count became clear; there was a lieutenant, a noncommissioned officer and eight soldiers. The lieutenant and sergeant were carrying machine pistols and the eight soldiers each were carrying rifles. The soldiers were leading, sometimes in single file, and then spread out when they saw the "injured rabbit." The sergeant was next and then the lieutenant. By using the injured rabbit trick, they were within my M-1 rifle range. So going down and rolling over into the prone position, the first shot hit the lead soldier. Up again and running then falling, the same thing happened. The second soldier was dead.

As any long-distance runner or well-trained soldier may tell you, you can think and even dream while running. There were eight Germans left. The M-1 rifle holds eight rounds in each clip. How to kill eight Germans with one clip? While running, the remaining six rounds in the M-1 were ejected and another clip with eight rounds was loaded. Thinking about it, these Germans probably had never seen an auto-reloading rifle such as the M-1.

There is a vast difference in automatic firing weapons and automatic reloading. Automatic firing weapons continue to fire as long as the trigger is pulled and it still has ammunition in it. Automatic reloading means each round is loaded and the trigger must be pulled to fire each round.

All of this simply means that the M-1 rifle can fire eight rounds much faster than the German soldiers could fire their bolt-action rifles and they would be surprised when I didn't work the bolt on my rifle.

Close to the high ground was a rock out-crop, at least twelve inches high, which could be used for cover. Reaching the out-crop, I spun around, dropped flat down behind the rock and started firing. The six soldiers and the sergeant went down, my last shot missed the lieutenant because he was in the rear and had time enough to run back and to the side. Going up into the high ground, there was a good spot to hide and watch.

The lieutenant dropped his machine pistol and picked up one of the dead soldier's rifles and ammunition. He started circling to go up in the high ground instead of following me. He was smart. Had he followed me up, I could have shot him. Now, it was up to me to stay higher than he was, so that he could be spotted and shot. He could not return to his unit unless he killed me. The hunt went on for several hours. There was a glimpse of him once, but not enough exposure or time for a shot. He fired at me one time and the bullet hit a rock nearby. It was getting late; something had to be done. Remembering cowboy movies, I started throwing rocks at different spots from time to time. Finally, he fired at one of them. Seeing the smoke and hearing where the shot came from, I started circling to approach him from behind. When I saw him, I fired. He had started turning and he fired but he was a second or two too late. His shot went wild. I don't know why, maybe it was anger or adrenaline, but I continued to shoot him until the M1 clip was empty.

After reloading, my search of his body started. He had many good things that could be used, a watch, a compass, a map, and a Luger pistol with extra ammunition, some food and water in his canteen. It was now twilight time. Finding a good hiding place, I ate his food and drank the rest of his water. Putting his bloody coat over me, I slept.

February 1943

At the crack of dawn, I buckled on his belt with the pistol, stuffed the other items in my pockets and headed back to the dead soldiers to get their food and water. This was backtracking some, however, food and water were the most important things.

In all the years since the war, the killing of this lieutenant has been one of my bad dreams. In my dream, he keeps on walking toward me on a narrow goat path. As each round hits him, I can see a puff of dust, but he keeps on walking until I can see a skull under his steel helmet instead of a face. Then I wake up sweating.

Going through the pockets of the six soldiers and the sergeant, I got some American cigarettes, two lighters and some food. Combining the water in their canteens into two of them and mine, then I drank the rest. I removed the lieutenant's belt and buckled on one of theirs with the pistol and the two canteens on it because they would not fit onto my U.S. belt. One of their blankets was rolled up and tied crossways over my shoulders. The days and nights were getting colder and colder.

The journey west continued and many miles were covered because I felt stronger with the extra German food and water. That night I had a sound sleep. At daylight, there were the sounds of heavy guns firing in the distance. After moving toward the sounds for about five hours, I could see smoke rising from burning vehicles. I could hear more sounds of a great battle; it took another two hours to reach a position in the high ground to see what was happening. It was a scene from hell. Bodies and burning vehicles were everywhere. These must have been the same Germans that I had seen making camp and then going forward on the road to attack an American position. Most of the Germans had moved on, heading west, but there were still a few German tanks with armored infantry down there. There was nothing that could be done except watch and wait. Looking at the German lieutenant's map, the road and the words Faid Pass, Kasserine Pass, and other names of places to the west could be seen even though the map was in German, this place would have to be Kasserine Pass. When night fell I slept off and on, but the noises and fires kept waking me up. Now and then a tank would explode. My heart was filled with dread because when daylight came, I knew that I would have to go down there.

The next morning, it was quiet. Some vehicles were still smoking. All the Germans were gone. Moving among all the dead soldiers, I started crying inside. There were a few dead Germans. The rest were American soldiers wearing my division patch, the Red Bull of the 34th Infantry Division. There were many American soldiers not only wearing the division patch, but also so many wearing the insignia of the Corps of Engineers. The Americans had dug foxholes and some were in them during the attack. The indentations of foxholes could be seen with tank tracks over them. American soldiers would have to learn the hard way. German tanks would go over a foxhole, lock one track and spin the other track over the hole and crush the soldier or bury him alive. Finding what I needed from the dead, reloads for M-1 rifle, two pup tent shelter halves with pegs and ropes, socks, an overcoat, blankets, a steel helmet and all the things that I had thrown away. After doing all of these things, the buzzards started landing to eat the dead. I shot some of them just to relieve my anger.

My journey west started as soon as possible to get away from this place. About two days later, there was a squadron of British tanks and some lorries with supplies and with 90-mm Bofors guns hooked to their trailer hitches camped by a cactus patch. It surprised them when they saw me coming. I know I must have been a sight. I was filthy from head to toe, my uniform torn and bloody and I am sure that I was stinking to high heaven. Taking off my steel helmet, I put on my tam o'shanter. I saluted the major in command (British Salute) and he said, "Where in the hell did you come from?" I took off both sets of dog tags and handed them up to him on the tank. He started shaking his head. Noticing their insignia, they just happened to be in the Royal Scots Regiment. Hastily briefing them about what had happened, I handed the major the German lieutenant's map. After the major and other officers looked at it, the major said, "I'll be damned, sergeant major, get me the highest ranking officer at division headquarters on the wireless; use the mayday signal if you have to." We continued to talk. In about three minutes, the sergeant major said, "We have a division colonel on the wireless, Sir." The major started talking to the colonel and read the map to him. Some of the German words that the major didn't know, he spelled out to the colonel. After they were finished, the major said, "That colonel is the division intelligence officer and he is already on the wireless to Corps Headquarters."

They gave me a mug of hot tea while I sat down. An open tin of Compo rations was placed in front of me. Without hesitation, I attacked the food, the chocolate bar first, then opening a can of sardines and placing it to my mouth and turning my head back, gobbled it down. All of them were watching me. Someone said, "Do you have any water, mate?" I replied, "About a half a canteen left, maybe I could have made it two more days." After gorging myself on all that food, the major wanted to know all the details about what happened and what I had seen. All of the officers had their notepads and maps out. Without mincing words, they were told everything I could remember, including how the officers and non-coms had abandoned us at Faid Pass.

When the conversation was finished, the major said, "Are you Commando?" I replied, "Yes, Sir, how did you know?" The major laughed and said, "You let me read your dog tags, your name and serial number is already at Corps Headquarters, what is your call sign?" I replied, "Alabama, then Stars Fell on Alabama." The major said, "Who was in command of the Commando School?" I replied, "Lord Lovett." Looking at his notes from division headquarters, the major said, "You and your statements have now been confirmed. Headquarters wanted to know these things. I'm sorry to put you through this." I said, "Sir, I understand, and your help is needed. The U.S. Army will send a message to my parents that I am KIA unless a message is sent to U. S. Army Headquarters, Algiers, and unless I go with you and find some U. S. Army unit, I will be charged with desertion." The major replied, "Don't worry we will do that."

It was now twilight. When I started taking out my canvass pup tent shelter halves and blankets to roll up in for sleep, the sergeant major came over to me and said, "Put all that back in your pack, lad, you will sleep in a tank where it is warm." I followed him to a tank and put all my gear in and lay down with blankets over and under me. The major was on the wireless for a long time. Being exhausted, my sleep was so deep that when I awoke the next day, we were already moving. My body and mind were hazy. So many things were happening so fast.

There was a place called Thala. It was a crossroad, but the only thing there was a cactus patch. The British tank squadron was racing to get there. Upon arrival, the squadron went past the cactus patch, did a complete left wheel of 90 degrees to form a battle line in the cactus patch. There was some concealment by the cactus. The squadron was facing south towards a long valley. The 90-mm Bofor's artillery were unhooked from the lorries and setup in firing positions. The main wireless operator was talking almost constantly with other units. He reported to the major that some British infantry, supported by artillery from the U.S. Army 9th Infantry Division, were digging in to the north of us. While we waited, I was able to wash my dirty body and clothes with water, and using some petrol to soak the bloody places on my uniform. The British laughed when they saw me standing there naked, going over my body, my clothes and my blankets dabbing white lice with petrol to kill them. One of the soldiers traded a Royal Scots cap badge for my Canadian Scottish cap badge. I usually wore a Royal Scots badge at Commando School and on missions.

An officer standing on top of a tank, using his field glasses spotted a large German panzer column miles away heading north towards us. The difference in well-trained soldiers and not so well trained soldiers in tough situations is amazing. We all had some hot tea, while the wireless operator notified the German position to other units. Everyone knew that when the panzers with armored infantry attacked, we could get some of them but not all. We would fight to the last man and go down firing. Even if we wanted to, there was no other place to go. The sergeant major gave me a spare Bren gun with extra clips. Moving out to the flank as far as I could go and still have some cactus for cover, I dug a foxhole and setup the Bren so that I could get enough angle to shoot the German infantrymen following behind their tanks. Noticing this, the sergeant major had some of the Bren gunners on the top turrets of the tanks take their pairs of Brens and move out on both flanks.

One of the officers let me use his field glasses to look at the Germans. Then a strange thing happened. When the Germans were about five miles from us, they formed a battle line to attack. Instead of attacking, they suddenly turned left 90 degrees and the column headed west. The major exclaimed, "They are heading to Tebessa. We have the road to Tebessa and we can beat them there." We were near the road from Thala to Tebessa, which was about fifty miles, and we could travel faster on the road than the Germans in the open terrain. Loading up fast, in about two and a half hours we were approaching Tebessa when we saw different groups of American soldiers. They had been pushed back by the Germans and looked exhausted, thirsty and hungry. They cheered when they saw the British tanks, even though there was only one squadron of us.

The British officers and noncoms immediately assembled the American infantrymen to form a battle line with the infantrymen digging in between their tanks and artillery. About a mile away, on the outskirts of the ancient ruins at Tebessa, was a U.S. Hospital. The U.S. flag and the Red Cross flag could be clearly seen. I requested that the major allow one of the officers and me to go in a jeep to warn them to leave. The major agreed. The hospital was the United States Army Medical Corps 7th Evacuation Hospital. This type of hospital was the forerunner of the Mobile Army Surgical Hospital (M.A.S.H.) used later in Korea. There were many wounded soldiers there and the hospital personnel were already worried because they could see the tanks and infantry forming up for battle. When the first lieutenant and I located the lieutenant colonel in command, we explained the situation to him. His thinking was that they were unarmed medics and therefore the Germans would not harm them and they didn't want to leave the wounded. We explained again, if the German column attacked, they would break through and at the very least, take all medical equipment and supplies for their own soldiers to use so they could not treat the American soldiers anyway. The real probability was the Germans would capture the doctors and nurses to treat German soldiers.

Finally, the lieutenant colonel agreed to load everyone they could on their trucks and travel northwest for about twenty miles on the road from Tebessa to Constantine and wait there. If the Germans broke through, they would continue on. If they did not break through, they would return. The first lieutenant said, "In that case, Sir, we will be here"

When the German panzers arrived and were in artillery range, they stopped and fired several rounds. The British artillery fired several rounds in return. To our amazement, the Germans turned around and left. This was the farthest west that any of Rommel's columns had reached and was another turning point in the African campaign.

The doctors and nurses returned to the hospital. The Americans and British made camp next to the hospital. The British and the hospital personnel gave the weary American soldiers all the food and water they could spare. The British used their wireless to relay to the U.S. Army our position and plight and spent several days resting there.

One evening, I jokingly said to the major, "Sir, the KR&R, according to my understanding, has provisions for rum rations for all soldiers at certain times of the year and at anytime after long and arduous duty." The major joked back, "But we don't have any rum." The captain said, "Sir, we do have some cases of Scots whiskey straight from Scotland." That did the trick. The cases of whiskey were brought from a lorrie; a sergeant did the pouring as all the soldiers lined up for their ration. Every man received nearly a mess cup full then a circle was formed as the sergeant major did the honors, as was the custom. He took a sip to nod approval, then he said the Gaelic words and made the toast to the King, "God Bless the King," which was repeated by all hands. Everyone started sipping. Some soldiers started singing, "Scotland, the Brave," "Danny Boy" and other Highlander songs. Soon everyone joined in. The American soldiers were listening. Some of the doctors and nurses came over and sang with us in the twilight. The sergeant poured them some Scots. Before we went to sleep, the major said, "Damn bloody good show, Alabama, damn bloody good show."

The British had noticed a strange thing. They didn't see American officers. When I was asked, I told them the U.S. Army had only a few and the new ones were ninety-day wonders. I also told them that I had been promoted to the rank of platoon sergeant, but I had accepted only the temporary rank. One of the lieutenants said, "Then you must be the commanding general of the Americans here." I replied, "I suppose so, Sir, but if true, then I am the youngest general in history, except for Alexander the Great, because I am still a teenager." They were shocked. The doctors and nurses had been looking at me in a strange way. They had seen me conversing freely with the British officers and noncoms. They had seen me arrive in the jeep with the British lieutenant to warn them. Then it hit me. When I came with the lieutenant and afterwards, I was wearing my tam o'shanter, not my steel helmet. The lieutenant was wearing his black beret, which was worn by all British armored soldiers, with the same Royal Scots cap badge that I was wearing. On my field jacket was the insignia of the U.S. Army 34th Infantry Division. When I was in the hospital mess tent eating, I had answered some, but not all, of the doctors' and nurses' questions. I asked a nurse for some paper and she loaned me her pen so that I could write to my parents. I was afraid that the U. S. Army would report me as missing in action.

The British left when they received a message telling them where to go to get supplies and regroup with their other tank squadrons. The U.S. Army Quartermaster Corps, Ordinance Corps and Medical Corps trucks arrived, bringing weapons and supplies. A convoy of Army ambulances arrived to carry seriously wounded soldiers to station hospitals and general hospitals. Oh yes, I got a brand new uniform, boots, socks and all that. Some of us went to see the ruins in Tebessa. The ruins do give one a strange feeling with the silence and thinking about the ancient peoples that lived there.

An army trucking company arrived. All of us bid farewell to the hospital personnel and expressed our mutual thanks to each other. The 7th Evacuation Hospital people did not forget the soldiers of the 34th Infantry Division during later battles in Africa and Italy. It was pitiful to see how few men were left that had started out in Ireland. There were other battles fought that I have not mentioned; such as Pichon and Fondouk, where the German panzers broke through the American lines and killed, wounded, and captured thousands of soldiers.

Winter & Spring 1943

General George Patton, with his foul mouth and show-off pistols, had landed with the Third U.S. Infantry Division at Casablanca to take command of the United States Army II Corps in Africa. He was sent to relieve the disgraced general who had built his bunker way behind the lines and failed to give leadership to the U.S. soldiers. The Allied forces were busy driving east to reestablish the original battle line. The Germans did not give up easily. They stopped at strategic places and forced the Allies to attack. A battalion of the 168th Infantry Regiment, 34th Infantry Division, was ordered to cross a valley and attack a German position on the high ground at dawn. By radio, they were ordered to stop during the night. Then later, they were ordered to go forward and attack, but it was too late. The lieutenant colonel in command replied to headquarters that it was too late and refused to give the order to move. Someone up high relieved the lieutenant colonel in command and gave a direct order to the second in command, a major, to attack. When daylight came, the battalion was completely exposed on the open ground and the German artillery slaughtered them.

Some of the soldiers of the 34th Division had received newspapers from their hometowns in Minnesota and Iowa. The Army did not send parents notices of men killed in action or missing in action except a few at a time. When a company was wiped out, the National Guard soldiers were mostly from the same small town. The parents had started noticing this as the "I regret to inform you" letters were piling up. In most of the companies, there were brothers, cousins, and old family friends. As a result the parents were complaining to their public officials about the large numbers of casualties.

For the American soldiers, hell started again. The communications were poor or non-existent. We marched in columns, more or less towards the east, across the vast wastelands, valleys, canyons, and plateaus. Without vehicles of any kind, as a matter of fact, vehicles could not go where we went. All we had of food and water and anything else was what each man could carry. These places were similar to the badlands of the Southwest in the United States. We traveled many times at night because the Germans still had air superiority and their fighters were strafing us during the daylight. During the nights, in total darkness, when we stopped for a ten-minute break and then proceeded onward, some soldiers would not wake up because they were so exhausted. They became stragglers in that wild land and were lost forever. When there was enough starlight or moonshine, the soldiers would look around, whisper to each other to move, and tap those who were asleep on their boots with a rifle butt.

One time, after marching all day, our column was in about the middle of a wide-open valley as twilight came. We were ordered to dig in. No one knew why we were in such a stupid situation. The freezing wind was going through our clothes from a thousand miles away without anything to stop it. The only thing we could do was dig, dig, dig, all night. We would take turns, getting in a hole and sleeping about ten minutes, then someone would wake you up to dig another hole. We were so cold that if we stopped moving we would die. The next day, insult was added to our misery. A German bomber flew low over us, headed westerly, then bombed the forward echelon of the 34th Infantry Division Headquarters; turned around and flew over us again headed east. Not a shot was fired at the bomber. We felt like the bomber crew was thumbing their noses at us. All we had was small arms. Everyone was standing in silence (disgust). A flight of buzzards flew over us, the symbol of death. Every soldier fired. Not a single buzzard was hit. Word was passed; the generals were angry because we fired. No one gave a damn what generals thought. Our morale was at rock bottom. If any generals had been with us, they might have been shot. All of us had been wondering where the American generals were hiding.

It is now time to write about the clothes we had and the clothes we did not have. We had lightweight long underwear, lightweight cotton socks, cotton fatigue (green) trousers and jacket, and lightweight field jacket with olive drab wool liner inside and suntan color outside that would shine in darkness. To go on patrol, the field jacket had to be worn inside out. We also had a lightweight overcoat. Keep in mind, that this was the best clothing we could have, but most of the time, we didn't have all of these items. The olive drab trousers and shirts were Class A uniforms and fit tight for dress wear; making it difficult to layer other clothes under them. The gloves were wool and lasted only a few days before our fingers went through them. The boots were short top with canvass leggings worn over them; the same as used in World War I. Some soldiers suffered from sores made by the legging tops rubbing against their legs, so they cut them shorter. Another problem was when the canvass leggings got wet; they would then freeze against our legs.

The clothes that we didn't have, but should have had, were: heavy long underwear, wool socks to layer with cotton socks, high-top boots, loose fitting wool trousers with many large pockets and held up with suspenders. Instead we had lightweight, tight fitting trousers, with small tight pockets, held up by a dress belt worn under a heavy weight web belt. We needed a wool cardigan sweater, a long, wide wool scarf for the neck and chest, a loose fitting wool jacket with many large pockets, inside and out, and a turn up collar. We also needed, wool gloves with leather gloves to go over them, or wool lined leather gloves, a balaclava, or at least a navy watch cap for our heads and ears. We also needed a long overcoat with large pockets and large turn up collar. It is hard to believe that we did not have at least a sweater, scarf, or anything to cover our heads, ears, and necks. It is no wonder that we suffered day and night from the cold weather.

After our wanderings, we finally formed a battle line facing east with all the companies spread thinly out. We dug in below a ridge and I started scouting at night again. Replacement soldiers and ninety-day wonders were coming in from the United States as fast as possible. A small group of replacements came to our battalion who had been in the United States Army for only thirty days! They had only two weeks of basic training, were loaded on fast ships to Africa, and then trucked to us. One of the best-kept secrets of the war was whatever happened to the "A" and "B" bags? The procedure was for soldiers to wear all of their field equipment and carry their two barracks bags. When they boarded ships, they would keep their "A" bags with them and their "B" bags would be stored somewhere in the holds of the ships; never to be seen again. The "A" bags would be carried by the soldiers to a Repo Depot (Replacement Depot) and be turned in; never to be seen again. However, at this time in Africa, the replacements were sent directly to the rear echelon of the division headquarters where they turned in their "A" bags; never to be seen again. One replacement soldier came to our company wearing his Class "A" jacket with all the shiny gold buttons because no one at division headquarters told him not to.

One afternoon, twenty Chinese came up the hill after they unloaded from a truck. They were all from China Town in New York City and had been drafted. They all carried a small Chinese-English dictionary booklet containing common words. None of them spoke English, except one could speak a little broken English. I thought this was good, maybe I could learn some Chinese. They all stayed close together while we were trying to get them to spread out and dig their foxholes. The next day, the Germans started firing some artillery at us now and then. We simply stayed in our holes and waited. The Chinese panicked, got out of their foxholes and tried to run huddled together. The German gunners fired a salvo making a direct hit on the Chinese.

When it was over, some of us crawled over to them. They were literally torn to pieces and, of course, all dead.

It didn't get any better. One replacement kept on begging and begging me to shoot him at night so he could get out. He would have shot himself, except there was a "General Order" passed around that anyone with a self-inflicted wound, accidental or not, would be court-martialed. Some soldiers had already shot themselves. I told the soldier that if I shot him it would probably kill him and I wouldn't shoot him anyway because we needed him to fight with us. Later, we were marching in a column and tanks were passing by us. This soldier tried to fake a stumble and then fall down so that the track on the tank would go over his leg. He was willing to give his leg to get out. The edges of the track caught his clothes and pulled his body on around and under the track as it rotated. He was squeezed like a bug with his insides squirting out. It was a gruesome sight. We marched on.

A replacement soldier came to our company. He was an Irish Catholic that had been drafted. His home was in or near Boston. He was married and his wife was pregnant. Their child was expected to be born in about two weeks when he was shipped out to Africa. All he could do was worry; then complain, then gripe and then bitch. He kept saying that he shouldn't have been drafted, or at least he should have been held back until their child was born. This went on, day and night, until all of us were ready to let him die. I would walk around at night humming, "The Bells of St. Mary's" He would scream and say, "I'll kill you." I would reply, "No, if the Germans don't kill you first, then I will." The others were tired of hearing him complain. It was time to do something. I said to him, "Let's take a walk." We sat down on some rocks. I started giving him a life or death lecture. "Everyone is tired of your griping and complaining and you are not pulling your own weight. No one can do a damn thing about your concerns. Your wife, your child, your family and your friends want you to come back to them. You have three choices. First, you will be dead if you don't shut-up and start helping everyone. Do you think these soldiers will protect you in combat? You know the answer already. Second, if you don't learn fast, you could go home without your arms and legs. Third, you could fight like hell, kill the enemy until the war is over and then go home. These are your only choices. Why do you think you're so special anyway? All of these men have their own problems." I pointed to one of the soldiers and said, "Do you see that man over there? He and his younger brother came to Ireland in January 1942, with the 34th Infantry Division. Shrapnel ripped his brother's stomach to pieces and he had to watch his brother slowly die in agony. Then, we had to leave his body for the buzzards and we had to write the letter to his parents, because he couldn't." Tears came in his eyes and he said, "I didn't know that." I replied, "There are a hell of a lot of things you don't know. You are young, strong and Irish. I like Irish, they are good fighters. Don't let your family be ashamed of you." He did change. He started helping, pulling extra duty and volunteering to carry heavy loads of food, water and ammunition up the hill when vehicles could not reach us. The platoon settled down and started good-natured joking as soldiers do.

It was subtle, but the old men from Ireland who had survived were learning from this awful on the job training. They no longer questioned my knowledge of combat. Some of them were beginning to understand leadership as corporals and sergeants. There were small running battles and skirmishes as we continued northward on the battle-line. One day a German fighter flew over our foxholes so low that I could almost see his eyes. He throttled his engine back and then glided over the ridges so that he was on top of us before we could see or hear him.

Cigarettes and other items were sent up to us from time to time. There were things such as large tubes of Barbosol shaving cream (we didn't have razors and couldn't spare water to shave) and large tubes of toothpaste (we didn't have toothbrushes and couldn't spare our water anyway). This was done by the intellectuals somewhere behind us. Our two cans of "C" ration beans per day was the only kind of "C" rations we could get because we were at the end of the line. Because beans were our main diet, some of the soldiers developed ulcers and boils on their bodies. When we had a bowel movement, we would dig a small hole in front of our foxholes to defecate in. Since we were on the verge of starvation, our feces were a small amount of pills like goat droppings. Toilet paper was non-existent, so we used weeds or anything we could find.

We carried extra flints for our cigarette lighters, but couldn't get any lighter fluid. To fill our lighters we would open the lighter; tie a string around it and let it down into the fuel tank on a vehicle and it would refill with fluid. Some of the replacements brought Zippo cigarette lighters made in the U.S. with them. We couldn't buy lighters or anything else because we didn't have a P. X. (Post Exchange).

Our battle line was on a high plateau, and sometime before this new position, our company had been sent a replacement that we called Barney. He had immigrated, with his parents, from Russia to Philadelphia when he was a young child. He had studied the violin most of his life. Someone said that he had played some with the Philadelphia Philharmonic Orchestra. Everyone liked Barney, but it was obvious that he would never make a soldier. Our company had acquired a captain and two ninety-day wonders. Without any talk about it, all the soldiers wanted to save Barney's life. So we all, except the captain, made Barney the company runner to take messages to and from the company headquarters to the platoons and squads. That way, he could stay at the company headquarters. Often he would forget to carry his rifle or forget where he left it. Every time the captain sent Barney back to us to stay on the line, the soldiers would send him back down to the headquarters with some kind of message such as, "We are hungry," "We are cold." Because we told him he was the company runner, he ran lickety-split everywhere he went. The captain relented because he knew the soldiers would never give up. Besides, there were times when a runner was seriously needed and Barney could help the company clerk; who would be overloaded with work after every battle.

One pitch-black night, there was a mighty storm with sheets of rain and thunder and lightening all around us because we were up high. In a flash of lightening, I saw Barney at my foxhole. He leaned over and told me something, but I couldn't hear because of the storm. He took off running. In another lightening flash, I saw him running the wrong way toward the German line! Leaving my rifle in the foxhole, I ran after him. He was fast. Guided by lightening flashes, I sprinted as if I was running a 100-yard dash. When close enough, I made a diving tackle to bring him down. Holding on to him, I was praying and cursing at the same time as we lay in the mud. Shaking my fist toward heaven, I was thinking, "Oh, Lord, why do you allow this?" Then I realized that this was not the Lord's will, it was the works of evil men. Then I cried in prayer, "Lord, help me save this young Jew, I am already in The Valley of Death and surrounded by evil." While I continued to hold onto Barney with one hand, we slowly made our way back to our line, moving only when I could see by lightening flashes. When we were back at our line, we laid down in the mud until dawn.

One day, another storm hit. This time there was no rain. It was large balls of hail, with thunder and lightening. We got in our holes and listened to the hail bounce off our steel helmets. When the hailstorm stopped, we got out and crunched around walking on the twelve-inch deep hail balls. Suddenly, without warning, it all melted, within seconds. All that water caused a flash flood flowing down the gully where our company headquarters was. It washed everything away down the gully.

Someone started shouting. One of the soldiers had stayed in his hole and when the hail melted the water caused the foxhole to cave in on top of the soldier. He was buried alive. All those who could get around the foxhole started digging with their hands. We were afraid to use entrenching tools (little shovels). As soon as his head was exposed, his helmet was removed and while two men were clearing the mud out of his nose and mouth, the others kept digging. While one soldier poured water from his canteen, the other used his handkerchief to clear the mud out. As soon as possible, his body was pulled out and his eyes, nose and ears were washed. There was an abandoned Arab thatched hut nearby. Soldiers picked him up and ran with him to the hut. I ran to the hut and set it on fire. Stripping his gear and outer clothes off, we moved them close enough to dry out. We kept moving his body around the fire to get it warm, but not too hot, knowing that he would die if he went into hypothermia. I sent a man to headquarters to tell the captain what had happened and to come back with the company jeep. The soldier was wrapped up in blankets and placed in the back seat with his head in the lap of a soldier. The jeep was driven off fast to carry him to the medics. We never knew if he made it.

Winter & Spring 1943

A nice day just didn't seem possible. Our latest ninety-day wonder seemed to be the type that would learn and make it. He recognized his lack of training and would listen. Just maybe the instructors at Officers Candidate School in Fort Benning were learning also. A good soldier cannot be trained in ninety days. An officer needs to be trained much longer than that. All the short training for officers and enlisted men in the United States Army was for cannon fodder. One day, when our cigarettes and stuff were sent up to us, there was also some gallon cans of stew and vegetables. One soldier had been talking about how his family owned a restaurant and how good he could cook a plank steak. He was elected to be our cook. Someone "borrowed" a two-burner portable stove that used gas. The stove was setup in a gully next to our holes. Our cook mixed everything up into British Compo Ration tins to heat it. All of us looked forward to a "hot" meal. The mess kits were rectangular shaped lightweight aluminum pans with folding handles. The only available way to clean mess kits was to scrub them with sand or weeds. Congealed grease wouldn't clean off. The mess cups, with folding handles, were also lightweight aluminum shaped the same as the canteens and fit into the same pouch before the canteen went in. Everyone lined up with their mess kits, while our cook dished out the hot meal. The lieutenant made some sort of casual remark. It was harmless and I can't remember what he said. A soldier, who had just received his food in his mess kit, slammed the food into the lieutenant's face; then dropped his mess kit and raised his rifle. This could not be allowed to happen. As I moved between them, I dropped my mess kit and pointed my rifle at the soldier's head. His eyes said he was ready to kill. As I stared him down, I shouted, "Don't anyone move or say anything." Gradually, the soldier lowered his rifle and the lieutenant stayed still and wiped the food off his face. I said, "Sir, let's take a walk" and with a nod of my head, the other soldiers gathered around the angry soldier so he couldn't fire. The lieutenant and I walked down to the company headquarters and I explained everything to the captain. The soldier had shown one of the first signs of insanity and wanted to take out his anger on anyone in authority. The captain agreed the only thing to do was to transfer the lieutenant immediately. The lieutenant thanked me and shook my hand. I went back up the hill. This captain was one of the good ones, and because he was good, he was soon promoted and moved on.

It was difficult to get and keep line officers (lieutenants and captains) because of casualties and there was a shortage anyway. After the captain left, we didn't have any. In a few days a first lieutenant arrived and of course, he became our acting captain. He had been a ninety-day wonder, but had been in the army long enough to get promoted from second lieutenant to first lieutenant. It became evident that he had never been in combat. To put it bluntly, he was arrogant and wanted to be a hero. In the infantry, armored, combat engineers and other combat units, all soldiers who killed the enemy were heroes. The lieutenant did not understand this. He ordered a three-day, thirty man combat patrol, which he would lead, and I would be the second in command. After explaining the problems involved, he still wouldn't listen. His thought was to go and capture a couple of Germans, bring them back and he would be a hero.

The German army didn't place infantry somewhere and leave them as the U. S. Army was doing. They always had transport, tanks and artillery near them. We prepared for the patrol and headed east carrying food and water for three days. The lieutenant read his compass often, but still didn't understand that you can't travel in a straight line in this wild country. He never did look up while we were on the high ground to find a peak or something to guide on. As a result, we traveled in blind canyons. When we stopped to rest during the night, the lieutenant would put his field jacket over his head as a light shield, use his flashlight to read his compass. As each hour passed, we were more and more worried. I had already quietly passed the word to save some food and water. Again, I showed them my rock that I was sucking, because we had some new soldiers that didn't know about this.

In the afternoon of the third day, we stopped to rest in a blind canyon. The lieutenant read his compass. The penalty for rebellion, desertion, or mutiny in a combat situation is death by a firing squad. Carefully approaching the lieutenant, I stood at attention, saluted, and said, "Sir, request permission to speak." The lieutenant replied, "Well, dammit, sergeant, go ahead." I said, "Sir, our three days are up. We are low on food and water, and any one tank or artillery piece could kill us while we are in this canyon. My request, Sir, is that I be allowed to scout ahead to return us to our battle line." The lieutenant replied, "Hell no, you smart-ass, we'll find the Germans." I said, "Sir, then it is my duty to survive to kill the enemy in accordance with my oath as a soldier and in accordance with the Articles of War. I cannot and will not give any orders or advice to these soldiers because they are under your command. I am leaving and if I make it back, I shall report to the highest ranking officer I can find." The lieutenant was dumbfounded. Reading his eyes, he knew he was not a hero. By the way, the canyon we were in was running north and south, not east and west. Picking an easy spot to climb out of the canyon, I started up. Looking back, all the soldiers were climbing after me in single file. When we reached the top of the canyon, I saw the lieutenant following the soldiers.

It was imperative to find a landmark; a peak or something to guide on before dark. Looking at my compass (which I had taken from the German lieutenant) there was a plateau with some ridges that could be followed to the east. A compass is good if you can travel in a straight line while on the plains or oceans. The sun and stars must be used also to survive in rough terrain. It takes years to understand this. The pioneers, going west in their covered wagons, guided on landmarks, mountain peaks and the like. When wagon trains camped for the night, the men would un-harness their oxen or horses and lay their wagon tongues pointed west or wherever they needed to go, so they could move before daylight and be headed in the right direction.

When I knew we were close enough to make our lines, I sat down to take a break. The lieutenant had eaten all of his food and drank all his water. Making certain the lieutenant could see; I ate my last can of beans and drank my last water. During all this time, I did not say a word to anyone. When we reached our battle line, no one talked; we were completely exhausted. It had taken a day and a half to get back. The other soldiers in our company wanted to know what happened. The first lieutenant went down the hill to company headquarters. The next day, he left in the company jeep. Since he was the acting captain of our company, the only officer he could report to was our lieutenant colonel commanding the battalion. Someone heard the conversation the first lieutenant and the lieutenant colonel had. It went something like this. The first lieutenant said, "I am not going on patrol again with that damn Houston because he left me. I am filing charges against him." The lieutenant colonel replied, "So I heard. He got you and the soldiers back alive, didn't he? If it hadn't been for Houston, you and the soldiers would be dead now. You screwed up. That company will never accept you as a leader. Charges should be filed against you for stupidity. My sergeant has already filled out the papers and I have signed them. One is an order relieving you of command and a complete report explaining why. The other is your transfer to regimental headquarters. The colonel there can decide what to do with you." The first lieutenant started protesting. The lieutenant colonel said, "I don't want to hear or see you again. Get in your jeep and drive your sorry ass to headquarters and maybe you'll get lost on the way."

The war went on. Crazy things happened. We didn't stay in one place very long. The battle kept moving north as the British 8th Army, under the command of Field Marshall Montgomery, continued to follow the east coast of Tunisia; attacking the Germans and Italians driving them to the north. Our company traveled some to the north and then turned to the east to reach a ridge to dig in and form another battle line. The Germans had a company of infantry already dug in back of the ridge and they had some artillery support. When we were within their range, the artillery opened fire.

Two soldiers dropped down in a small patch of weeds. A shell exploded a few feet in front of the weed patch. We knew they were goners, but two heads popped up and one said, "Man, that was close. Where did it hit?" One soldier starting screaming, "I'm hit, I'm hit, medic, medic!" Someone crawled over to him and said, "Joe, you damn yard bird, that's not blood, that's water from your canteen." Shrapnel had ripped open his canteen and when he felt the water running down his leg, he thought it was blood.

When shrapnel hits your body, it takes a few seconds before you feel anything. The first sensation is like a sting because the shrapnel is so hot. When shells hit the ground, they burn the earth. First, it is white hot, then red hot and then the glow goes away. Another shell suddenly exploded and shrapnel hit my right foot. It cut a gash across my instep and other pieces cut my big toenail and lacerated the rest of my toe. It felt like there was water in my boot. We crawled back down the hill and got away from the artillery fire.

I found a combat medic who stopped the bleeding and cleaned the wounds. Then he poured sulfanilamide powder on the wounds and bandaged them up. All soldiers had been given packets of sulfanilamide powder and some sulfanilamide tablets to carry. The instructions were to pour the powder on wounds and for the wounded soldier to swallow some tablets, the number depending on body weight. Sometimes, soldiers would be carrying up to a hundred pounds of gear and not knowing their body weight anyway, we would poke the tablets in their mouths according to how serious their wounds were. When their wounds were very serious, they got more tablets.

At another place, we dug our holes below a ridge. We heard machinegun fire from a German fighter. One of our Piper Cubs (L-5s, we called them Paper Cups) popped up and over the ridge flying only a few feet above the ground. A German fighter was after the Piper, but couldn't get a clear shot because the fighter was fast while the Piper was flying very low and going very slow. The German pilot came in fast for a quick shot, then went around to try again. The Piper pilot put his wheels on the ground and while the aircraft was still rolling, opened the door and rolled out. The German pilot hit the Piper with his machinegun and it started burning while the pilot ran towards us. By then, we had opened fire on the German so he left. He would have surely killed the American pilot if we hadn't been there.

The instep on my right foot healed with only some scars left, but as you may imagine it was difficult to keep my right toe clean. It would get infected and swell up so I would cut my boots some more. There were four other soldiers in our company who were having problems with swollen feet and needed larger boots as I did. They were all Swedes from Minnesota and were in the same battalion I had been in when I was in Ireland, good guys. We complained enough so that we were finally given a jeep to go to the rear echelon of the 34th Infantry Division to get new boots. After our feet were measured, we waited there for the Quartermaster Corps to get us new boots. We all needed size 13-EEE.

The colonel on the general's staff in charge of training was the one I had met in Ireland. He was now the senior officer at the rear echelon. The brigadier general was at the front echelon. The colonel was sincerely pleased to see me. He said, "Well, Sergeant Alabama, who doesn't want to be a sergeant, some people have heard about you. How in the hell have you been? Sit down, let's talk." We talked for a long time about what had happened, etc. He told me he was up for promotion to Brigadier General. I said, "Sir, that's great, we need more leaders." He was aware of the foul-ups by some high-ranking American officers, but couldn't talk about it.

I asked the colonel if he knew where my two combat engineer friends, 1st Lt. O'Farrel and Staff Sergeant McDonald were located. The colonel called in a sergeant and told him to find out where they were. Their unit was the U.S. 19th Combat Engineer Battalion. After a while, the sergeant returned with a strange look on his face. He said, "Sir, the 1,200 men of the 19th Battalion were wiped out at Kasserine, except for 100 or so that escaped, the lieutenant and sergeant were KIA." Sitting there, shaking my head, I couldn't say anything. The colonel said, "They were brave men. They were trying to lay a minefield to stop the main column of Germans, but were too late."

The sergeant said, "Sir, there is something else, there is a sergeant in personnel that has some information about the lieutenant and sergeant." The colonel said, "Tell him to come over here." In a few minutes the personnel sergeant came in and handed the colonel some papers and said, "Sir, the lieutenant and sergeant gave me this recommendation and report to type up. When it was ready for their signatures, they were gone and never had a chance to sign it." The colonel read the papers out loud. They had recommended me for the Medal of Honor and the report explained how we blew up the German ammunition dump. I said, "Sir, I don't need a medal, both of them deserve medals." Of course, an unsigned recommendation is not valid. Normally, an officer has to witness the action to recommend a high medal. The colonel instructed the personnel sergeant to prepare the papers using the same information for medals for both of my friends and for acting Sergeant Houston to sign and he would counter-sign. Then the colonel said, "I'll see what I can do." My sleep was not good that night. I wanted to talk to my friends' families. I prayed what I was taught as a child, by Methodist, Baptist, and by the sisters of Saint Mary's of Loretta.

Winter & Spring 1943

While we waited for our new boots, two strange looking soldiers arrived. They were wearing German boots, some British battle dress trousers, and other things, but they were wearing the U.S. Army field jackets with the U.S. Army Big Red One patches (1st Infantry Division) on them. These two soldiers had enlisted in the United States Army with me at the British Depot in England. These were some of the ones who had deserted the U.S. Army somewhere. We talked. This is their story. After the 34th Infantry Division invaded Africa, they got "lost" and then "found" the 1st Infantry Division (regular army). Being good soldiers, and not liking the National Guard "Saturday night" soldiers, they volunteered to serve in the 1st Infantry Division. They became the Number 1 and Number 2 scouts. The commanding general of the 1st Infantry Division, and all the others, liked their work and their knowledge of combat. However, the commanding general of the 34th Infantry Division demanded and demanded that they be returned to the 34th for court-martial for desertion. The two soldiers didn't seem to be concerned about it because they knew the judges for a general court-martial would be regular army officers. Besides, how can anyone be charged with desertion by going into combat? I never knew what happened, but I think the charges were eventually dropped.

The rear echelon of the 34th was located in a small French village. It had a main dirt street with some commercial buildings similar to the old west of the United States. All of the commercial buildings were vacant because of the war. The U.S. Army had occupied the vacant ones (I am proud of the fact that the army of the United States always pays the owners of property.) There were houses at the ends of the main street, plus some back of this on sub-streets. French Roman Catholics had occupied these houses since long ago. There were some Arabs living there also.

Some of the French people had heard me speak to some of them in my broken French. These were isolated people and none of them could speak any English. One day some of the older men and women came to me and asked for help. After much gesturing and conversation, they were telling me that because of the hated Bosch and the Italian Fascists, they had not seen a Priest for several years. Children had been born and not christened and the Holy Sacraments had not been taken. All of the older boys and young men had fled. They had received a message that a Priest was coming. The help they wanted from me was to escort them across the valley to their secret meeting place. An elderly man said in French, "Sir, you are a great soldat American and you can protect us. The people have great fear. The journey will be a long day and we will carry food and water for everyone. I replied in French, "I understand, but my colonel must give permission."

When I entered the colonel's office, he said, "Now what's up?" I replied, "Sir, the people of this village want me to escort them to their meeting place across the valley, and I'm getting tired of waiting for my boots." The colonel said, "Maybe I can do something about your boots, but what else are you talking about?" I explained about the Priest coming and the things the people wanted to do and that I didn't want to eat their food, they had so little. The colonel said, "Go with them. That's a good thing. Tell the sergeant in the kitchen that I said to give you all the food you can carry." I replied, "Thank you, Sir."

There were some Arabs in the village that owned horses. Not good horses, they were all skinny. It was a long way to cross that valley to the hills. The best way would be to ride a horse. The negotiation to buy (really rent) a horse and saddle started while some of the French people watched. As I counted out French francs, every now and then stopping and showing them to the Arab, he finally agreed. The French were shaking their heads, meaning it was too much. Mounting the horse Arab style, I got his attention by tapping his head with the flat of my bayonet. He ran so I simply guided him around in circles until he gave up. A French family agreed to keep the horse in their yard until the Priest arrived. Giving the French family some money, I asked them to buy grain and feed him well.

One evening, the Priest arrived, together with his assistants, in an old French truck. It was agreed that we would leave at daylight the next morning. After breakfast, the cooks packed four musette bags full of food; such as sardines, salmon, corned beef, hash, Spam, crackers and bread. Tying the straps together making two pairs of bags, I placed them behind the saddle on the horse as if they were saddlebags. Many Americans came to watch the strange procession. The younger children were placed in the truck, together with food, water and wine. There were no children less than three years old because the young men and most of the young women had left when the Nazis occupied France. It looked like children who were about eight years old and above would walk. The column started off with me leading on the horse, then the truck, followed by all of the others. A World War I veteran had given me the compass bearing to follow to reach their secret place. This procession crossing the valley was a strange sight.

Calling for a ten-minute break after the first hour, as soldiers do, I realized that the children and elderly needed a break every thirty minutes. It was about five miles to the hills and it took four hours to get there. In the hills, some of the men led us to the mouth of a cave. The mouth was large enough to lead the horse in after I dismounted. The inside of the cave was huge with many rooms. There were signs everywhere that people had lived there through the ages.

The people gathered together in the large area and sat down because they were tired. The Priest said some Latin words and then when the Lord's Supper was prepared, the people passed by to be blessed and to receive the Lord's bread. The Priest offered the Holy Sacrament to me, but I declined. He blessed me anyway, and we drank some wine together later. The children were christened and a small room was setup as a confessional. The women prepared the meal and we had lunch with many happy smiles. They knew most of the American food that I had brought, but a few items, such as sweet potatoes and Spam, were unfamiliar to them. They asked me to explain. They understood that sweet potatoes were another kind of potato that grew in the ground and Spam was a kind of ham. They liked it. American soldiers called Spam on toast S. O. S. (stuff on a shingle).

The confessions were taking a good while. Getting worried, I reminded the Priest how long it took to get there and that it would take longer returning because everyone was tired. We needed to reach the village before dark because of the danger of being attacked. He agreed and hurried the confessions. Everything was packed up and we left. After a while, all of the very weakest were packed on the truck. It was awful for me to watch but there were never any complaints. This was a great thing for them. Looking back, I saw a small boy stumbling along, so I turned back and lifted him up on the horse, in back of the saddle, and he put his feet in the musette bags. He held onto me with all his might until I finally got him to relax. With over two miles to go, I saw that there was no way we could make it before dark. Then, I could not believe what I was seeing. In a cloud of dust there was a convoy of trucks heading towards us at high speed. American soldiers jumped out of the trucks, picked up the children and elderly, and loaded them. It is not easy to get into the back of a 6x6 truck because of their height. At the village, there stood the colonel and other officers with field glasses, watching. The people started singing. It had always been apparent to me, even in Ireland, that this colonel really was a good guy.

The next morning, the people, led by the Priest, assembled in front of the colonel's office and started singing. The colonel, all officers, noncommissioned officers, and men came out from wherever they were. The Priest and the people blessed and thanked "mon colonel" and all the Americans. They sang the French National Anthem and other songs. They didn't know how to sing "The Star Spangled Banner" of the United States. Neither does anybody else, either foreign or domestic for that matter. The Anthem of the United States of America has always been and will be an embarrassment. It should be changed.

The colonel finally did get the quartermasters to send our boots so we loaded our jeep to return to the front. As we reached the end of the village, we noticed an abandoned house with a Red Cross flag on it. We stopped and looked around. The door had a padlock on it, but there was no one there. Popping the hasp off with a bayonet, we went inside. What a wonder! There were cases of chocolate candy, cookies and such, stacked from the floor to the ceiling. Why hadn't the Red Cross man distributed these items to us, the soldiers? The American Red Cross needed some distributors. Case after case was loaded on the jeep for proper distribution. This was my first bad experience with the American Red Cross.

On down the road, we passed by two Piper Cubs, with their crew's setting-up a new camp. These were the 34th Infantry Division artillery spotters and reconnaissance aircraft. The story was going around about these sergeant pilots receiving credit for destroying several German fighters. They did this by flying slowly around mountains and down into canyons. When German pilots tried to line up on them to fire, they would crash because the German planes couldn't pull up or turn quickly enough. The new American Red Cross distributors completed their tasks upon arrival back to the battle line. Someone said the American Red Cross man complained and complained, until finally a high-ranking officer told him he had better shut-up.

Winter & Spring   1943

The crazy war went on as the battle line moved north, ridge by ridge. We were issued some brand new untried equipment; walkie-talkie radios, bazookas and antitank mines. The walkie-talkie radios didn't work because someone had to be listening for calls and the batteries were usually dead. Our GI flashlights were thrown away when the batteries went dead because we didn't have any more. With fresh batteries in the radios they still didn't work after tapping them against a rock. The bazookas were made to fire rockets. They were made out of sheet metal like a stovepipe. To aim, you would look at different notches on a vertical piece of metal. One flashlight battery fired the rocket when the electrical current ignited it. At the prone position, one soldier would load the rocket in the barrel making sure the electrical contacts were in the correct position. The other soldier would aim and pull the trigger. The rockets that did fire burned some soldiers with the back flash. The procedure we developed was to count to three and if it didn't fire, lay it down carefully and run. There was no way of knowing if the rocket was activated or the battery was dead. The other problems were; how could the infantry carry this hunk of metal and rockets or get new batteries? How could two infantrymen lie down in front of an advancing tank with an 88mm big gun and a pair of machineguns? If anyone could do this, then make a direct hit the rocket would just bounce off the tank. Some more of our experts in Washington!

The antitank mines were just as crazy as the other items. They were rectangular shaped sheet metal canisters with "V" crimps in the top where the two detonators could be inserted. The detonators were the same size and shape as 12volt buss fuses and contained nitroglycerin. The mines were set to explode with 300 pounds of pressure. Soldiers were to run out and lay them down in front of their holes! The two detonators clinked together if they were in the same pocket. You have to be psycho to carry nitro anyway. The mines were cumbersome and hard to carry. Sometimes they would fall off our web belts. They were not powerful enough to stop a tank. One fell off the belt of a soldier in another company. He had left the detonators in the mine. They were marching in single file. The soldier behind him stepped on the mine and since his weight, plus all his gear, weighted over 300 pounds, it exploded and several men were killed.

We were hungry; we were always hungry. One day there was a scrawny, skinny cow wandering around in front of our battle line. Soldiers started talking, to them that cow looked just like a platoon of Germans. The artillery spotter on the line with us was also hungry. He agreed and performed his duty. He called the artillery, not on a walkie-talkie, but signal corps lines. First, you must bracket the target, then fire for effect. It took twenty rounds to hit the cow. The artillery spotter gave the order to cease firing. The Germans had run. We had fresh meat that night.

An Arab caravan approached our battle line from the east. We spotted them by using field glasses as they passed through the German battle line. I selected soldiers who had BAR's (Browning Automatic Rifles) to go out with me to act as escorts through our line. Giving them a short lecture, I said, "Half of you walk along with them on the right flank and the other half get on the left flank. Don't get too close. The Arabs have every right to be here. There shouldn't be any trouble. Do not fire unless the Arabs fire first. Be nice." One of them replied, "Now, Sarge, we are always nice. We went to Sunday-School." Everyone laughed. When the caravan had gone completely through our line, their leader rode his camel over to another soldier and me, and gave each of us a scrawny chicken with their legs tied up. I gave the Arab two packs of Lucky Strike cigarettes. One chicken would not even provide one bite for a squad and we usually shared with a platoon consisting of three or four squads. The soldier and I flipped a coin. He won and I was glad because I didn't have to figure out how to share two chickens with all those men. I don't know what he did with them.

An Arab man approached our line carrying a small boy on his back. Someone signaled him to come on in. Believe it or not, American soldiers had been given a standing (on-going) general order to shoot any Arab that came within two hundred yards. The Nazis paid them a bounty for information or whenever they turned in an Allied soldier. But, so did we. A mine had injured the Arab boy's arm and U.S. hospital personnel had placed a cast on his fractured arm. The Arab father had been given instructions to return with the boy to the hospital at a certain time. When the father and son returned, the hospital had moved. The father had been carrying the boy for days, searching for Americans. The combat medics tried to remove the cast with ordinary knives, but couldn't. There was the smell of gangrene. The medics mixed sulfanilamide power with water and poured it in the edges of the cast so that it would run down the arm. They also gave the boy some sulfanilamide tablets. All this time, the boy never cried. After giving them some food and water, the medics arranged for a jeep to carry them to a hospital. The "A"rabs, "B"rabs and "C"rabs (1st, 2nd, and 3rd class Arabs) as the soldiers called them, had some beautiful children. All soldiers seemed to like dogs, children and especially orphans that we saw from time to time.

While changing our position again, we came upon a river. The river was full from winter rains. One-half of our company stripped down, washed our bodies and clothes while the other half formed a defensive perimeter around us. When the first half finished washing, the second half took their turn. We never had towels; we walked ourselves dry using body heat the same way we did when it rained on us. When we finished bathing, we filled our canteens upstream and then headed off downstream. After passing several turns in the river, we came upon a bunch of bodies; some on the banks and some were floating in the water. All of the bodies were bloated and they must have been dead for several days. They were German, Italian, and American soldiers. Dead cows, horses, camels and other animals have a terrible stench. The stench of human bodies is different and so much worse. Buzzards were eating the bodies that were not in the water. Some of the new soldiers, that had never seen dead men up close, were vomiting. We left that place at double time.

Small groups of German tanks, sometimes with Armored Infantry with them, sometimes not, would pass by while we hid in the rocks in the hills. If they caught any of us too far out in the valleys, it would be too bad. We saw some German tanks that had wooden crates of captured American cigarettes, food, etc. tied to them in the back of the turret over the engine. If we could only set the crates on fire, the engine air intake would suck the fire into the diesel engine. The engine would explode or start a fire inside the tank. The U.S. Army standard ammunition for M-1 rifles and BAR's were lead cartridges. We could get armor piercing (A. P.) steel cartridges also, but we needed tracer ammunition that had a chemical that burned when fired. Machinegun ammunition came to us with the belts already loaded and every fifth round was a tracer for the machine-gunners to aim with. Unpacking some machinegun belts, I removed sixteen rounds of tracers (enough for two 8 round M-1 rifle clips) and replaced the tracers with lead cartridges. Showing other soldiers how to do this, they were cautioned to always replace them with another cartridge when removing the tracers because a machinegun will stop firing when there is a missing cartridge in the ammo belt. My personal preference was to carry some M-1 clips of tracers in one pocket and some clips of A. P. in another. Lead slugs will not penetrate the gear worn by soldiers as well as A. P.

For infantrymen to try to destroy a tank by any means is ultra dangerous. One day, we were moving north staying on high ground next to a valley. Four German tanks approached in single file in the valley close to the high ground. It just happened that there was a deep gully in the back of the rocks that my platoon was hiding in. I said, "Pass these instructions. Load Tracers, we will all fire one clip at the last tank after it passes us. Then jump down into the gully for cover." About thirty-six soldiers fired eight rounds each of tracers into the wood crates and then jumped and slid down into the gully as the "Screaming Meemies" screeched over our heads. Smoke was rising in the direction of the tank. Then there was an explosion. The Germans stopped firing in our direction, so we climbed and crawled to higher ground. Peeping over rocks, the tank that we fired on was blown apart, still burning, and the other three tanks were standing by. The tank that we fired on was destroyed, including the crew. This was the only opportunity we ever had to destroy a German panzer. A new design German "Tiger Tank" moved near us one time. At the time it was the most awesome tank in the world.

Sometimes we received mail and parcels. It was difficult to receive mail because we were constantly moving but when we did, we would try to hunker down to enjoy it. A few of the old soldiers left from Ireland received newspapers from their homes in Minnesota or Iowa. These newspapers were the only contact we had with the rest of the world. Everyone read them. They had news (propaganda) about the Pacific Theatre, Europe and the Home Front. My mother sent me another parcel and guess what, it was a box of Whitman's Sampler. My platoon consisted of twenty to thirty-six men, depending on casualties and on replacements. Whitman's Sampler chocolates were a delight even when there was plenty of all kinds of food. Seeing the look in those soldiers' faces when they saw my chocolates, I didn't have the heart to eat all of them. Each man in my platoon picked out one piece and I ate the rest.

When any of us went to our headquarters, way behind us, we would occasionally see some civilians hanging around. They wore U.S. Army uniforms without any military insignia. They wore patches on each shoulder with white letters that spelled "WAR CORRESPONDENT". None of them ever came close to our battle lines except one whose name was Ernie Pyle. I saw him one time at our company headquarters just down the hill from our line. He walked over to three of us, introduced himself, and offered us a cigarette. He insisted that we call him "Ernie." I left because I needed to go back up to our line. The other two soldiers told us later that Ernie wanted to talk to combat infantrymen, not officers or soldiers to the rear. Ernie asked them where they were from, what they did and where they had been. He wrote all of this down in a little notebook.

A few days later, another sergeant and I were a good distance ahead of our column scouting when we saw a large French plantation with huge olive groves, vineyards, and the like. The two-story mansion was beautiful. It was constructed of brick, with a copper roof, wrought iron porch rails, and everything else. There were trees, shrubbery, a garden, and many smaller buildings around the mansion. Everything was closed and locked and we couldn't find anyone there. The largest building, other than the mansion, was high and looked like some type of garage with large doors. There were some smaller regular size doors and the sergeant with me was able to pick the lock on one by using some wire and nails we found in a tool shed. We were amazed when we went in. There was a Ford Trimotor (a three engine aircraft). Adolf Hitler's personal aircraft was this same model and I had seen one at the Municipal Airport in Montgomery,

Alabama, which was used to carry passengers during the beginning of Eastern Air Lines during the 1930's. We started dreaming. The sergeant told me that he had just gotten his private flying license when he joined the Army. He didn't have much experience, and I told him I had some solo experience. Could we fly this aircraft to America? We finally gave up on our dream, because somebody would certainly shoot us down and it wouldn't have enough fuel anyway. We re-locked the building and moved on.

The Germans and Italians retreated to the north. Now and then, they would stop and form a defensive battle line. There were some good size battles, near a place named Goubellat, involving the 34th Infantry Division. The Germans had buried some American soldiers who were KIA. They made some make shift crosses with the dead soldiers' names, ranks, and serial numbers on them except they added "T-42" to the serial numbers because they thought that was a part of the serial number. The U.S. dog tags contained: name, rank, serial number, next of kin, T-42 which meant the date of a soldier's tetanus shot, and the worst tragedy of all, religion. There were three categories of religion; "P" meant Protestant, "C" meant Catholic, and "H" meant Hebrew. The Nazis did not consider Jews to be prisoners of war (POW). They tortured them to death. Some of the American Jews, who were infantrymen, tried to beat out the "H" in their dog tags, but couldn't. Some of the Jews swapped dog tags with dead American soldiers, which we encouraged. After all, this meant death or survival. It is no wonder that American infantrymen became so bitter. Our great leaders with some exceptions, in the U.S. Army, didn't have one grain of common sense.

The Allied troops reached the coastal plain with the infantry following the armored divisions. Between Goubellat to the south and Mateur to the north, there was a great running tank battle in the plains. The British 8th Army, under the command of Field Marshall Montgomery, had finally linked up with the troops of the British V Corps, the Free French XIX Corps and the United States Army II Corps. The Allied Supreme Commander in Algiers, General Eisenhower, issued the order for all Allied Forces to be under the command of Field Marshall Montgomery. This infuriated the potbelly General Patton, and started a long-standing feud of jealousy. The Allies did win, driving the Germans and Italian tanks further north. There were many destroyed tanks and British Bren Gun carriers scattered alongside some railroad tracks. Searching a British tank that had not burned, I found a Thompson sub-machinegun and a bunch of loaded ammo clips. Because it was better for close-in fighting, I kept it; taking my M-1 rifle apart and scattering the pieces, I left.

SUCK A ROCK 32: Somewhere in North Africa, Tunisia

Spring 1943

There was a high plateau rising from the coastal plains near Mateur. It was several miles in length and breadth. It could be seen as far as the naked eye could see. On the military maps, it was designated "Hill 609." The Germans and Italians had heavily fortified the top of the plateau with their infantry dug in and supported by artillery. They planted mine fields going up the slopes using antipersonnel mines such as the "Bouncing Betsy." The canister was loaded with steel balls and was buried with three wire prongs sticking above ground. They are very hard to see. When a soldier stepped on one, the wire prongs would go down and activate a spring. Then when the soldier moved his foot, the spring would send the mine 7 feet high and it would explode covering a wide circle of ground. Thus the GI's named it the "Bouncing Betsy." The enemy did not plant antitank mines on the slopes because tanks could not climb up them.

The things that I am writing about now are the happenings of my company of infantry only. The entire 34th Infantry Division had formed up together to attack Hill 609. The division had spread out about 22 miles from the plateau to make a coordinated advance. An infantry division consists of about 15,000 soldiers plus supporting units. We moved forward at night and before daylight hid in weeds or rocks. The heat became fierce during the daylight because it was spring and we were down from the mountains. The enemy had complete control for miles around the plateau with their artillery.

As we moved forward, our hearts were filled with dread. The only way to defeat the enemy on top of the plateau was with infantry. There was some good news, and we prayed that it was not just another rumor. The U.S. Army artillery had received more weapons and men and was assembled back of us. They would race forward to support us when we were in position below the plateau. The U.S. Army had large artillery; such as the 105-mm rifles and the 155-mm rifles that were not effective in the badlands because by the time they could be setup, the enemy would be gone. These weapons could hit targets twenty miles away with good artillery spotters. Without question, Hill 609 had to be captured, as this would split the Axis forces between Bizerta to the north and Tunis and the Cape Bon Peninsula to the east.

During the night, we crawled silently to the base of the plateau and dug our foxholes. If anyone hit a rock digging, they would simply move over and dig. In the darkness, one soldier moved too far up the slope. There was a flash of light and then the noise of an explosion. He was in the minefield and a Bouncing Betsy got him. He screamed in pain. The German machine gunners zeroed in on that spot.

The dying soldier was one of the original National Guard men in Ireland, as was his cousin who went wild. The cousin was going up to help him. The soldiers closest to him tackled him and tied him up with pup tent ropes. The Germans were using the dying soldier for bait. Crawling backwards, when there was some moonlight, I found the sergeant commanding the weapons platoon and convinced him to fire his mortars at the dying soldier's position. The small mortars started firing and were hitting mines everywhere a shell hit.

This started a chain reaction. When the commanders of the big U.S. artillery saw the flashes of fire, they gave the order to fire on the slopes and the top of the plateau. The enemy returned fire with their artillery. This was exactly what was needed for the infantry to get to the top of the plateau. The artillery would have to perform saturation fire up the slopes at certain spots to clear the mines for the infantry to go up. I can't really explain what it was like during that night and all the next day. With friendly fire and enemy fire over our heads, the entire earth moved and we held onto the ground with our fingernails while down in our foxholes. There were loud explosions as far as we could see.

The next day, we stayed hidden in our foxholes. After dark, some jeeps reached us with "C" rations and water and passed our orders up and down the line. The infantry would crawl up the slopes through the paths in the minefields cleared by our artillery and then wait just below the crest until the crack of dawn. Our heavy artillery would start shelling the top of the plateau at 0100 hours and cease firing at the crack of dawn. Then all of the infantry on the battle line would attack simultaneously. We got as many men as possible spread out just below the crest where there were not any mines.

It is not possible to describe all of the battle that followed with thousands upon thousands of infantrymen locked together in close combat, and at times, hand to hand and bayonet to bayonet. We did surprise the enemy. They didn't believe we could reach them that fast. Soldiers on both sides knew they had to win or die. We caught many of them in their foxholes. Some had started walking after the artillery ceased firing. We killed many of them on our first charge. Then we were too close to reload. Both sides fixed bayonets and crashed together. With my Tommy gun, I was able to fire longer because it held thirty rounds. I started to reload, but there was no time. Suddenly, a German appeared in front of me ready to thrust his bayonet. Crashing into him, I used my Tommy gun to block his bayonet thrust, but he was able to hit me in the mouth and nose with a partial swing of his rifle butt. Dropping my Tommy gun, I popped my fingers in his eyes. When he let go of his rifle to protect his eyes, I grabbed it and hit him with the butt on the side of his head just below his steel helmet. When he was falling backwards, I reversed the rifle and drove the bayonet into his throat. Picking up my Tommy gun, I reloaded and started firing. There were many targets, but I concentrated my fire to help any of our soldiers who were having trouble.

The battle raged on. Our first charge cleared out our immediate area. The surviving Germans retreated so we all sat down to catch our breath. My nose was bleeding; I stopped some of it with my handkerchief. Then I took out my one bandage from the pouch on my web belt, and used it to compress my nose by tying it around my head. Suddenly, I had a strange gut feeling. All of those years of training paid off. Remembering that whenever the Germans retreated, they always regrouped and counter-attacked. In British training, it was called "consolidate for a counterattack". They were the best army in the world at this, and usually they would win because they could do it so fast. I started screaming and the other soldiers stared at me as if I were crazy. I said, "GET READY FOR A COUNTERATTACK! RELOAD! GET IN YOUR HOLES! TURN THEIR MACHINEGUNS AROUND AND RELOAD THEM." It took them a few moments for them to understand. We got ready just in time.

Wiping the blood and sweat off my face, I watched my captured German watch. We were all tired and breathing heavily. When the second hand on the watch approached the three-minute mark, we could see them. Talking softly now and humming songs to calm everyone I said, "They are coming fast. Stay down in the holes. Don't let them see anything. There will be at least two lines, maybe three. If we fire too quickly at the first line, then we will have to fight the other lines again. We want the first line to be about thirty yards from us before we fire, then we can hit their back-up lines. I will give the order to fire."

To understand this, if only one soldier opens fire at the wrong time out of fear or whatever, then the battle is lost. Taking my steel helmet off and putting my tam o'shanter on, I could see better between some rocks I had pushed together. My concern was the second or third line position. There was a third line. The decision was to fire at 25 yards (75 feet) at the first line.

I gave the order to fire. With automatic reloading M-1 rifles and some of the German machineguns, the first line was wiped out in a few seconds. The Germans seemed surprised, but the second and third lines continued to charge. The American soldiers continued to reload and kill. For the first time, I was now proud to be an American soldier.

All that day, we continued to advance and fight across the top of Hill 609. As far as we could see, to the left and right of us, the soldiers of the 34th Infantry Division were fighting. All available combat medics were tending to the wounded. In large battles, such as this one, it was common for the soldiers to get separated from their squads, platoons, companies and battalions. All that mattered was to keep pressing forward. Picking up food, water, and ammunition from the dead, we continued forward across the top of the plateau to the downward slopes on the north side. We had started our attacks from the south. The drivers of U.S. jeeps had found paths to go up and down the southern slopes and brought us supplies and carried the wounded back.

The nights were spent laying down and rolling up in German and Italian blankets. The night wind up there was cold. Starting down the northern slopes after daylight, large base camps of Germans and Italians could be seen in olive groves. Evidently, they didn't know that they had lost the battle. Smoke from cooking fires could be seen. When we were close enough to fire effectively, we stopped and waited for the weapons platoons to catch up with us and setup their machineguns and mortars. When the firing started up and down the line, it was a sight to behold. The enemy was running around to get to their vehicles to retreat. Many of their soldiers and vehicles were hit. When the firing stopped, there was not a leaf left on the olive trees.

After moving on about two miles to the northeast, we came upon a squadron of British tanks. There were about 40 American soldiers with me and some had minor wounds. The British medics patched them up. Then the British gave us hot tea, compo rations and water. Not even thinking about it, I was still wearing my tam o'shanter with the Royal Scots cap badge on it and carrying my Tommy gun. That is why the British soldiers were staring at me. I talked to the sergeant major and then the major in command and others. When I explained that I was commando and all of that, the major said, "Our Bren gunner in our lead tank was KIA and we are short handed all around. We could use a good Bren gunner."

Suddenly, the lead wireless operator shouted, "Our orders are coming in, Sir." The major climbed in the tank and we could hear some of the conversation going on. The major got out of the tank and explained the orders to everyone. The U.S. Army II Corps were ordered to capture Bizerta, which was a major shipping port. The British V Corps were to capture Tunis and the Cape Bon Peninsula, together with the British 8th Army who were continuing to advance to the north along the East Coast of Tunisia. The Free French XIX Corps were to occupy and place all of the cities and villages in Tunisia under French Martial Law. Also, they were to kill or capture all Axis soldiers and Vichy French.

Then the major said, "We have been ordered to leave at once and drive towards Tunis. Other squadrons will join us on the way. The infantry and artillery units will follow the armored divisions as fast as possible. The recon. units (reconnaissance) on land and in the air have reported that German and Italian forces are retreating towards Tunis and Cape Bon. The major objective for the armored units is to capture the aerodrome in Tunis before the Jerry's can blow it up."

Spring 1943

    As the squadron prepared to leave, I decided to go with them. What the heck, I was tired of walking, being hungry and thirsty and sleeping in a hole. I approached the major, saluted (British salute, of course) and said, "Sir, if I can help, then I'll go with you." The major replied, "Thanks, you can help. I understand that you have served with a tank squadron before." I told the U.S. soldiers that I was going with the British and they should continue moving to the northeast because all U.S. troops were headed that way. Placing what little equipment I had and my Tommy gun in the lead tank, I climbed in and we roared off. One of the crew handed me a tanker's helmet with earphones. The earphone and mike were necessary to talk to the crew and the other tanks because of the noise. As we moved, the hatch was open and I commenced stripping down my pair of Bren guns to clean them, check their operation and reload. The crewman nearest to me handed me some cloths and gun oil and then pointed to the Bren gun ammo clips. The Bren guns were full of dust.

    When my guns were ready, I said on the intercom, "Sir, this is Alabama, request permission to test fire my Bren guns." The major replied, "Jolly good idea, Alabama. Permission granted." Then the major said "Commander to all hands, check your weapons and supplies. When the lorries re-supply us, we'll have to do it in a hurry. We have a hellava long way to go." The squadron captain had platted our course to Tunis on our maps, which we were following. Late afternoon we passed through some scattered Axis tanks that had run out of fuel, broken down or something. The crews were walking to the east toward Tunis. The infantry would capture them.

    We started noticing something else. The wireless operators back of us were very busy. Squadron after squadron of tanks were joining our column back of us. It was just one of those things that happen. Because our squadron was further north and east of the others, we were the lead squadron and since I was in the turret of the lead tank, I thought I should start talking like a scout should. The coordination between all these British forces was excellent. There was a parallel column of lorries racing ahead of the tanks, fuel lorries, water lorries, food lorries, ammo lorries, and others. The lorries were faster than the tanks. When the lorries reached our squadron, we stopped and got out of the tanks. Everyone had some food, water, and of course, some hot tea, as the lorries filled our fuel tanks with petrol and loaded other supplies. The soldiers on the lorries worked fast and in sequence; pulling up to each tank and loading whatever was needed. The attitude of the soldiers had changed, they were joking and all of that because they knew that Africa and the Middle East would be won.

    The lorries stayed in place, and as each squadron reached them, they did the same thing. There should be some kind of medal for these soldiers for making hot tea in a compo ration tin so fast. After going to the latrine (there was none; just go where you can) and changing drivers again, we were off after the Jerries. All of the tank crews were trained to swap positions. In battle they preferred to use their main positions. As a matter of fact, I had been awarded a Class III Internal Combustion Engine Driver's License by the British. So I offered to take a turn at driving. The major said no; we need you on the Bren guns. The drivers of tanks have limited vision and must have some help. We were all exhausted, but the adrenaline was flowing.

    The darkness of night had come upon us. Pushing the mike button, I said, "Major, Sir, request permission to be 1ˢᵗ Scout and talk." The major replied, "Alabama, you are the 1ˢᵗ Scout. Keep talking and report what you see." My reply was simple. "There are enemy tanks running ahead of us. I can see their exhausts and I am following them." On and on we went through the darkness. I kept on reporting. Sometimes the enemy tanks were in a column formation and then they would change to a line formation. I talked on and on. Then I couldn't see the exhausts from some of the enemy tanks. Maybe they had turned around to fire or another thought came to me, they may be out of fuel. I said, "Sir, some of the Jerry tanks and other vehicles are stopping. They are probably out of fuel. Recommend all guns ready to return fire. If they are SS, they will try something." One of our squadron officers said, "Alabama, who was in command of the commando school when you first went there?" I replied, "Sir, Lord Lovat, a good commander. He's probably a general by now." I wondered why he asked that. Later, they told me that our transmissions were being relayed to London by wireless.

I continued to talk on the intercom as we passed more and more Jerries during the night. At daylight I said, "Sir, there must be thousands of Jerries walking. They are exhausted and beaten, they have all dropped their weapons." I started singing "There'll be Blue Birds Over The White Cliffs of Dover" and "Stars Fell on Alabama." Looking at my map, we were on the main road from Mateur to Tunis and we should see the aqueduct built by the Carthaginians to bring water from the mountains 75 miles away to ancient Carthage. It was built without a transit or bulldozer, but it sloped perfectly. Maybe old Hannibal eyeballed it himself.

When the aqueduct was in sight, I said, "Sir, we are preparing to pass under the aqueduct. It is a good place for snipers. I will fire some rounds along the top of it and then close my hatch. I have memorized from my map the route through the city to the aerodrome." The major said, "Well done, Alabama. All tanks do not stop for anything. Proceed to the aerodrome as fast as possible." The streets were empty and it looked like a ghost town as we roared through. All of the civilians were in hiding.

I said, "Sir, we are approaching the aerodrome. It looks undamaged." The major said, "All tanks, do not damage the macadam. Form two columns, one on each side of the macadam, using the grass." After two or three minutes I said, "Sir, there is one aircraft left and nothing else... HOLD IT!" There was a Jerry pilot running from the control tower to the aircraft carrying what looked like a musette bag. I brought him down with a three round burst with my Brens. I said, "Sorry, Sir, I shot a Jerry pilot running to the aircraft and I see some smoke in the control tower." The tank crew ran in and put the fire out. The Jerry pilot had been burning papers, which he had stayed behind to do. It was ascertained later that the Jerry pilot was a squadron leader, a major. The musette bag contained papers, which were picked up by intelligence people when they arrived later.

We were a tired mess of soldiers. Squadron after squadron of tanks and lorries came in and wheeled around facing the runway. Other British forces were ordered to proceed northeastward up the Cape Bon Peninsula to capture the rest of the Axis forces. Some of the soldiers had "liberated" vino from the Eyeties (Italians) in Mateur and elsewhere. We drank vino. A great sadness came upon me. A great victory was ours, starting with El Alamein. French West Africa and Morocco on the Atlantic Ocean, Algeria, Tunisia, Tripolitania, Libya, Egypt, Ethiopia, Somalia and the Near East were now liberated from the Axis powers. The Suez Canal was now safe and would save thousands of miles for Allied ships. However, the war would go on and on.

The British soldiers were meeting and greeting friends and relatives from other units while I drank alone. What I really wanted to do was to go home. In great despair, I started thinking that if I could get the German aircraft started, I would fly it home. It was a Focke-Wulf fighter with a longer range than Messerschmitt fighters. Telling some of the soldiers that if they would start the engine and pull the wheel chocks after I got in it, then I would fly it. Some of them were top-notch mechanics. They had to be in order to maintain and repair all of the equipment. The vino was flowing and they were enthusiastic about it.

I climbed in the cockpit, and they started the engine by reaching in and throwing the correct switches and when the wheel chocks were pulled, I taxied onto the macadam, turned to line up on the runway and took off. At 200 feet, I banked and flew a box pattern around the aerodrome, landed and took off again. (This is called touch and go practice). After doing this three times, I climbed to about 1,000 feet and headed west. What little brains I had left were saying you can't make it. You will be shot down or more likely give out of petrol somewhere in the desert. Turning back, I realized that I had disappeared from the sight of the soldiers at the aerodrome. On the final approach to the runway, I could see the officers and men lined up on both sides and it looked like they were cheering and waving their arms. Upon landing, I opened the canopy, climbed down out of the cockpit, leaving the aircraft on the runway with the engine running, walked over to the grass and said, "I need some vino. It's a Long Way to Tipperary."

I sat down on the grass. Soldiers gave me mess cups full of vino, more than I could drink. It was similar to the times when I returned from commando missions or raids. After debriefing, we tried to get drunk. When I am hyper, I can't get drunk. I was crying inside and out. It had been six months since we left the ship in November and that seemed like a lifetime ago. The crew of "our" tank came over and sat beside me. Combat soldiers don't want to talk much. It is all in their eyes. Sipping vino together, the sergeant in command of "our" tank said, "Alabama, we thank you for your help. You were with us when your training was needed." One of them said, "Alabama, you are a bloody good soldier."

The next thing that happened was when the major commanding our squadron came to talk with me. I was getting up to salute when he said, "Alabama, don't get up, I have some friends here to see you." The other officers and the sergeant major of "our" squadron were with him. That is not all. It was a surprise to see the people from the Royal Scots tank squadron that I had gone to Tebessa with. The major and other officers, the sergeant major and the sergeant who had penned the cap badge of the Royal Scots Regiment on my tam o'shanter greeted me.

We all gathered around, had some vino together and talked. Before dark, we had food and tea. Then after dark, everyone was ready for the major broadcast from the BBC, London. The BBC did broadcast worldwide and the time depended on Greenwich Mean Time. All of the wireless operators turned up their receivers so we could listen.

The usual news broadcasters came on and talked about the war situation in the Pacific Ocean and other places in the world. The Prime Minister, Winston Churchill, came on and delivered another one of his great short speeches. With my fading memory, I can't recall the exact words, but he did speak about the victory in Africa and the Allies would win the victory in Europe and the rest of the world. The axis powers would be destroyed on the land, on the sea and in the air.

Then Petula Clark came on, singing some popular songs and talking to the brave allied soldiers, sailors and airmen around the world. She praised the Allied forces in Africa for their victory and then said we have a song for one of them; then she sang, "Stars Fell on Alabama."

Rolling up in a blanket, I went to sleep. The next morning, many noises woke me up. Latrines were being installed, (canvas attached to poles in the ground for some privacy) with slit trenches dug. Temporary showers and mess tents were going up. Field Marshall Montgomery and his staff had arrived. Tents, folding tables and chairs were being setup. R.A.F. officers and men arrived in lorries and went to work on the control tower, setting up communications equipment and the like.

It is easy to imagine how filthy we were. My wool pants and field jacket were torn; my wool shirt had blood on it from my broken nose. They offered me a complete new British desert uniform. I accepted new socks, underwear, cotton trousers and shirt, but decided to keep my U.S. Army field jacket with the Red Bull (34th Infantry Division) patches on it for identification purposes, and my tan U.S. Army boots. The British boots were black. Of course, the only head gear I had was my tam o'shanter; my steel helmet was left on top of Hill 609.

After showering and putting on new clothes, I tried to clean my jacket with some petrol. It was still a mess. Finding someone with a mirror, I looked at my front teeth. The bottoms were chipped on both of them. Later in the morning, a regimental sergeant major came to me and said, "The Field Marshall has asked to speak to you." The regimental sergeant major led me into the Field Marshall's tent. The Field Marshall was seated at a table and other officers were seated at tables or standing. The R.S.M. saluted and said, "Pte. Houston or acting sergeant Houston, also known as Alabama, is here, Sir." I saluted, the Field Marshall returned our salutes and said, "At ease." Then he and the other officers slowly looked me over from the tam o'shanter on my head down to my boots.

Then he looked straight into my eyes and smiled. He said, "Alabama, we know you are a bloody good soldier. London knows you and we thank you for your service. You are welcome to serve with us at anytime. Is there anything we can do for you?" I replied with a smile, "Thank you, Sir, as you may have noticed I have been supplied with a new uniform. It is necessary for me to leave in the morning to find my U.S. Army division and I am worried about what the U. S. Army might do." He replied, "Alabama, good luck, and if you have any trouble with your commanders, my Chief of Staff will let me know." He nodded toward a general. I said, "Sir, with your permission, I wish to thank the Royal Scots tank squadron who saved me when I was near death going from Faid Pass to Kasserine and beyond." The R.S.M. and I came to attention, saluted, did an about face and left. The RSM said, "Alabama, the Field Marshall would like to recommend you for a high medal." I replied, "Sir, please tell him and the others, thanks, but a medal would cause me to have a great deal of problems." He said, "Will do." We shook hands and parted. The Axis powers signed an unconditional surrender of Africa and the Middle East on May 13, 1943 in the Cape Bon Peninsula. I was 19 years old.

SUCK A ROCK 34: Somewhere in North Africa, Tunisia

May 1943

The next morning, I prepared to leave. They gave me a musette bag to sling across my shoulder and to carry my stuff. They really loaded me down with a shaving kit, toothbrush, soap, facecloth, two packs of 50 Cape to Cairo cigarettes, reloaded clips for my Tommy gun, and food from compo rations. Items such as chocolate bars, tins of sardines packed in olive oil, hardtack and the like. I stuffed my pockets and bag full. I kept my U.S. Army web belt with the U.S. water canteen. U.S. and British web belts, etc., don't match, so I put an extra British canteen full of water in my bag.

When loaded up, I started walking toward the city. After a short distance, a jeep pulled up beside me. There was a sergeant driving it and in the other front seat was the R.S.M. The R.S.M. said, "Get in lad, It's a Long Way to Tipperary." When we arrived at the main part of downtown Tunis, I said, "Sir, I'll get out here and thanks."

Everything was quiet on the main streets. Now and then, there would be some military traffic. After wandering around for a while, I decided that I deserved a few days leave. Looking at my British Army map, I found a park with some buildings and gardens. It was closed, but obviously it was a place for outdoor dining and drinking wine while the orchestra played on weekend afternoons and evenings. I spent the night there in one of the buildings. During the night, there were sounds of firing in the streets.

The next day, people started coming out on the streets and I met the Cohen family. Madame Cohen had two daughters, Collette, who was about 18, and a younger daughter. Her husband was a captain in the Free French Army and her son had escaped the Nazis and Fascists by going through the battle lines with some other French young men and boys to join the Free French Army. I told her I had met some of the Free French soldiers and she would be hearing from them in a few days.

She invited me to spend the night with them in their apartment. I accepted; they were afraid. Madame Cohen had been astute enough to save up food for a time like this. She prepared a home-style supper such as I had not seen in a long time and I shared some of my food with them. When I handed each of them a chocolate bar for dessert, tears came in their eyes. It had literally been years since they had chocolate.

They wanted to talk some more when they found out that I was an American soldier from Alabama. They had never seen an American soldier. I slept on the sofa in the living room with a chair jammed under the front door knob, and my Tommy gun lying beside be. After dark, the firing and killing started again. Tunis, as a place of last refuge, was filled with people who hated each other. There were Nazi Germans, Fascist Italians, military and civilians, French loyalists, French collaborators, Arabs, B-rabs, C-rabs, and all kinds of other people in Tunis at this time. If anyone had tried to come in that front door, I would have pulverized them. None of us slept well that night.

The next morning, after assuring Madame Cohen that I would return before dark, I started walking around. They couldn't thank me enough. It is too difficult to describe the fear of these three unarmed women. Nearing the main boulevard in Tunis, Avenue Jules Ferry, there were the sounds of British Bren guns and rifles. A battalion of Gurkha soldiers, from Nepal in India had arrived. They were in the British 8th Army and had reached the city and started killing their mortal enemies for centuries, the Muslims. They were shooting Arabs in every direction; even shooting the ones on the streetcars.

A jeep raced up and stopped in the middle of the melee. A British major got out and ordered the sergeants and corporals to fall in with their men. There were a lot of them. A battalion is four companies of soldiers. The Gurkas obeyed immediately. They are very good professional soldiers. Their families in Nepal depended on their pay for their livelihoods. All of the Gurkha officers for the Gurkhas are British. When the soldiers had all fallen in at attention and line-by-line, the major addressed them. The major was livid with rage and shamed every one of them. He said, "We kill soldiers. We do not kill civilians." He gave the order, "By the right, quick march" and marched them out of the city.

That afternoon, I returned to the Cohen's apartment. When Madame Cohen learned that I had bought and eaten some kind of cookie from an Arab street vendor, she scolded me saying the food was not sanitary. That night was the same as the night before. At daylight, there were convoys of trucks and other vehicles carrying Free French troops and sergent chefs of the Police Militaire. The French brought in the Senegalese soldiers and it was easy to identify them. These tall, strong, black soldiers, with their long rifles and long bayonets and long knives, would establish law and order. I will always fondly remember them. One of them saved my life when I was on patrol with them at Faid Pass.

When the French loyalists saw these things, they came out in droves, lining the sidewalks and cheering. The word was being passed along that American soldiers would perform the victory parade in Tunis on that day. Saying goodbye to the Cohens, I explained that it was necessary to see the parade and find my U.S. Army unit. They understood and none of us thought we would ever see each other again. Making my way to the main streets, I saw crowds forming on the sidewalks. Maybe, this was not just another rumor. Absent from the crowds were the collaborators and Italian civilians.

The sounds of a military marching band were heard. In all of my service in the United States Army, I had never heard a U.S. Army marching band. The people around me were all female. They would glance at me, but were afraid to make eye contact because I was wearing a strange uniform. Other than the British insignia and parts of their uniforms, the only identification that I had was my worn out field jacket with the Red Bull insignia of the 34th Infantry Division and the American flag under that.

As the band passed, playing military marching songs of the U.S. Army, the British Army and the French Army, everyone cheered and waved. The honor guard passed, carrying the flags of the Western Allied Nations. Then I saw the guidon (flag) coming. The 34th Infantry Division was selected for the parade. Watching the guidons and their bearers, I was doing a mental count down. The 133rd Infantry Regiment, with three battalions; the 135th Infantry Regiment, with three battalions; the 168th Infantry Regiment, with three battalions; my regiment was the 135th Infantry.

The soldiers were in massed formation (close order) the same as if they were marching in New York, New York. As the soldiers passed, I was ready when I saw my battalion and my company approach. In those days, I had a great voice to command. According to the Veterans Administration doctors, after the war, I lost my voice screaming at soldiers during the war. They were correct. It is difficult for me to speak now.

When my company guidon appeared, I shouted the command, "Eyes Right." Several lines of soldiers, in massed formation, obeyed. There were only a few of the "old ones from Ireland" left. The big guy, who had thought I wanted to take his B.A.R. in Ireland and all I did was test fire it because the training colonel wanted me to, was there. We became friends later.

The soldiers whispered up and down the lines looking at me. At least, they now knew I was alive. I gave the command, "Eyes Front" as they marched on.

When the parade ended, the girls and young women started talking to me. None of them spoke English. When they asked my age, I thought about it. It was May 21, 1943, my birthday, and I was now twenty years old. When I told them it was my birthday and I was now twenty, they all lined up to give me a "souvenir"; that is, a hug and a kiss on each cheek. The last one in line just stood there looking in my eyes. She was taller than the rest and certainly was a daughter of Abraham and Sarah. Something clicked between us. She told me she had just turned twenty and her name was Rosette Attelan. Then she hugged and kissed me on both cheeks and there was a mutual reaction, we kissed lips to lips. The others laughed.

My body was shaking and trembling. Women and girls do smell and feel different. All of us soldiers had become used to being dirty, nasty and smelling bad. It had been too long for us to live like animals. When my shaking stopped, they asked many questions. These people were isolated from the Allied world for years. Their schools had been closed; their radio stations silenced, and their local and European newspapers shut down. The only news they could get, other than Axis propaganda, was from the B.B.C. London. To do that, they must have a wireless receiver and if they were caught with one, they would be executed.

Rosette introduced me to her younger sister, her aunt and cousins who were refugees from Bizerte, and others. They asked my name and I replied, "Collier Houston and my secret name with the Resistance is "Alabama." They shook their heads. After repeating this several times, I gave up and in French said, "My first name is Daniel." Their eyes lit up and they smiled.

All of this conversation was in their French and my broken French. Some of them said my accent was Parisian. I told them I had been in Northern France. Then they understood that I had been with the "French Resistance People." Rosette's home was in Gafour, Tunisie. When the Germans and Italians came north, her father sent her, her mother and sister to her grandmother's home in Tunis. Her father was a World War I veteran and worked for the French National Railway System. He and some others sabotaged the railway engines by taking out critical parts so the Axis soldiers couldn't use them. Then they went into hiding.

Rosette's aunt, being the senior lady present, invited me to go with them to grandmere's house. The grandmother's name was Madame Zaborie. Her husband had died several years before. She was a native Hebrew of Africa and spoke only Hebrew or Arabic, which were about the same language. After meeting the others, it was obvious that Madame Zaborie was the family matriarch. There were not any males of any age, except myself, in the house. That is what war does to people.

Madam Zaborie started preparing the evening meal and telling the others what to do. Seeing this, I opened my musette bag and presented all my food to her. There were many "Ooh la las." When I handed the sardines packed in olive oil to the Madame, she gave me a great big smile and then turned away as tears appeared in her eyes. Everyone became silent. Olive oil was scarce because of the war, and it was used for so many food preparations. The main use was for cooking oil. I gave them all my food, including some kitchen matches and one of my two cigarette lighters. I knew I could get more food the next day when I would leave. I showed the Madame how to use the cigarette lighter and told the others how to refill it.

After supper, we sat around the large table and talked. Grand-mere had many questions. She talked in Hebrew and the others would translate her words into French for me. She wanted to know how I got there from America. She had a sister who had emigrated to Chicago years before. Did I know her sister? It took a while for me to explain these things. We all went to bed. I slept on the floor in the parlor (a small sitting room).

After eating in the morning, I told them that I had to find my army unit. After hugs and kisses, I started walking and soon got a ride on an army truck headed to Mateur. There was a U.S. Army camp near Mateur. It was part of the Headquarters of the 34th Division. Finding the first sergeant, I asked him if Roy Palmer was there. He said, "Hell no, he's already gone with the general to Oran and I don't want you guys to get together, no telling what you'll do." I replied, "Well, stuff it up sergeant," and I left. There was another camp on the east side of Mateur with about a hundred soldiers of the 34th Infantry Division in it. They had all been separated from their companies since the battles at Hill 609 and Bizerta. I camped with them.

There were abandoned German and Italian vehicles everywhere. Many of them were operational if they had gas. Of course, astute soldier boys from America knew how to fix that. Some of them took huge German half-tracks and raced around with them on the hills and plains. Some of them tried out other vehicles. That is how they continued to get supplies from a U.S. Army Quartermaster Depot. When I started asking about the depot and how I could get there, one soldier came over to me and said, "Hey, Sarge, I'll take you there." He started shouting, "Hey, you guys, the sergeant is here."

Standing there dressed in mostly British uniform, with my tam o'shanter and other clothes, the only identification I had was my torn field jacket and boots. Many soldiers gathered around me. There were four soldiers who had been in Ireland and they were talking about me to the others. I also recognized some replacements that had been with me somewhere. I said, "Thanks, I went into Tunis with the British tanks. Now I need a uniform, pup tent and everything else." The soldier took me to the depot in a "liberated" Volkswagen. While there, I got new clothes, helmet, pack, web equipment, pup tent and the like. I kept my Tommy gun.

There were several rumors going around. The remainder of the 34th Infantry Division would move to join the other units of the 34th camped outside Oran. The 34th would be re-supplied, receive many replacements to bring the units back up to full strength and train. The 34th had several thousand casualties to replace. Some of the companies, and at least one battalion, had been wiped out. As an example, the 1st Armored Division had been destroyed for all practical purposes and were replaced by the 2nd Armored Division on the battle lines. That is how fierce the fighting had been.

Another rumor was that the 34th Infantry Division combat infantrymen had gotten so angry with the "Sun Tan" military police in Oran that they carried their weapons into the town and killed some of them. The infantrymen called the military police "Sun Tan" because they had already been issued summer cotton uniforms and had arrived from the United States as regular military police. None of them were combat soldiers and when combat soldiers got a pass and went to town, the military police would arrest them for not wearing a tie or some other stupid nonsense. Combat soldiers did not have ties or much of anything else. We were still wearing olive drab wool uniforms; the same as we had worn when we came to Africa.

As a result of this, the commanders in high places decided regular military police could not control combat soldiers and therefore other military police companies in other cities would be formed using combat infantrymen. The new companies would be "Provisional Military Police

Companies." Provisional means temporary. A provisional military police company would be formed in Tunis using combat soldiers from the 34th Infantry Division.

While these things were happening, a jeep with a sergeant driving and a major in the front passenger seat, turned off the main road and bumped up the open ground to our camp. We gathered around and saluted as the major got out. He looked mean and lean and he was wearing military police insignia. He told us he was looking for a few combat infantrymen that were not afraid of anything, mean as rattlesnakes and could ride a motorcycle. I said, "I qualified to ride a Norton motorcycle with the British, Sir." He replied, "What's your name." I said, "Private, or acting sergeant, I don't give a damn which, Daniel C. Houston, Sir." He looked at some sort of list and said, "Were you one of those soldiers who enlisted and came from the British to Ireland?" I replied, "Yes, Sir." He said, "A staff Brigadier General said I should look you up. Are there any more of you here?" I said, "No, Sir. Some of them are dead and I've lost touch with the others."

The major looked around and said, "Can any of you others ride a motorcycle?" A total of seven others said they either could or would try. The major said, "I don't have time to baby sit or give on the job training. When the motorcycles arrive, any of you who can make it to my office in Bizerta will be hired." He gave us directions to his office and left. The next day, eight Harley Davidson motorcycles arrived on a truck. They were unloaded and the truck left. The others watched while I started mine. I explained the kick-start, throttle control, spark control, front and rear brakes, clutch and gear shift. Three of them were somewhat familiar with all this and started their engines. The other four had trouble starting, so we helped them.

With all eight engines running, I said, "Let's make a trial run down to the road and back." It was not easy because the ground was rough with rocks here and there. Three of them and I made it down to the road and waited for the four others. They kept falling and obviously would not make it. So, the four of us who had made it, went back up; took down our pup tents, tied everything on the rack of our motorcycles and headed for the major's office in Bizerta.

Most of the city was destroyed by intense shelling. The major's office was in a partially destroyed building that had some rooms intact. The major explained some of our duties and told us to go to supply and get whatever equipment, including weapons that we needed. Also, we would need windshields on our motorcycles with the words 'SPECIAL MILITARY POLICE' stenciled on the windshields and sides.

"You are now authorized to represent me and give direct orders to all officers and enlisted personnel. If anyone gives you any crap, especially officers, tell them that. You also have complete arrest powers. My title is: "Provost Marshall, Mediterranean Base Sector." I serve under the command of the Allied Supreme Commander, General Eisenhower. I am the commanding officer of all military police. You may get your food and whatever you need from any U. S. unit. As you see, we don't have a cook." He also told us that the only staff he had or needed was a sergeant and a corporal who were his clerks. He introduced us to them. He said he wanted me to be his sergeant in command of the odd job motorcycle force. He said, "I'll make that a permanent rank if you want it." I replied, "Acting sergeant would be fine, Sir."

We went to a supply depot to get everything done. A captain asked who was going to sign for all of this. I said, "I will, Sir." We got new M-1 rifles, GI 45 caliber auto load pistols with Sam Brown Belts, ammunition, a pair of leather saddlebags to go over the rear wheels on the Harleys and leather gun scabbards to strap on the front wheels. I used two gun scabbards, one on each side of the front wheel, one for my Tommy gun and the other for my M-1 rifle.

The Harleys would be our homes and we had to prepare them to ride long-distances at high speed. Our procedure was to wrap our blankets and clothes in pup tent shelter halves (canvas) and strap them on the rack over the rear wheels and hang two canteens of water over them. Eventually, from experience, we wore fighter pilot's helmets (light ones with goggles) fighter pilot's jackets (light ones), fighter pilot's light gloves, jump boots, and sunglasses. When we started working with tank columns, we wore tanker's cotton coveralls with hoods because of the dust and flying rocks.

When we finished at the supply depot, I signed the captain's receipt thusly, "Sergeant Daniel C Houston, Corps of M.P., for the Provost Marshall." The captain seemed surprised because all of this was new. The Provost Marshall hired six other motorcyclists from the combat infantry, making us a force of ten Special Military Police. A Provisional Military Policy company had been formed in Tunis using combat soldiers from the 34th Infantry Division.

The Provost Marshall instructed us to go to the Military Police Headquarters, Tunis. The captain commanding had been notified. All civilians were now under French Martial Law. We were to report to the sergeant chefs of the police militaire to work with them. Our new mailing address would be the M.P. Company in Tunis and we would receive our pay there. We could bunk and eat there at their barracks whenever we wanted to and we should go by there to check on our mail and pay.

Early Summer 1943

The Military Police Company in Tunis had established their barracks in an unfinished building with a courtyard and three stories of empty rooms at the end of the main boulevard, Avenue Jules Ferry. This Avenue was wide and divided with shrubbery and electric streetcars in the center. Our motorcycle gang was given one room per man, the same as the other military police. We left extra blankets (to sleep on) and other stuff on the concrete floors of our rooms so we wouldn't have to unload and reload stuff. Our mail was kept in the office on the first floor until we came by to pick it up. All of the officers had private apartments. The cooking, eating, and meetings were done in the courtyard. A cooking fire was going at all times because some military police were on duty at all times. The place was easy to secure since the only entrance was the main door into the courtyard.

Scouting around alone, I found the Free French sergent chefs of the police militaire. They had set up their headquarters and living quarters in an obscure apartment. They could have lived in luxury, but didn't. Broken down tables, chairs, and beds were all they had. They were tough, hardened old soldiers. The youngest was probably 30 years old. When I parked my Harley and went inside, as instructed by the Provost Marshall, I spoke to them in my broken French. They smiled. A feeling came over me that we had met somewhere before. They explained that the mission was a raid on the Kasbah and this was like a top-secret commando mission.

The old walls of the old city contained the Kasbah. Translating Kilometers to miles in my mind, the wall around the Kasbah was about fourteen miles. There were some larger entrances and then some secret ones. Inside the Kasbah were some German and Italian officers who had not surrendered, plus all kinds of collaborators. They must be captured or killed.

On a certain night, the Kasbah would be completely surrounded by Senegalese soldiers with fixed bayonets and orders to kill anyone trying to escape from the Kasbah. U. S. Army trucking companies would put the Senegalese in place and then the trucks would be used to transport prisoners to a French prison. U. S. Army infantrymen would protect the truck drivers and guard the prisoners while they were being transported. To enter and search the Kasbah would be teams consisting of three soldiers in each team; one would be a French sergent chef of the Police Militaire in command, another would be a British "Red Cap" (Military Police) and the third one would be a United States Army Military Policeman. No doubt about it, this would be a large coordinated operation by the Allies. All military personnel would be given strict orders to kill anyone that threatened them or tried to escape. Enemy soldiers in the Kasbah would be armed and wearing civilian clothes.

The afternoon before the operation, the teams were assigned and given maps marked to show where each team would enter and search. The U. S. Army trucks were in position at the French Senegalese camp. During the night, everything went as planned. When the Senegalese were in position around the walls and at the entrances to the Kasbah, the teams moved into their positions. My two partners were a sergent chef that I had met and a British Red Cap. I rode my Harley following the sergent chef and Red Cap, who were riding a "liberated" German motorcycle with sidecar, to our assigned entrance.

At the crack of dawn, we entered the Kasbah and started searching. The buildings in the Kasbah had an unimpressive solid doorway, which opened into a central courtyard surrounded by several stories of apartments with walkways and balconies with railings overlooking the courtyards. The apartments had a few heavily fortified windows looking out over the very small streets and alleys. It didn't take long before shots and screams were heard. The sergent chef shot the exterior doors down and we entered each building and searched each apartment.

The British Red Cap and I were surprised at the things we saw. Good-looking women had photos of their German and Italian Officers who had been living with them. Some had other Nazi and Fascist mementos and pictures of Hitler and Mussolini. We lost count of how many plaster of paris busts of Mussolini we saw.

As we approached each apartment door, the sergent chef gave the order to open the door. If the door was not opened immediately, he shot the lock off and we rushed in. The minute he saw a Mussolini bust or other Nazi or Fascist item, he would grab them, walk to the railing and drop them in the courtyard. The courtyards became messy.

When we exited each building with prisoners, there would be French soldiers waiting to escort them to the trucks. There is no way to know how many truckloads of men and women were carried to prison that day. It was almost dark when the operation was over. This was a long hard day.

From time to time, we were sent to small towns or villages in Algeria and Southern Tunisia to assist the French in capturing or killing German and Italian soldiers. We were mainly used for this because we could travel far and fast on our Harleys. On one of these missions, when we were traveling fast through the mountains; one of our guys missed a curve in the road and drove off the mountainside. We stopped, but there was nothing we could do. Our force was now down to nine. We would lose others.

Law and order were gradually established in Tunis. I was able to see Rosette and her family. Whenever I received a Whitman's Sampler from home, I would take it to them. Rosette and others in her family went with me to dances sponsored by the U. S. Army Air Force. Rosette and I went to several movies. It was strange to hear Bogart and other actors and actresses speaking French. The sub-titles were in English. It seemed that all the French people wanted to see "CASABLANCA" and "TO HAVE OR HAVE NOT". These movies had a profound effect on the morale of the French. In the war years, they had never seen anyone stand up to the Nazis and French Collaborators the way Bogart did.

Someone called our Military Police Headquarters and asked for a motorcycle escort to escort Miss Vivian Leigh (British actress who starred in "Gone With the Wind") and her party from the airport to a theater on Avenue Jules Ferry. She was scheduled to perform for the British troops. We escorted them from the airport all the way to the backstage of the theater. Miss Leigh thanked us and invited us to stay for the show. We declined because we were hungry. We had not eaten since that morning at daylight.

Occasionally, I went by to see the sergent chefs. We would drink some wine, eat and talk. They asked many questions about people and things that I had seen. These were not ordinary police militaire. They never talked about themselves, but I was certain some of them had served with the Surete Nationale in Paris and also had served with the Resistance. They became my mentors and guardians and at times I would go places with different ones, riding in the sidecar of a German motorcycle. It was wild riding with them. They would go through the marketplaces and narrow streets at high speed. If people didn't get out of the way, they would be hit.

Madame Cohen's husband, Captain Cohen, and their son with the Free French Army returned. They invited me to have dinner with them. Captain Cohen and the son thanked me for helping their family. After dinner, we talked some. Captain Cohen asked me what I thought about the Communist Party. I told him that I really didn't know anything about them. He invited me to go to a meeting with him at a certain time and place and I accepted.

When I told the sergent chefs about this, they said they were glad that I had accepted and for me to observe everything. At the meeting, I didn't see or hear anything specific about Communism. It seemed to be an organizational meeting with about thirty French Army officers there. All of this I told to the sergent chefs later.

Sometime later, Captain Cohen and family invited me to go to the theater as their guest. The great American singer who lived in Paris, Miss Josephine Baker, was scheduled to present a show for French Army Officers. Since I didn't have a "Class A" uniform, I borrowed one from one of the three Swedish American soldiers whom I had met in Ireland. They were now in the military police company and were with me to get new and larger boots. The show was great and Miss Baker received much applause. She was an icon of France before the war. After the show, many of us went to the outdoor restaurant to dine and listen to the orchestra.

During these times, there was a huge build up of the United States Army Air Force in Africa. Mainly, long range bombers with some fighter escorts. The P-38 fighter was used more than other fighters were because it had twin engines and longer range. The U. S. 12th and 15th Air Force were flying from bases in the Mediterranean area while the 8th Air Force was flying from bases in the United Kingdom.

General Hap Arnold established his headquarters in Tunis in a large complex of buildings called (to my memory) "Lucie Carno." Hearing the name of General Hap Arnold brought back memories. The pilots who came to Maxwell Field in Montgomery during the 1930's were now the commanders in World War II. Some of the names I remembered besides General Arnold was General Chenault of the Flying Tigers in China, Major Bethune and Captain Hauptman, with his beautiful wife, who lived in our neighborhood.

Some of the sons of the pilots were in the Boy Scouts with me and later some of the sons and daughters were at Lanier High School with me. The pilots flew their P-12's (double wing Pursuit Aircraft) to the south of Montgomery to a shooting and bombing range in the Florida Panhandle. This range became the huge Eglin Air Force Base, larger than the State of Rhode Island. Some wives would drive down to this isolated place to be with their husbands. In the 1930's, ladies did not travel alone. One of my brothers accompanied Mrs. Hauptman as she drove their Cord automobile, with the top down, to Florida. (I wasn't old enough.)

Other important things happened in this part of Florida during World War II. Colonel Jimmy Doolittle and others planned and trained for the Tokyo Raid. Naval Aviators from the nearby Pensacola Naval Air Station trained the bomber pilots to take off from the deck of an aircraft carrier. The first missile ever fired in the United States was fired from Topsail Hill in South Walton County over the Gulf of Mexico. It was a captured German missile.

General Arnold's office was upstairs at the "Lucie Carno" under heavy security. On the ground floor was an auditorium, complete with balconies; and in another small area, with another entrance, was a medical aide station. In my wanderings about, I met the 1st lieutenant in command of the aide station. He had a medical degree, but had not completed his residency. Doctors who had completed all requirements were at least captains. During lonely nights, we talked and drank coffee. His first assignment was at Maxwell Field. When he found out how long I had been gone and where I had been, he became concerned about me. He didn't know that there was no rotation system for the infantry like the air force had.

The Air Force held dances in the auditorium on certain evenings with a good Air Force band playing. There was a problem, not with the Air Force, but with the American Red Cross. A female employee of the Red Cross decided to run the show. The dances had been open to any military personnel who happened to come by.

The American Red Cross occupied the best building on Avenue Jules Ferry and the American civilian employees of the Red Cross lived in a small hotel. Soldiers could go by the Red Cross and get lemonade, coffee, cookies and things like that, but they had to pay for whatever they had. Keep in mind, the U. S. Army paid for everything, and the food was furnished by a U. S. Army bakery. The Red Cross Director had a U. S. Army car and a civilian driver. All of his expenses were paid by the Army and he had a great salary.

The Red Cross decided that soldiers would have to go to their office in order to get a ticket for upcoming dances. The problem was soldiers only had two or three-day passes and hadn't heard about getting tickets anyway. The Director talked the Military Police Captain into assigning two military policemen to take up the tickets at the dances and keep the nasty combat infantrymen out.

One night, Rosette and I were going to a dance when I noticed some soldiers outside. They told me they couldn't get in because they didn't have a ticket. Explaining to them how the Red Cross had started requiring tickets, I said, "All of you wait here, I'll be back." I went inside and got a bunch of tickets that had been turned in to the military police and went back outside and gave each soldier a ticket. They grinned. One of them said "Thanks, Sarge."

In a little while, the female Red Cross employee started screaming at me. She was boiling with anger and saying what all she was going to get done to me. Being fed up, I got angry right back and in a loud voice, so that all the soldiers and airmen could hear, I told her what the Red Cross was doing. When she tried to scream some more at me, I said, "Why don't you explain how you send more money home than you are paid?" (The sergent chefs had told me that she made much money entertaining U. S. officers.) The soldiers and airmen applauded. She turned beet red and left. All of the soldiers and airmen felt the same as I did about the American Red Cross. This was the second strike I had with the Red Cross.

The Director of the Red Cross didn't know that I was under the command of the Provost Marshall. He tried to get me in trouble with the military police captain, but it backfired. His civilian driver assistant was wearing a U. S. Army Air Force flight jacket. It was illegal to buy or sell any U. S. Army equipment or supplies. I asked the driver where he got the jacket. He wouldn't answer me. Instead, he went into the Director's office and I followed. The Director told me to leave him alone and blah, blah, blah. I said, "He will answer the question," and I left.

When I explained to the sergent chefs, two of them followed me back to the Red Cross building on their German motorcycles. I put my S. M .P. (Special Military Police) brassard on my arm and carrying my Tommy gun, we went into the Director's office. Seeing us, the Director changed his attitude from belligerent to conciliatory, to begging. The sergent chefs didn't even listen. They arrested the driver; handcuffed him, and put him in a sidecar and then took him to prison. The Director never knew how close I came to arresting him on charges of aiding and abetting a criminal and interfering in military matters.

The sergent chefs sent a message to Allied Supreme Headquarters, Algiers, requesting the assistance of the U. S. Army C. I. D. (Criminal Investigation Division) of the Military Intelligence. By the time a message was received stating the arrival time of two agents at the airport, the sergent chefs had already gathered a lot of evidence about a black market ring. Under the Napoleonic

Code, people will talk to save themselves. We three drove our motorcycles to the military police vehicle compound and picked up two military police jeeps. Taking our weapons with us, we drove the two jeeps to the airport and picked up the two agents. One was a first lieutenant and the other a master sergeant. After we arrived back at the sergent chefs' headquarters, I explained everything I knew about the situation to the two agents. When they heard about the Red Cross Director, they became angry and indicated he would be given certain instructions. The investigation was now in their hands. I left.

Sometime later, the sergent chefs told me that the entire black market ring had been arrested and were being tried. Some of them were U. S. military personnel and some were civilians. The leader was a U. S. Army captain. They had made a lot of money dealing in all kinds of stolen goods.

Early Summer 1943

Our Special Military Police motorcycle group was ordered to report to the Provost Marshall in Bizerta. We were seated around a large table in one of the rooms in the Provost Marshall's office. There were British army maps on the table. The major explained that everything he told us was Top Secret and reminded us of our oath when we were sworn into the army. General Eisenhower's staff was the only others who knew about the upcoming operation.

The Allies were preparing to invade Sicily. The main forces would be the U. S. Army and the British 8th Army. The U. S. Army was forming a new corps and the main loading port for the invasion would be Bizerta. The British and other U. S. Army units would load at other ports. Pointing to a map, he gave us instructions and our orders. There is only one road into and out of Bizerta. The port had been divided into staging and loading areas with code names. We were told to memorize the locations and names of each area.

The Provost marshal said, "Since space at the port is limited, the Navy will dock their L. S. T.'s (Landing Ship Tanks) one at a time at each loading area with their bow doors open. You will guide each convoy to the proper area and as each L. S. T. is loaded, it will pull out and another L. S. T. will come in. The timing and coordination is absolutely critical; otherwise, the convoys will get stacked up on the one road."

"You guys will be working alone and I will tell you again, don't let anyone for any reason break into your convoy. Senior officers will try to intimidate you. The only officer you will take orders from is me. This is a War Zone and a critical combat operation. You are authorized to arrest, give orders to or kill anyone to protect this operation."

"All unit commanders will receive general orders to follow you and they will not know where they are going. You will receive orders from me as to when, where, and what units to meet and guide to the docks. Sergeant Houston will teach you how to find coordinates on your maps. (This was a surprise to me.) You can use this room to study and bunk in. Go study and memorize the code areas at the docks. I'm gonna work your tails off, and I am counting on you to do your jobs. You say you are mean combat soldiers. Now is the time to get meaner!"

The first time I saw the harbor at Bizerta, after the 34th Infantry Division had captured the city, it was a horrible looking mess. There were vessels of all kinds. There were only a few yacht type vessels not damaged or sunk. The Germans and Italians had confiscated privately owned yachts for their own use. I thought, if only I had a place to run one and leave it, I could go home with it after the war. There were some bodies in the water that had floated up from the sunken vessels.

When we rode to the harbor, the changes were amazing. The U.S. Navy and the U.S. Army Corps of Engineers had been working night and day. The harbor was cleared, docks repaired and the large buildings formerly used for warehouses and the like had been converted to Navy repair shops and to handle military supplies. There were sea-going tugs, repair ships and even a squadron of U.S. Navy P. T. boats docked there.

Our nine member motorcycle special force (we laughed about that) continued to study our maps, memorize roads and get our gear ready to move and live alone. The major gave each of us our orders to pick up military units and lead the convoys to the docks. He also told us this would be the last time we would receive our orders at his office. He gave us the time and coordinates for our next meeting.

The procedure was good and simple. Each one of us would arrive just before daylight at our assigned unit, go to the commanding officer, and have breakfast with him while explaining the convoy and loading orders. The units will be ready to move soon after we arrive. Keep the convoy in formation, if a vehicle breaks down, push it off the road and leave it.

We always headed the convoy out at daylight so that the one the greatest distance from Bizerta would arrive last and before dark. It was too dangerous to run convoys on a single road at night. The convoys went fairly well. The only problems at this time were Arabs with their donkeys pulling two wheel carts. All of us had the same problem; we would go back and signal the Arabs to use the shoulder of the road, but they would ignore us.

When we told the major about this, he told us to order a tank or a 6x6 truck to push them off the road. Finally, the Arabs got the message; their bluffs didn't work. Sometimes they or their donkeys were killed. Then U.S. military vehicles started breaking in our convoys. Most of them would pull over, stop and wait for the convoy to pass when I went back and signaled for them to pull over. The problem was taking the time to go back, because I would have to go full throttle to get back to the front of the convoy to guide them on the correct roads. If there was any oncoming traffic, the only way I could do this was to go in and out of the lines of tanks and trucks at full speed.

Our Harleys' maximum speed with a windshield was 93 miles per hour at 0400 hrs. (4:00 A.M.) when there was more oxygen in the air. By accident, I learned that I could shift gears without using the clutch. One time I was riding alongside a British dispatch rider on a Norton without a windshield. We were on a long, level, straight road and there was no traffic. We signaled each other to go full throttle. My Harley Davidson topped out at 93 M.P.H. and stayed there. The Norton gradually pulled ahead of me and topped out at 106M.P.H. The dispatch rider told me this when we stopped to have a drink of water and a cigarette. I gave him a pack of Lucky Strikes, which he appreciated because they were better than Cape to Cairo.

A jeep full of officers got in one of my convoys. When I signaled them to pull over, they ignored me. The vehicle behind the jeep was a tank. All of the tanks were running at full throttle with their hatches open. I didn't have time to stop and arrest them. The machine gunner, in the turret of the tank, saw what was happening. I signaled him to fire over and to the side of the jeep. That got their attention. They pulled over so fast the jeep almost rolled over. The soldiers in the convoy that saw this gave the officers a finger as they passed them.

Another time, a command car, with five officers in it, broke into my convoy. I went back, signaled them to pull over which they did, but they got back in. I did the same thing again and they got back in again. By then, I was ticked off. The Provost Marshall was right. The officers did not believe I had the time to do anything about it. I went back, pulled my Tommy gun out of the scabbard and fired a burst over their heads. They pulled over. I shot holes in the radiator of the command car. The senior officer was a full colonel in the U.S. Army Air Force and with him was a major, a captain and two first lieutenants. The colonel was arrogant and shouting, "M.P. I have a staff meeting to get to and you are interfering." I replied, "Sir, the Provost Marshall, by command of General Eisenhower, has issued a General Order that no one will be allowed to break into any of these convoys and this is the third time you have done this. All of you are under arrest. Now, spread eagle with your faces to the ground." They didn't seem to believe what they were hearing. I fired a burst over their heads and they got down. One at a time, I got their identification cards; then I got their dog tags.

It was fortunate that I got back to the front of the convoy just in time to lead them to their loading area. I remember the code name for that loading area was "Houston." When the convoy was loaded onto the L.S.T's, the officers' I.D. cards and dog tags were turned in by me to our major. After he heard the details, he was almost jumping up and down. The major always cursed a lot. He said, "You did exactly the right thing. I'll fix their cans; they are arrogant S.O.B.'s and they'll not get away with it." When I left, he was already on the phone talking to a staff general in Algiers.

All of our motorcycle force heard what had happened. The colonel's commanding general was ordered to place the five officers under open arrest and escort them to a hearing at the Provost Marshall's office. A general from the Judge Advocate General's office at Allied Supreme Headquarters was at the hearing. The Provost Marshall told the five officers that he was filing charges against them for a general court-martial and based on the charges they faced, he would recommend a minimum sentence of twenty years in Fort Leavenworth or a maximum sentence of a firing squad. Then he gave them a choice. They could accept the punishment that he was authorized to specify and there would not be a court martial. If they chose a court martial, they would be immediately placed under close arrest and taken to prison in Algiers to await trial. They decided to accept the punishment specified by the Provost Marshal.

The general from the judge advocate general's office instructed the sergeant clerk to draw up certain papers for them to sign. Then papers were drawn up specifying the punishments. The colonel who was in command was reduced in rank to 2nd Lt. The major who was second in command was reduced in rank to 1st lieutenant. The captain and the two first lieutenants were ordered to forfeit one month's pay and allowances because they were junior grade officers. (All majors and ranks higher were senior grade officers and should know better than to disobey a general order.) The punishment was reviewed by a board of general officers in Algiers and it was upheld.

Being near Tunis, I stopped by M. P. headquarters to get some pay and to see if I had any mail. My pay, a letter from home and a parcel were there. The parcel contained a box of Whitman's Sampler, which I shared with my great task force of eight. In my letter, my mother told me that her sister's son, Sergeant Jake Lindsey, was in Africa in an armored infantry battalion. I had convoyed the first echelon of that unit to Bizerta that morning and I was to pick up the second echelon the next morning.

It is a difficult thing to remember everything in proper sequence. Jake was my first cousin and named after our grandfather, Jacob Ramer, who had been the sheriff of Covington County, Alabama. His mother, my mother's sister, was Lena Ramer Lindsey. My grandmother, Georgia Ann Meadows Ramer, was living with Aunt Lena in Defuniak Springs, Florida, when she died. She is the one that taught me about sucking a rock and many other things. She died while I was gone to the war.

When I arrived during the darkness the next morning to convoy the second echelon of that unit, I said to the lieutenant colonel, "Do you have a Sergeant Jake Lindsey?" He replied, "Yes, but he went with the first echelon yesterday." I never did see Jake.

After our first convoy orders were given to us at the Provost Marshal's office in Bizerta, all of our meetings were at different places where we were absolutely alone. No one could see or hear us. The Provost Marshall gave each of us our orders and gave us the coordinates and time for our next meeting. Most of the time, we met before daylight about 0400 hrs. (0400 A.M.). From time to time, one of our riders wouldn't be there. The major would then tell us he was dead. Of the ten riders that started out together, five of us survived and one of our survivors lost his leg. A bunch of soldiers in a 6x6 truck had gone berserk on vino. When the M. P. tried to stop them, they ran him off the road and when he crashed his leg was caught under the Harley. We all learned that the best procedure, under those conditions, would be to stay back of the truck and shoot them.

All of us were weary. I stopped at hospitals, when one was nearby, to get food, water, and some sleep. When there was no hospital, I hid off the road and slept on the ground. We only had time for four or five hours sleep per night. The riding was so rough. I got an Arab leather worker in Tunis to make all of us a leather belt like a girdle. We strapped these on under our shirts to hold our insides together. The leather worker had made me several leather shoulder holsters to hold German Lugers.

For instance, many roads had shell holes in them. By the time you can see one at high speed, it is too late to slow down. The only chance is to go full throttle and jump it. The old Harley Davidson's were heavy and not made for jumping. Fortunately, somehow I made all the jumps. Army truck drivers could not see a motorcycle back of them. When I started to pass one of them, the driver suddenly turned left. There was no road there, only wide-open spaces. With no time to brake, I turned the front wheel and laid the Harley down on the crash bar and turned loose. My body skidded about 35 feet while the Harley flipped completely over, skidded and came to rest. My body was bruised and skin was burned off. The only things that saved me were the boots, heavy gloves, helmet, leather jacket and such. Later, I stopped at a hospital to get my skin patched up.

One of our riders tore the heel and sole completely off of one of his jump boots while skidding on it. I pulled up and stopped back of a 6x6 truck, which had stopped for a bridge crossing. The bridge had been blown up by the retreating Germans and the Corps of Engineers had installed a one-lane pontoon bridge. British Red Caps (military police) were stationed at each end of the bridge directing one-way traffic. The truck in front of me had stopped too close to the bridge, so the Red Cap motioned for the driver to back up, which he did. Motorcycles do not have a reverse gear. As the truck backed slowly toward me, I jumped off. The truck went over the Harley and crushed it. The driver apologized, but it wasn't his fault. Soldiers helped me unload my gear and salvage what I could. Then the truck driver carried me to a supply depot to get a new Harley and other items. This kind of happenings does wear a body to a frazzle!

After a convoy that I was leading had been loaded at the docks, I drove my Harley into the large building housing the Navy machine shops. My Harley had started skipping some when I throttled up. Driving up to a Navy lieutenant, who seemed to be in charge, I saluted and said, "Sir, my Harley has started skipping and I need the help of one of your Engineman." He replied, "Of course." Pointing at a sailor working on an engine, he said, "That sailor over there will help you, just tell him I sent you, and by the way, I've seen what you guys have been doing. I wouldn't have your job." I saluted and said, "Thank you, Sir."

The sailor was bent over working on an engine as I rode up and said; "The lieutenant said it is O.K. for you to work on my Harley." He turned and looked up and as we made eye contact, he started trembling. He softly said, "Chief, don't talk to me. I've been in trouble and I'm being watched." We recognized each other. He had been in my platoon at N.O.B. Norfolk. I bent over, pointed to the carburetor and such to explain the problem with my Harley. Softly I said, "We are O.K. no one knows who I am, and no one will bother us. As you can see, I am a Special Military Police Officer and my boss is in command of this operation." He calmed down and we talked about what had happened at boot camp. He told me that every man in the platoon knew I had done the right thing. Those two drunks would have killed that boy. When each man was called in to testify at the inquiry, they all told the truth as I had instructed them. It was fortunate that the lieutenant and chief were still drunk as skunks when the corpsmen (medics) took them to the hospital and it was evident that they had beaten the hell out of that boy. When the doctor from the hospital, a lieutenant commander, testified at the board of inquiry that ended the proceedings. The lieutenant and chief were permanently relieved from duty and received some other punishment.

While the Engineman worked on the carburetor, changed spark plugs and other things, he told me the platoon graduated and then some of them went to various schools and some were assigned to ships in the Pacific and Asiatic Fleets. Many of them had gone down when the Japanese first attacked in China, the Philippines and Pearl Harbor.

The Engineman tested the Harley engine and when finished, we shook hands and wished each other good luck. He never did tell me about his trouble. There were imprints on his fatigue jacket sleeve where his stripes had been removed.

My stomach was in great pain. After several bowel movements, there was nothing left in my stomach, but I still needed to go. There was a loop road that went south out of Bizerta and then made a loop returning to Bizerta. A number of hospitals had set up along this road, so the place was called "Hospital Row." There were "General Hospitals," "Station Hospitals" and "Evacuation Hospitals" waiting to be shipped to Sicily and Italy at the proper time. The 7th Evacuation from Tebessa was there. Whenever I could, I had been stopping at some of these hospitals to shave, shower, eat and so forth.

The pain in my stomach continued so I went to see the lieutenant colonel in command of the 7th Evacuation. He said, "Son, you have amebic dysentery and we all have it. Paregoric is needed, but there is none. The pain is great, but it'll wear off." He gave me some kind of medicine to drink and a bottle of aspirin. It was agony squatting down over a slit trench in the boiling hot sun trying to have a bowel movement with an empty stomach. I kept on drinking all the water I could hold and eating salt.

Just before daylight one morning, I was on my way to pick up another convoy to lead it to Bizerta. I stopped to go to the bathroom, eat some rations and smoke. At false dawn (when you can see some light, but the sun is still below the horizon), I looked at my orders from our major as to when and where we would meet the next time. The orders were to meet the next morning at 0400hrs. on July 5th. Therefore, today was July 4, 1943. I thought about how many holidays I had missed.

A great big red ball of fire (the sun) was rising above the horizon. There was a large lake and as the sun cleared the horizon, it looked like a lake of blood. There were no clouds in the sky; it was absolutely clear. There were no signs of life of any kind. No birds, no insects, no grass or trees, although I could see for many miles in every direction. I tried not to look at the lake of blood and wondered if I were losing my mind. Leaving that place at full speed, I went on. Sicily was invaded by the U. S. Army and the British 8th Army in July 1943. The U. S. Army 82nd Airborne Division was flown from Africa to Sicily to make the first combat jump of the U.S. Army in World War II.

Summer 1943

The four remaining members of the Special Military Police motorcycle force did get a break when the invasion of Sicily started. We continued to do odd jobs. The activity at all the ports in Northwest Africa never did slow down. U.S. Army troops of all kinds, including infantry and armored divisions with equipment and supplies, continued to arrive from the United States. There was a tremendous build-up of the Air Force. No one talked about it, but everyone seemed to know that Italy would be invaded from Africa and Sicily as soon as the Sicilian campaign ended.

Whenever there was an opportunity, I continued to scrounge food and such at the 7th Evacuation Hospital on Hospital Row. One of the nurses and I had become friends and several times she rode on my Harley with me to Ferryville to get some good wine. She was from Mississippi and her name was Delta. Delta was older than I was, but what the heck, everybody was older than I was. Officers would arrive in the late afternoons to pick up their dates (nurses) on Hospital Row. They drove U.S. vehicles and German vehicles. Whenever officers saw Delta and me together, they would give us nasty looks because enlisted men were not supposed to date officers. We out-stared them until they looked away. Sometimes, I slowly and deliberately rearranged and checked out my weapons while they watched. Taking my shoulder holstered Luger out of my saddlebag, then strapping it on, swapping places with my Tommy gun and M.I. rifle in their saddle scabbards after checking the loads, gave them an eye full. The officers were mostly desk jockeys anyway. The doctors and other nurses told them not to mess with Delta or me.

Delta told me she was getting a ten-day pass and if I could get one, we could go on a tour. That was so unusual that I wondered how she managed that. She laughed and said, "Maybe because of long, hard, arduous duty. Alabama, don't you realize the respect the colonel and all of us in the 7th Evacuation Hospital have for you for helping us at Tebessa? You came from out of nowhere in your strange uniform with those British tanks." I said, "I'll go ask my major for a pass."

My major laughed, gave me a ten-day pass and said, "Alabama, remember you are responsible for her safety." I saluted and said, "Yes, Sir, and thank you, Sir." When I left, the major, the sergeant and the corporal were laughing and talking about us having a "Cook's Tour." A "Cook's Tour" was a tour of Europe and other places that rich Americans took before the war.

Our first stop was at a U.S. Army supply depot to get supplies and other clothes for Delta. Nurses had already started wearing GI uniforms, the same as soldiers, especially those in Evacuation Hospitals. We got Delta some jump boots so she could lace them tight to protect her ankles, pilot's leather jacket, gloves, and helmet with goggles and sunglasses. She took her lieutenant's brass off and tucked her hair under her helmet. The soldiers at the depot were wondering what was going on, but didn't say anything.

We became young again, swimming in the Mediterranean and camping on the beaches. At Carthage, near Tunis, we explored the ruins and went swimming. In the Kasbah, I introduced her to the Arab and Jewish merchants that I knew. Delta was having a ball. She had a great personality and was interested in everything and everybody. The perfume merchants gave her all kinds of perfume to take back to her friends. They explained how a small vial of pure essence could be mixed to produce many bottles of perfume. The only things that Delta had to pay for were a beautiful leather ladies' pocketbook (nurses had GI pocketbooks), handcrafted silver and gold jewelry and a hand woven rug to send home. The reason for not paying was all the merchants knew that the only way Americans could come to their market in the Kasbah was with an M.P. escort, so I was a special friend.

It was a joy to me to see the expressions on her face and in her eyes. It is difficult for people to understand the impact that war had on the young nurses. Delta had been gone from home for a long time. She didn't want to leave the market place, but I insisted it was time to go. We tied the rug on top of everything on the rack and went to see the sergent chefs.

When I introduced Delta to the sergent chefs, they were delighted. They insisted on taking us out to dinner and dance at the open-air restaurant in the park. We bathed and got ready to go. Delta got to ride with one of them in a sidecar on his German motorcycle. While sipping good wine, we ordered our dinner. Delta wanted to try all kinds of food and the sergents obliged. The music was beautiful and Delta and I danced several times; then she danced with each of the sergents. While we enjoyed our dinner, we told the sergents how we had first met at Tebessa.

Of course, Delta didn't speak French, but I interpreted the best I could and the sergents helped every now and then. They did understand English, but would never use it with me because they insisted that I learn French.

After we returned to the sergents' headquarters and living quarters, there was a noticeable change in them. It was certain they had enjoyed this brief moment in their bleak everyday lives. I could see something in them that I had never seen before; how much they missed their wives, children and families in France. They could not even write a letter to them. We sipped some wine and talked some.

Suddenly, the sergent that I had always thought I had seen somewhere said in English, "Alabama, do you remember a Free French sergent in the commando with you that you called Pete?" I replied, "Of course, he is one of my close friends and partners." The sergent said, "He was my younger brother and was killed in action on a raid. I was there in our family farmhouse when you came in with Pete that night. After you left commandos, there were so many people tortured by the Gestapo that someone talked. Many were tortured and murdered. Pete did not surrender; he killed all he could before they got him. I didn't want to tell you, but you have the right to know."

My body was shaking and with my hands over my face, I bent over trying to hold back the tears. Oh, Lord, should we all die? My mind was flooded with memories. It took a while for me to look up. Every sergent chef looked me straight in the eyes and I knew why they would kill anyone that bothered me. We were bonded as brothers for life by the bloody war. When Delta and I made eye contact, she was sitting up stiff with horror in her eyes. Delta and the other American nurses, doctors, and medical people had seen and treated wounded and dying soldiers and had become hardened to those things. But they didn't know about the other horrors of war. Delta and the others had thought about me as a wild, sometimes crazy, maybe brave American soldier but did not know some things about me.

The sergent looked at Delta and said, "Tell your people to take care of Alabama, he is a commando and a special soldier." Another sergent gave me instructions in French. We were to go to a small hotel. All arrangements had been made. We were not to pay for anything. The room is in our name and you are protected. The lady's rug will be sent to her home; it is too much for you to carry on your motorcycle. Delta wrote down her home address. When we arrived at the hotel, we were given the great treatment. My Harley and weapons were brought in and protected.

138

When we were in our room, we couldn't sleep. We were both hyper. I had to get things off my mind and she had to get some understanding in her mind. In the first place, she and the others had wondered at Tebessa how an American soldier could wear a British tam o'shanter, but they had forgotten that. There were some things I could tell Delta and other things I couldn't. I cautioned her over and over to never say anything about the sergent chefs or commandos, because if you do their families could be murdered.

The next day we continued our tour. We spent the nights in small hotels in small towns on two occasions. The other nights were spent sleeping on the ground. Two things amazed Delta. One was how friendly the French people were to us. Sometimes, we stopped at small cafes to eat. People would come over and talk to us and give us wine. The café owners would not let us pay. They also would give us some food and water to take with us. She and the other nurses had never met local people.

The other thing Delta kept talking about was how infantry soldiers lived on the ground or in holes no matter what kind of weather. I taught her how to tell time and direction by using the stars, the Big Dipper, the Little Dipper, the North Star, the Morning Star and others.

On and on we went as the Harley roared across mountains and plains. I thought about taking her to the ancient city of Kairouan, at the crossroads of ancient caravan routes. One route ran north and south and the other one ran east and west. I decided not to go there because Kairouan was a Muslim Holy City and there might be trouble if someone saw Delta (a woman) dressed like a man. I had heard that Kairouan was one of the cities for Holy Pilgrimages. I wanted to go to see the French farm family that I had spent the night with on the high plateau, but I knew I couldn't find them because at the time I was there I didn't have a map. The location was on a small rarely traveled mountain road.

Again, Delta was amazed seeing the sights in the mountains and plains. On two occasions, we saw mirages shimmering in the distance. Stopping at an oasis, she wanted to spend the night there. I warned her it was not safe; good people would come there, but also bad people. We swam and bathed in the water and left.

Turning towards the west, we went to the ruins at Tebessa, in Algeria, and after stopping there, we headed northward in order to end our tour back to Bizerta. On the way, I showed her the awesome plateau called Hill 609. She said she remembered the long convoys bringing wounded soldiers, wearing the Red Bull insignia of the 34th Infantry Division, to the hospital. They worked day and night patching them up and then sending them to station hospitals and general hospitals. They worked on many of them while they were lying in the trucks. There were so many wounded that we gave out of stretchers and were giving out of medical supplies when a convoy arrived bringing more medics and supplies.

In the late afternoon on the tenth day of our leave, we arrived at Hospital Row. The nurses and some doctors gathered around as we unloaded the Harley. Delta couldn't wait to tell them about our tour. They all went inside the mess tent and sat down at the tables. They were all talking as Delta was showing them the things from the Kasbah. There were so many "oohs" and "ahs." that it sounded like Christmas in July, or a bunch of high school seniors planning their prom.

I parked the Harley next to a supply tent and carried all my weapons inside. There was a GI folding cot inside the tent that I slept on when I was there. Medics were not allowed to carry weapons and weapons were not allowed in hospitals except military police were required to carry weapons at all times because they were on duty at all times. Anyway, I didn't want to show weapons, so I used the supply tent. We brought back all the good bottles of wine we could carry. My Tommy gun was short, so I placed four bottles of wine down in the saddle scabbard and then replaced my Tommy gun over them.

It was still daylight when I finished unloading and squaring away all our things. The talking and squealing from the mess tent was heard up and down Hospital Row. Nurses from the other hospitals came over. I took a leak, then a ten-minute break as real soldiers do. When I walked into the lieutenant colonel's office, he was busy filling out medical reports. He stood up. I saluted and said, "Sir, I wish to thank you, take your pick from these wines." Opening a musette bag with different kinds of wines, he picked one. He said, "Sit down. Don't thank me, you have helped all of us commanders on Hospital Row."

He opened the bottle of wine and said, "We'll have the first drink together and we'll talk. The only reason I allowed Delta to go with you was because of what you did for us at Tebessa, but that was not enough, I violated rules, but your major had already told me you could handle anything. It turned out to be a good thing. These nurses have worked hard and needed something to think about."

One bottle of wine was given to the head nurse (a major), one to the cooks, one to the other personnel, and the rest to the doctors and nurses. The nurses chattered most of the night. I went to sleep. After breakfast the next morning, I was ready to leave. The nurses hugged me and gave me friendly kisses. When Delta hugged me and gave me a real kiss, the others applauded. She was about to cry. I said, "Please don't do that, maybe we'll survive." War is cruel and filled with bitterness and sorrow.

When the three other Special MP's and I met with the major, he told us that the planning to invade Italy was underway. He would need us later on for some special jobs; he would let us know when. He said, "Go to Tunis and stay with the military police company there. Help them and the French police when you are needed."

In Tunis, Rosette and I started seeing each other on a regular basis. We went to dances, some movies and swimming. Gradually, her family allowed her to go out with me without her aunt or someone as a chaperone. Sometimes we would walk to the park and all around the city. The sergent chefs kept a watchful eye on us. They liked Rosette. They knew her father and family. They always welcomed us when we went by to see them and insisted that we carry some good wine to her grandmother's house.

Rosette and I decided to get married. Her family and everyone we knew approved. But we had a problem. We were both twenty years old and I couldn't marry without parental consent unless we were twenty-one. No priest, rabbi, or mullah would marry us without consent. Rosette could get parental consent. Maybe I could, but it would take a long time to receive it. None of that mattered anyway, because the U.S. Army wouldn't recognize our marriage unless I was twenty-one.

Her family told us that we could be engaged and marry after the war. Her mother and father married when he returned from World War I. So we were engaged. I went with Rosette and her family to some of the Jewish festivals at the temple. We met many friendly Catholics, Jews, Muslims and whatever.

The only reason there is so much religious hatred in this world is because wicked leaders preach and teach hate to their followers from the time they are born. Religion has always been used for the evil leaders to obtain riches and power. There are many good people of different religions. One time I was at a U.S. Army supply depot in Tunis. The Army hired many Jews and

Muslim civilians to work there, which was a good thing because they could feed their starving families and relieve soldiers for other duties. Some of the civilians wanted to paint my name "Daniel" on both sides of my Harley. It became apparent that both Jews and Muslims wanted to do this. So, I gave the command. The Muslims would paint one side in Arabic and Jews would paint the other side in Hebrew. Honestly, I couldn't tell any difference in the writing, but they were happy.

Somewhere south of Tunis, my head started spinning with fever. I was getting weak. There wasn't a hospital nearby. The closest place I could reach was Madam Zaborie's. When she took one look at me, she started giving orders to the others. They took my gear and clothes off down to my waist and laid me face down on a table. I couldn't see what they were doing exactly. Grandmere was placing what seemed to be hemispheres of clear glass suction cups on my back. She poured some kind of solution in each cup and when placed on my back, it formed a suction action.

I could feel heat from the cups and it was a good while before they were removed. While I lay there, I was given some kind of medicine to drink. After the cups were removed, they wrapped my throat and chest with towels soaked in some kind of solution and placed me in a bed, covering me with blankets. I went to sleep, but I remember sweating a lot.

Losing track of time, I think I was there about two days, and I have never forgotten what a great lady Rosette's grandmother was. During our dinner conversations, we sometimes discussed religion. Grandmere said, "How can a virgin girl have a child?" Someone interpreted that into French for me. She was referring to Mary, the mother of Jesus. After thinking about this, I replied, "The same way Moses and the Children of Israel passed through the Red Sea on dry land." When someone told her this, she looked at me and grinned. It would have been good if my knowledge of the Bible had been better at that time. Their rabbi had told me that they believed Jesus was a prophet, but not the Son of God.

When I felt steady enough to ride my Harley, I went to a Station Hospital in Tunis. Inside the entrance, I told the duty sergeant I needed a doctor. A nurse came and guided me to an examination room. After undressing to my waist, she took my blood pressure, temperature and the like. I still had some fever. A doctor thumped my chest and listened to it. When he saw the red circles on my back, he exclaimed, "What in the world is this?" I explained. He called other doctors to come in there. I explained again. Some nurses came in to see what was going on.

After poking and listening to my chest and back, they took some X-rays and told the lab people they wanted to read them right away. They gave me anti-biotic, and after reading the X-rays, the lead doctor, a major, said, "We all agree you have pneumonia and whoever did this saved your life." While they moved me to a bed, I could hear them discussing ancient remedies and medicine. After my temperature went down to normal, I was released.

A few days later, Rosette and I were walking down a main street that ran into Avenue Jules Ferry when she remembered something she wanted to tell me. The first American soldiers that the people of Tunis saw were American Prisoners of War that the Italian Army forced to march through Tunis. The Americans looked bad; they were dirty, their uniforms were torn and some of them were wounded. The Italian women and children threw stones at them and spit on them. The Italian soldiers were trying to show how good and brave they were. I told her about the British and U.S. Army saying, "It is better to be captured by the Germans than by the cowardly Italians."

One night, about 0300 hrs., I returned to M. P. Headquarters and went into the courtyard. The M.P.'s on duty told me that a soldier, who said he was my brother, was asleep in my room. It turned out that he was my brother, James (Samuel James Houston). He had a pass and had been searching for me for several days. James was in the United States Army, Combat Signal Corps., attached to the 34th Infantry Division. They were the soldiers that strung thousands of miles of wire for combat telephones. The ones you see in movies that are hand cranked. They also set up and operated radio (wireless) communications. It was a great pleasure to see James, but I became angry because my parents had told me in a letter that James had lost a kidney. No one should be in combat with only one kidney. We talked until after we had breakfast in the courtyard. His pass ended that day, so I asked one of the M.P.'s to take him back to his unit in a jeep so he would not be in trouble for returning late. Most M.P.'s did favors like that because we were all infantrymen from the 34th Infantry Division. Later during the war, I received a letter from my parents telling me that James had been wounded by artillery fire in France and was hospitalized in Paris.

The military police company in Tunis sent patrols in jeeps into the Kasbah daily. They picked up dead U.S. soldiers that had been murdered and robbed. For this reason, the Kasbah was posted "OFF LIMITS" to all military personnel. The signs were at all of the entrances. At night, the only things that moved were criminals. Even during daylight, a soldier alone could be murdered in a hidden alley. Another problem was all strangers would get lost and couldn't get out. It took me a long time to learn the small streets and alleys. There were no street signs or lights. All of the Kasbahs, in the different cities, were the ancient walled cities. New cities were built outside the Kasbah walls. My advantage was having a map of the Kasbah at Tunis when we did the original raid. The only way military personnel could legally enter the Kasbah was with an armed M. P. Some of the military would come to the M. P. barracks and ask if one of the military policemen would take them into the Kasbah. Military police would do this if they had time.

One night all of us were awakened by loud voices in our courtyard. A small-time, not too well known, actor from Hollywood with a group from the U.S.O. (United Service Organization) was insisting that an M.P. take them into the Kasbah because he was important. The military police on duty were trying to explain there is nothing to be seen in the Kasbah at night. The actor didn't believe them and started using threats. All of us picked up our weapons and went down to the courtyard. The M.P. told him to go to H---, he was stupid and crazy. The group left.

The general's staff decided to take more action to prevent the deaths in the Kasbah. A J.A.G. (Judge Advocate General) major and his staff set up an office near the military police jail to handle court martials. A new first lieutenant, who was a motorcyclist, was assigned to the military police company. We came up with a good plan. Driving our Harleys, all together, down the narrow streets very slowly, the soldiers heard us and ran. At certain places, military police were waiting in their jeeps. The soldiers ran right to them and were arrested and carried to the jail in trucks.

The ladies of the oldest profession came out and watched us. They wanted to give us a free souvenir. Whenever they saw M.P. brassards they said, "Ouu, la, la, Mademoiselle Promenade." Just kidding us, of course. There were three brothel districts in the Kasbah, one low class, one middle class and one first class. The ladies in the low class brothels lived in cribs while the ladies in the first class ones lived in elegance with fine bars and such.

The military police jail was overloaded with prisoners, so prisoners were placed on the flat roof of the jail. Infantry surrounded the jail and the J.A.G. office. The prisoners, several hundred, were lined up from the J.A.G. office to the jail. The major spent about three minutes with each prisoner. The objective was to teach the soldiers a lesson, but not sentence them to prison. The major sentenced each of them to forfeiture of pay. After sentencing, the soldiers were taken back to their units by truck and the M.P. in charge turned over the papers to their commanding officers.

Late one afternoon, I stopped at a main entrance that led to the markets in the Kasbah. The British Consulate was located just outside the walls there and a British sentry was on duty at all times. They were friends. I parked my Harley and said, "How are things?" The sentry said, "Two doctors and three nurses went in a while back. That's their jeep over there."

I thought, oh no, oh no; it would be absolute darkness within minutes. Pulling my Tommy gun out of its scabbard, I ran. My heart was pounding with fear for them. It was twilight when I saw them milling about and talking. The merchants had already closed and locked their shutters. I pointed the way and shouted, "RUN, DAMMIT, RUN!" They looked startled, but started moving. I moved, but stayed behind them. It was now pitch black dark. I shouted again, "Run for your lives!" and I heard their shoes hitting the cobblestones faster. Now and then, I stopped, faced backwards and froze. I sensed, more than I heard some movement. Just in case, because the robbers could throw knives, I laid flat down and fired. I fired three round bursts high, low, and to the side, then ran. When we reached the sentry, the doctors and nurses were gasping for breath. I said to the sentry, "Thanks, Mate." He replied, "Glad to help." The nurses were shivering. They heard the firing and the danger was sinking in. One of the doctors was a lieutenant colonel, the other doctor was a captain, and the three nurses were first lieutenants. I instructed them to follow me to the medical station at the Lucie Carno.

The first lieutenant, in command of the station, was there. When he heard what had happened, he was furious. He was not only their junior in rank, but also their junior as doctors. They stood silent as he chastised them. Then we all sat down and drank coffee; lots of coffee. The first lieutenant explained his anger. Unarmed doctors and nurses have no business being on the roads at night. You are doves ready to be plucked. What really shook the group up was when he explained what would have happened if Alabama had not, by accident, found out you were in the Kasbah. He said, "You two doctors would have been murdered and stripped down for them to take whatever you have. You three nurses would be kept alive and sold; never to be seen or heard from again." The doctors and nurses said they had never heard of these things, and simply thought it would be a good trip to shop in the Kasbah. This was true; many military personnel did not know what was going on, especially hospital personnel because they were isolated.

The lieutenant colonel thanked us and said, "It is time for us to go." The first lieutenant doctor replied, "Sir, you will not leave until daylight. You can change my order because you outrank me. My friend, Alabama, is a Special Military Police Officer whose commander is the Provost Marshall of Africa, and he is authorized to give general orders. If that is not enough, General Hap Arnold's headquarters is just above us and if I call, some staff officer will tell you the same thing." The lieutenant colonel apologized.

Everyone settled down to spend the night. Thinking about the British system of a rum ration after long, hard, hazardous duty, I went to my saddlebags and brought in four bottles of great wine. After we had a first sip, I said, "Shame on you doctors, you don't observe things." The doctors started looking around, but missed my point. The nurses were squirming around hiding their feet. The nurses were in some pain because they either lost their shoes or kicked them off while running. They had worn their dress shoes. Their feet were cut and bruised from the cobblestones. Some of the medics stationed there assisted the doctors while they cleaned the nurses' feet, sprinkled sulfanilamide powder on the cuts and bandaged them. None of their cuts required stitches.

The first lieutenant told the doctors some things about me and that I should be Z.I.'d. (Meaning transferred to the "Zone of Interior," the Continental United States) because I had been gone too long. (The only way this could be done would be by a Medical Review Board). He told them about my great right toe continually getting infected. The lieutenant colonel looked at it and said, "I can fix it. Come to see me any time." He gave me the number and location of his station hospital.

One day I parked my Harley beside the lieutenant colonel's office (a tent). He greeted me warmly and introduced me to some of his staff and said, "When do you want me to operate?" I replied, "Now would be fine." We went over to the surgical tent. I sat in a chair with my foot propped up in the air. The doctor gave me some shots in my toe and foot. He said, "If you have any pain, let me know. I can give you something more powerful." My foot was numb; I said, "I'm OK."

While this was going on, the nurses heard I was there and came over to say hello. The operation was simple and quick. The doctor made cuts on each side of the messed up toenail, folded the skin back, and removed the toenail and most of the root. He then folded the skin back down and sewed it in place. When finished, I got ready to leave. The doctor laughed and said, "You're not going anywhere. In a little while, your toe and foot will swell up, you'll not be able to walk except by hobbling." He told his sergeant to take care of my Harley and weapons. I was assigned to a cot in the surgical ward. They had a type of basket made of wire that was placed under the covers on the cot so that the covers did not touch my foot.

That night, I awoke shaking with a chill. The cot I was on was rocking. I couldn't speak. Someone called a nurse. They piled blankets on me. After a while the chills stopped and I went back to sleep. Just before daylight, I started sweating with fever. I heard some doctors and nurses talking. One of them said, "He has malaria." After daylight I was moved to the "malaria ward." There were two rows of cots with soldiers on them who had malaria. All of us had extreme chills and when the chills stopped, there was a little time before fever would start again. In the time in between chills and fever, we drank all the water and liquids we could. Also, we ate something when we could. Quinine was not available. The Japanese had cut off quinine and some other medicines. Atabrine didn't seem to help much. Every now and then, someone died when their fever went too high and stayed too long. A young soldier's temperature reached 109 degrees and he lived, but his brain was cooked. The whites of our eyes turned yellow. Everything possible was tried in order to break our fevers. Lots of aspirin were used and they would strip us naked and pour water on us. The young doctors in the military had never seen or treated tropical diseases. There were soldiers in the Pacific Theater with tropical diseases. Some of them were strange; such as elephantiasis. Messages were sent back to the United States asking old doctors about treatments.

One night, a John Wayne movie was scheduled for the hospital. A crew traveled around to hospitals and showed different movies. They would hang a movie screen on the side of a 6x6 truck and after dark show the movie. I wanted to go, but all the nurses said, "No." After dark, I slipped out and sat down on my steel helmet to watch the movie. In a few minutes, I was unconscious. I awoke the next morning lying on the ground with the sun in my face. I went back to my ward and received a real scolding, which I deserved, by the nurses. People had been looking everywhere for me.

The chills and fevers gradually subsided for the survivors in the malaria ward. The survivors were moved to a "Recovery Ward" as new patients with malaria came to the malaria ward. The station hospital was located next to an air base. All of the patients, except a very few, were in the Air Force. The soldiers who served in the ground crews had never seen combat and enjoyed tricks like the Boy Scouts did. One evening, I was going to bed and realized that my cot had been short sheeted. That means folding a bottom sheet so that your feet will not go all the way down. Simply shaking the sheet out, I lay down and went to sleep. They were disappointed because they thought I would struggle and all that. They didn't realize how good it was for me to have a cot to sleep on and a tent over my head.

One evening I came back from chow early. I went to the latrine and with a razor blade shaved the bristles off a toothbrush in very small pieces. With the small pieces on a piece of paper, I sprinkled them in the sheets on the three ring- leaders cots. They itched, tossed and turned all night. I asked them the next day if they slept well. They continued to itch until they showered and changed the sheets. They knew I had done something; but they never did figure it out.

All of the doctors and nurses were kind to me. The captain that I met in Tunis said, "You are a lucky man. If you had gone down with malaria in some wild place, you wouldn't have made it." Other patients in the hospital wondered about the connection between us, but no one ever told them. As my strength improved, I started watching the bombers take off and land at the air base. Sometimes I went to the control tower and watched. The bombers took off at daylight and returned in the evenings. This was just one of the many air bases. After they took off, they assembled into their formations over the Mediterranean. There were so many, we couldn't count them. The 12th and 15th U.S.A. Air Forces bombed targets in Sicily, Italy, France, Austria, Yugoslavia, Greece, Czechoslovakia, Germany, and the toughest target of all, the oil fields at Polesti in Rumania. The 8th U.S. Army Air force stationed in England was also bombing some of these targets.

The aircrews earned my respect; not from what I heard, but from what I saw. The gunners not only had to withstand the cold, but also had to stay on oxygen for hours. The bombers had to fly at high altitudes to clear the mountains. The U.S. fighters flew cover for them for part of the way and then had to return to refuel and meet them on the way back. The anti-aircraft guns protecting Polesti were the best in the world. German fighters attacked the bombers on their way to the targets and then on their way back. Some of the bombers were shot down by the anti-aircraft guns, during their bomb runs, and some were damaged. The damaged bombers were sitting ducks for the German fighters.

When the bombers returned to the air base in the late afternoons, it was an awful sight. The aircrews were exhausted; even the ones that landed safely. Time after time, damaged aircraft would appear, just barely clearing the rolling hills, and then belly land on the runway. The ground crews worked feverously clearing the wrecks off the runway. A bomber landed with the tail section almost shot off. All that I could see holding it on was the control cables. There were dead and wounded on many aircraft.

Hollywood went to war. Many elitist thought Hollywood would help the morale of the poor, dumb, real soldiers. Just imagine how these aircrews felt when they saw a picture of Clark Gable commissioned as a captain air gunner. The picture showed him firing a machine-gun one time in Miami. He was a good actor, but not a machine-gunner.

Summer 1943

The lieutenant colonel commanding the station hospital had notified my major in Bizerta that I had malaria. After saying good-bye to the people at the hospital, I rode back to the military police barracks in Tunis. There was some mail from home and a parcel with a Whitman's Sampler inside. Rosette and her family were worried about me because they had not seen or heard from me. One of the sergent chefs told them I was in the hospital. At first, they thought I had crashed on my Harley.

When I returned to my major's office in Bizerta, he told me that plans were being made to invade Italy. The 34th Infantry Division would go in. There were a number of new divisions that were arriving from the United States plus some of the divisions that were in Sicily that would go in. The major told me to stay in Tunis until he called the other three motorcyclists and me to come back.

One afternoon, I happened to be near a U.S. officers' club. One of our military police stopped me. He wanted me to lend him my G.I.45 pistol and Sam Brown belt. He had gone somewhere and didn't get back in time to go by our barracks and get his, and he was going on duty at the officers' club. I said, "Sure." I handed him my Sam Brown belt when I removed it from my saddlebag and unhooked my pistol from my web belt, which I was wearing, and handed him the pistol. He had his brassard in his pocket.

None of us liked to wear our brassards and weapons around civilians when we were off duty. It was late afternoon and some civilians brought chairs out from their apartments to sit on the sidewalk, talk, and enjoy the coolness of evening. They were about 100 feet away and I decided to chat with them for a little while. My Harley was parked so that the M.P. could watch it. The M-1 rifle and Tommy gun were on the Harley and my Luger, with shoulder holster, was in the saddlebag. The web belt that I was wearing held a G. I. flashlight (the heavy metal kind) and an M.P. Billy club.

I sat down with the civilians and we talked. In a few minutes, it was twilight. Suddenly, from out of nowhere, appeared a first lieutenant from the 82nd Airborne and a 1st Lt. pilot. They were cursing and shouting. They wanted to fight. It was apparent they were berserk on vino. I jumped between them and the civilians as they rushed in. I shouted, "Halt." That diverted their attention to me. The closest one, the Airborne Lieutenant, was swinging at my head. I dodged his fists, drew my Billy club and hit him hard in the temple. The Billy club splintered and broke, he went down hard. I was glad that he was the first one because I saw the large combat knife strapped on his leg. The civilians ran inside their building.

Within seconds, the pilot moved in swinging and cursing. I dodged; the splintered Billy club with its sharp point was still held in my right hand, attached to my wrist by the strap. The human mind works by low voltage electricity. The speed of electricity (and light) is 186,000 miles per second. I didn't want to kill the pilot by sticking the Billy club in his throat, but I had to stop him. I drew my flashlight from my belt and hit him with it. He appeared stunned and I thought I could talk him down. I stuck the sharp Billy club in his face and said, "Do you want this in your throat?" He cursed and swung his fist again. He was too far-gone to reason with. I hit him in the head with the flashlight again. It was now dark. The pilot ran. The flashlight still worked. I caught him and he swung again. I hit him again. My flashlight was taking a beating. Using a come-along hold, I maneuvered him to the main street. I flagged down a British 1500 wt. Lorrie and asked the sergeant to take us to the military police jail. I told the sergeant and the soldiers with him that the pilot was berserk on vino. The pilot started cursing and swinging again. The soldiers picked him up, slid him in the back of the lorrie and sat down on him.

The military police at the jail locked him in a cell and because he was an officer, the duty sergeant called a lieutenant to come and calm him down. Two M.P.'s and I went back in a jeep to find the other lieutenant. We stopped at the officer's club and I got my Harley and we started searching. We found him in the middle of a dark street. He had been stripped and robbed. The M. P.'s rolled the body up in blankets and a canvas shelter half and carried it to the morgue. War is crazy. I had gotten soft and didn't have a weapon on me. I went to the officers' club and told the M.P. there what had happened. Looking inside, I saw officers and nurses drinking and dancing. I left, and the band played on.

Rosette and I went to dances, movies and the like whenever we could. I talked with French people most of the time and I would dream in French. Sometimes days would pass that I didn't hear or speak English. A message arrived instructing my group to return to Bizerta. We knew our jobs in Africa were ending. The provisional (temporary) military police company in Tunis was notified that the company would be disbanded and the personnel would return to the 34th Infantry Division.

Rosette and I went to our last dance together. We were at the Lucie Carno and went up to the balcony to dance. We danced and danced. We sang some French songs and the American song, "As Time Goes By," in French. We cried. We never saw each other again.

The next morning, we four cyclists packed our gear and went to Bizerta. Our major told us that his office would be moving on soon and we would be transferred back to our units in the 34th Infantry Division.

Three notable things happened about this time. As the Sicilian Campaign was ending, the general commanding U.S. forces, General George Patton, was relieved of his command for going nuts and hitting a U.S. soldier who was a patient in a U.S. Army hospital. He was a pain in the behind for the U.S. Army and the Allies. Patton spoke to an infantry division and said, "With your blood and my guts, we'll kill the Nazi S.O.B.s". Some of the members of the press (war correspondents) wanted to make Patton a hero, so they started calling him "Blood and Guts Patton." He had a foul mouth and I never knew a soldier that liked him. There were rumors that he never gave any soldier a clear shot at him. Any good commander could have accomplished what Patton did with armored divisions in France.

Bob Hope started his famous U.S.O. (United Service Organization) shows in Sicily. His show was awful; dirty jokes and strip-teasers (actresses) from Hollywood. The powers that existed canceled his shows and said that would not happen again. Bob Hope was never a good actor, singer or whatever. Somehow, he changed his act, hired good joke writers and was allowed to continue his U.S.O. tours. Combat soldiers never did like him and some even hated him because his shows were always way behind the combat lines. He added to the agony of combat soldiers and he became rich and famous. We never saw him because we were just cannon fodder.

Glen Miller and some of his musicians volunteered to join the U. S. Army. Major Glen Miller and his band became the No.1 band of the United States Army Air Force. This band played in concert for all U.S. military forces in the United Kingdom. They were in a C-47 aircraft headed for Africa. The aircraft disappeared over the Atlantic Ocean somewhere west of France or Spain. The Luftwaffe was in command of all air space over France and adjacent Atlantic waters at this time. All soldiers liked Glen Miller and his band and we were saddened when they were lost.

During the last meeting of my Special Military Police Force with the Provost Marshall, he didn't curse much. We had all become close as soldiers. As our mentor, he knew everything we had done. We sat around the table in his office, together with his sergeant and corporal. He said to his sergeant, "Now, bring out the good wine." As we sipped the wine, we talked about things that had happened. American soldiers didn't know how to drink wine. They would go into a wine bar and drink whatever was served. It was easy to guzzle down, even when it was rot- gut, full of impurities. When they went outside into the sun, the wine went to their heads.

The major said he had the authority to promote me to the permanent rank of platoon sergeant, or give me a field commission with the rank of lieutenant. He said, "Will you accept either of these?" I replied, "Thank you, Sir, the only way I can survive is to be a private and then an acting sergeant or whatever is needed in combat. I have been an acting company commander in combat. The only way I can save myself is to train and help soldiers survive. Your offer to make me a lieutenant in the military police is tempting, but I started in the infantry and I would be ashamed to quit now."

The major said, "I understand, would you other three accept the rank of sergeant?" The other three cyclists were great soldiers. We had survived many things. They looked at me and at each other. When I spoke, they understood. If you became a noncommissioned officer or a commissioned officer, you would have to obey all of the stupid orders and crap from above or face a court martial. None of us would have survived the battles in Africa if we had obeyed orders or waited for orders that never came and when they did, it was usually the wrong time and place.

The other three cyclists agreed the rank of corporal would be O.K. The sergeant typed orders for each of us to carry. The orders transferred us back to our former units in the 34th Division. We were to report to a Repo Depot (Replacement Depot) and we would be sent from there to our units. The major told us to ride our Harleys to the Depot and turn in whatever equipment we didn't need. When we arrived at the depot, it was raining and all of the tents were surrounded by mud. In the headquarters tent, we found the duty officer, a captain, and handed him our orders. He gave the orders to a corporal to record and told us to turn them in to our commanding officers when we reached our units. He also told us which tent to stay in and since it was getting dark, wait until morning to see the supply sergeant.

There were hundreds of replacement soldiers there staying in rows of tents. Of course none of them knew where or what units they would be assigned to. We rode our Harleys to our tent, took our weapons off, and went inside. It was not a pleasant sight. The replacements were nervously milling about. I could feel and smell the fear.

It was eerie in that place. There was a soldier standing at the entrance. He stopped me and said, "Sarge, do you believe in Jesus?" He looked awful. Rainwater was dripping off his steel helmet; his face was gaunt and his eyes were sunken. There was flickering light from a naked light bulb hung from the ceiling of the tent. It was gently swaying as the rain drummed on the canvas tent. I replied, "Yes, I do." He said, "The others won't listen; we are all going to die and need to repent." I said, "They are under pressure. Their minds are mixed up and all you can do is to keep trying."

We found some cots and put our gear down. The replacements started looking at us and figured out that we were trained soldiers because of our uniforms and the like. They had never seen a Tommy gun. We were not wearing our brassards, but we were wearing our G. I. pistols. Soon they gathered around us and started asking questions, such as, "What's it like in combat." There is no way to explain combat. I finally said, "Start thinking about the only way to survive.

We all need to kill as many Germans as we can. The more we kill, the sooner the war will be over. Watch and listen to the older guys. Learn everything you can, as fast as you can. Stop thinking about other things. Think only about killing Germans"

We were tired, so we went to sleep. The next morning, we ate and then went to the supply sergeant. We turned in our equipment and got some more items. What we needed was the equipment carried by combat infantrymen; such as a combat pack. I kept my M-1 rifle and my shoulder holstered Luger pistol.

The captain informed us that we, along with some replacements, would be going to the 34th Infantry Division by truck the next day. When I arrived at my original company, I reported to the captain and searched for anybody that had been in Ireland. There was only one; his name was Pitts, now Platoon Sergeant Pitts. He was my friend who had deserted in the Philippines and was sworn into the U.S. Army with me at Thursley Surrey, England. We stood on the Company Street looking at each other. Pitts broke the silence. He said, "I'll be damned, I'll be damned, Alabama, you made it." I replied, "Yep, and so did you." We sat down by his pup tent and jawboned for a while. The first sergeant joined us and they both said, "We sure could use your help."

They explained the situation to me. All of the soldiers in the company, except a few, were replacements that had never been in combat. The few that had been in combat were replacements that had some experience during the last stages of the African Campaign. The officers were ninety-day wonders, or had been. The captain and one lieutenant had some experience during the last part of the campaign. The company had two platoons, without sergeants, who were commanded by corporals. There were not enough experienced soldiers to fill all the ranks. The first sergeant said, "It would be good if you would accept the rank of platoon sergeant. I'll speak to the captain about it." Sergeant Pitts laughed. Then he explained to the first sergeant about me not accepting rank. I said, "I'll accept acting sergeant only. Unless my last commanding officer, the Provost Marshall, changed it, I'm still an acting platoon sergeant."

The first sergeant said, "That'll be O.K. I'll ask the captain for permission for the company clerk to record it. The only reason I'm the first sergeant is because I was one of the first replacements to the 34th Infantry Division and I survived. I am scared to hell with this. I know it takes about ten years to become the tough "Top Soldier." I'll be leaning on both of you. You are the only help I have." Sergeant Pitts and I eyeballed each other. Memories came to us. This man would be a great soldier if he could survive. He didn't shoot bull and he was not thinking of himself. His worries were how to protect green soldiers. Everyone knew this war would go on and on. We couldn't help thinking about how many of the soldiers we were looking at would not survive. We told the first sergeant, "You have our help." We packed up, ready to leave for Italy. It was no longer a secret; we knew where we were going.

Late Summer & Early Fall 1943

Hollywood movies are great. They always have music, flags waving and sounds that we never made. The music would tell what was going to happen. Combat soldiers never heard music, never saw flags and never made unnecessary sounds. We moved under darkness for cover and silently as possible.

The first Allied troops to invade Italy were units of the British 8th Army. They crossed over from Messina in Sicily to the toe of the boot in the Italian peninsula. Then other 8th Army units invaded Italy at the heel of the boot at Taranto. At the same time, units of the newly formed United States 5th Army, under the command of General Mark Clark, and with 8th Army units, invaded at Salerno Bay. If my memory is correct, the first U.S. Army divisions to invade Italy were the 36th Infantry Division (Arrowhead) and the 45th Infantry Division (Thunderbird).

I wrote to my parents and to Rosette, but couldn't write very much because of censorship. I did tell them that I was O.K. and if I didn't write for a while not to worry. Also, I told my mother to please send a Whitman's Sampler. I wrapped up my tam o'shanter and mailed it home. While I write this book, my tam o'shanter is at rest in my closet. The writing inside is faded, but I can still read "1940" and it still bears a burn mark on the top edge. This is called a near miss and I still can't recall if it was made by a bullet or shrapnel.

Many U.S. divisions of the 5th Army started landings south of Naples at Salerno Bay. The beachhead was secured after fighting off fierce German counter-attacks. My regiment of the 34th Infantry Division went in at Salerno. As the Allied Forces built up, a battle line was formed to head north. The Germans fought every yard of the way. Some days and nights we made some progress driving them back. Then sometimes we were driven back. This was the first invasion by the Western Allies of what the Germans called "Fortress Europe." The Germans used their regular army, including the officers and men from the Afrika Korps, and had no intention of losing. There were about one million soldiers locked in deadly combat.

The Allied battle plan for Italy was for the British 8th Army to advance to the North in the Eastern part of Italy while the U.S. 5th Army advanced to the North in the Western part of Italy. One of the great Allied victories was when the 8th Army captured Foggia to the east with its great airfields. This was early in the Italian Campaign and enabled the allied bombers and fighters to increase their effective range deep into middle Europe. Good news was rare. We all celebrated when Naples was captured. The town and harbor had been severely bombed and shelled. By working night and day, the harbor was cleared. The supply soldiers had been doing back-breaking work carrying supplies from landing craft across the beaches. Convoys of Liberty ships arrived in the first shipping port the Allies had captured. The ships carried tanks, heavy artillery and everything else.

At this time, the only way the infantry could get supplies in the mountains was for them to carry them on their backs. The toughest things to carry were wooden cases of ammunition. We were exhausted. The infantry soldiers had to attack, fight off counter-attacks, go forward, go back, and spend two hours on watch and two hours off for twenty-four hours per day. That is not all. We hunkered down in our holes and if you didn't have one, you scratched out one, while artillery fire rained down upon us. To me, this was Africa all over again except there were more soldiers, both friend and foe and the distances were shorter. The shrapnel sounded like hail hitting our helmets. Some were smaller than needles, and some were large as a fist and the white hot metal would slice a steel helmet.

The U.S. Army hired Italians with donkeys to carry supplies to us in the mountains. This worked for a while; then the problem started. Whenever the Germans fell back, they already had the coordinates mapped for roads, mountain passes and mountain trails. They would randomly fire a shell to these spots. After the Germans started random firing at certain mountain trails, the Italians quit. The situation was critical. The 5th Army headquarters sent an emergency request to Washington, D. C., A.S.A.P. (As Soon As Possible) send mules.   The Supreme Powers in Washington understood how critical the situation was and immediately started action on General Mark Clark's request. Government agents bought mules in Missouri, Arkansas and other places. These were genuine All-American farmers' mules. The mules were shipped to New Orleans by railroad and U.S. Army trucks. Arrangements were made for fodder and water for the mules.

The Chief of Naval Operations in Washington ordered the U.S. Navy Captain of the Port of New Orleans to prepare Merchant Marine ships (Liberty Ships) to carry mules to Naples, Italy. During wartime, all of the United States Merchant Marine personnel and ships become under the command of the United States Navy. There were Liberty Ships loading or preparing to load at the docks in New Orleans. Some were going to the Pacific and some were going to Europe. The Captain of the Port ordered three Liberty Ships to be modified to carry mules. Horses and mules are difficult to carry in ships. They must remain standing or they will die. They get sick and need fodder and water and they defecate where they are standing. The Captain ordered extra crews to handle the mules. The mules would be placed below the decks, but there was a problem.

Normally, a fully loaded merchant ship didn't need ballast because they could load freight all the way to the bottom. To explain this, I will use an example. The trading ships that came to America from Europe about two hundred years ago, carried bricks for ballast low down in their hulls to reduce the possibility of capsizing in a storm. They carried cargo to America, but they carried more cargo back to Europe. For that reason, the bricks would be unloaded and that is why the wharf docks at Savannah, Georgia, are paved with these bricks. The ships carrying mules needed ballast. The Captain of the Port handled the problem. On the docks were cases of beer scheduled to be shipped to the Pacific. The beer was loaded as ballast.

In the meanwhile, Platoon Sergeant Pitts was hit in the palm of his right hand by a machinegun bullet. It was patched up in the hospital, but he didn't have much grip in the hand because the bullet broke the bones. Because he had served in the Philippines where they used mule trains, he was selected to work the mules. Sgt. Pitts rounded up farm boys to work the mule trains. Pitts told me this story when he led one of the trains up the mountain to our company. I was glad that he would make it through the war, but I missed having him in our company. We, like all the line companies, had many casualties. Some were dead and some were wounded severely and would not return. The Italian civilians in the battle areas were starving. Long lines of women, with baskets on their heads, were going somewhere, maybe near Sorrento, to get apples to bring back to their families.

It was suicide to take new replacements on patrol, so I was doing patrols at night alone. We needed to find river crossings and mountain trails. One night I found a place to cross the Volturno River without a bridge or swimming. Scouts on patrol from other units also found other places. One cold, rainy night in October the 3rd Infantry Division, the 34th Infantry Division and the 45th Infantry Division made the first crossing of the Volturno River. The current was strong from the rains, and at the deepest spots, the water was chest high. We held our rifles high and kept moving. There were something like thirty thousand of us GI Joe's that crossed the river.

We never knew when Thanksgiving came or went. Whenever I awoke from sleep, it took my brain a few seconds to figure out what country and place I was in. There were always rumors. A big one was that we would be home by Christmas. This happened before every Christmas. There was a new division on its way to relieve us and so forth. Bing Crosby's and other's Christmas songs were banned because they were bad for our morale.

The Allies continued to attack. Yard by yard, the progress north was slow; it was one mountain after another. The 34th Infantry Division finally captured Mt. Trocchio. From the mountain to the north, we could see the Rapido River Valley. Across the valley was Cassino, a town below the Abbey on Monte Cassino. This place would become another living hell for Allied infantry. The Germans formed a heavily fortified battle line at Cassino. The line ran east and west along the Rapido River. They called it the Gustav Line and Lord Ha Ha, in his radio broadcast from Berlin, bragged about it and said the Allies would never break it. He said the same thing about the Gothic Line to the north later during the campaign. The Germans held the high ground with infantry, tanks, artillery, minefields, and booby traps in front. They used all kinds of mines, Schu mines, concrete mines, Bouncing Betty's, "S" mines, box mines and Teller mines for tanks.

After one of our attacks, we read the insignia on some of the dead and wounded Germans. They were German paratroopers. In the meanwhile, the Allies invaded at Anzio. This was a good plan. It was like an end around in football and would out flank the western end of the German Gustav Line. In addition to the British, the 1st Special Service Force, the 1st Armored Division, the 3rd Infantry Division and the 45th Infantry Division landed against light opposition. As they went inland, for some unknown (never to be explained) reason, they were ordered to stop. This was like the battalion in the 168th Infantry Regiment that was ordered to stop and then go too late and come under heavy artillery fire in the open daylight in one of the battles in Africa. When the invading force at Anzio stopped, the Germans had time to surround the beachhead with tanks and artillery. This happened in January and the fighting continued at Anzio and Cassino until late May 1944.

From "Somewhere in England," I received a letter from my friend, Bruce Lewis, telling me that his younger brother Gerry was in Italy. Gerry was in the Seaforth Highlanders, which was the Canadian Regiment that formed the First Special Service Force with the U.S. Army. They trained somewhere in Montana for mountain fighting to go into Norway. They were sent to Italy instead. There have been many "Special Service Forces" since then, but this one was the very "First." A movie was made about the First Special Service Force. It was called "The Devil's Brigade." The shoulder insignia was an arrowhead with the point up. The letters "USA" were horizontal across the top and the letters "CANADA" were vertical.

I knew that Bruce's father had died before he left Canada and the only family he had left was his mother and his brother. Later, I received another letter from Bruce telling me that Gerry was KIA in Italy. After that I received a letter from my friend Lornie Roussain, "Somewhere in France," telling me that Bruce was KIA in France.

After I returned home from the war, I found out that Bruce's mother in Sault Ste. Marie had died before Bruce was killed. When the postman tried to deliver the notice to his mother that Bruce was KIA, there was no one to deliver it to. The neighbors told the postman about Mrs. Lewis' friendship with my mother. So the postman sent the notice to my mother. My mother was so grieved about this, she didn't tell me until I returned home.

The "Stars and Stripes" (an Army newspaper) started publishing in Italy. It contained cartoons by Bill Mauldin and featured two dog soldiers named Willie and Joe. All soldiers called each other "Joe," which started the expression "GI Joe." Mauldin's cartoons joked about officers and other trials and tribulations of Willie and Joe. Some high-ranking officers tried to stop the cartoons about them. However, they were overruled because the jokes were good for morale. After the war, Sergeant Bill Mauldin published a book of his cartoons entitled "Up Front."

One of the best, if not the best War Correspondent ever, Ernie Pyle, came around talking to soldiers. He would come almost to our foxholes. We first met him in Africa and he wrote many dispatches about the 34th Infantry Division. He called us the old tired division from Ireland. The 34th Infantry was on battle lines longer than any division in the history of the U.S. Army. Ernie Pyle was appreciated by U.S. soldiers all over the world. During the last days of the war in the Pacific, a Japanese sniper on Okinawa killed him.

Ernie Pyle was responsible for the creation of the "Combat Infantry Medal" and the new rank of "Private 1st Class" of the Infantry. He complained over and over again about the rank and pay of combat infantrymen. Why should an air gunner be at least a corporal, receive flight pay, and be on duty while in the air, when a soldier on the ground fired machine-guns as a private and was on duty twenty-four hours a day? Also, all combat soldiers received the lowest pay, the least food and water, and the worst living conditions of any of the U. S. military branches of service. He continued to state that the infantry was the only branch of service that could lose or win the war.

A book was published containing some of his dispatches. A movie named "The Story of GI Joe" was made starring Robert Mitchum. It was so real that the Hayes censor office for Hollywood would not allow it to be shown. Then they relented. The movie "Saving Private Ryan" was fairly realistic, but not as much as "The Story of GI Joe" which was only shown for a short period in 1946 or 1947. Then it disappeared

During the months of fighting at Anzio and Cassino, the Germans had a huge gun installed on a railway flat car that could fire twenty or so miles. We called it the "Anzie Express". The Germans fired at targets during the nights and at daylight the gun would be gone. It took a long time to find out where it was hidden. They had built a railway sidetrack and hid the gun in a tunnel during daylight. The Allies tried to hit the tunnel with bombs, but failed.

The U.S. Army Air Force came up with a brilliant plan. The P-38 lighting fighter had twin-engines and could carry a bomb. A bomb was installed on a P-38. After practice runs, the pilot headed the P-38 straight toward the tunnel, released the bomb then climbed straight up. The bomb went into the tunnel, exploded and wrecked the big gun. This was called skip bombing.

About this time, the Army developed another field ration. This one was named "K-Ration" and was better than the "C-Ration" used in Africa. It was packed in boxes similar to Cracker Jacks and there was one for breakfast, one for lunch, and one for dinner. The one for breakfast contained powdered eggs with Spam chopped up in the eggs, powdered coffee and the like. As usual, the wizards in the U.S. assumed that the infantrymen could stop, build a fire and cook or heat these rations. At least, we could chew or suck on them.

One of the good things the Army did was to issue morphine. Combat medics carried morphine, but the medics went down fast, just like the other soldiers. Each company was supposed to have at least one combat medic, but there were never enough of them. So the Army issued morphine to all non-coms. It was packed in a cardboard carton like shotgun shells, with every other one reversed so that each one would fit. The morphine was in a square type tube like toothpaste, with a needle attached instead of a cap. The needle had a cover over it to keep it sterile. The morphine saved many lives. It was easy to use. All we had to do was remove the cover over the needle, stick it in and squeeze the morphine out of the tube. One of the notable soldiers that was saved in Italy was Lt. Bob Dole. We also used it to kill the pain in dying soldiers. There was a soldier whose body was torn apart when we were in the Waddies of Africa. There was no help for miles and we had no morphine. Our company was beat up and we were on the run. This soldier would never make it even in a hospital. He was not able to hold his rifle to his mouth to shoot himself. In his agony, he said, "Sarge, shoot me, please don't leave me for the buzzards to eat while I'm alive." I walked away, turned, made eye contact for a second, his eyes thanked me; then I shot him in the head. In another of my bad dreams. I can still see his eyes. Later, I filled out a report that he was KIA.

SUCK A ROCK 40: Somewhere in Italy

Fall & Winter 1943-44

My mind and body were wearing out. The Allies attacked different places on the Gustav Line at Cassino and along the Rapido River trying to break through the battle line and drive the Germans back. The Germans counter-attacked and we would end up back where we started. Good sucking rocks are found in and around riverbeds. They have been ground smooth by the flow of water through the ages.

General Hap Arnold gave the order to bomb the town of Cassino and the Abby on the mountain. The Air Force reduced both to a pile of rubble. The German soldiers had good cover while the bombing was going on and when the bombing was over had excellent firing positions in the rubble. We attacked again, but failed. Tanks could not maneuver in the piles of rubble. The U.S. Army Graves Registration personnel were overwhelmed with the great number of bodies. The Army had issued "mattress covers" which were made of white cotton with a hole in the top. If and when soldiers not on a battle line could find hay or grass to stuff in the mattress covers, they would have something to sleep on. Grave's personnel took the bottom dog tag off of each body and then drove the top dog tag into their teeth. Then each body was placed in a mattress cover and the top of the cover was tied up. The soldiers doing this wore facemasks and gloves because of the smell and fear of disease.

My company was close by during one of these operations and could not avoid watching. A bulldozer dug a large hole, pushed the piles of bodies in the hole and then covered them with dirt and rocks. Years later, the bodies were placed in cemeteries with neat crosses or the Star of David in rows and rows. Of course, many mistakes in identification were made.

Because I have survived, it's my duty to write some of the things soldiers talked about. To the families of the dead boys and young men, they fought for America under the worst possible conditions. The way they were buried or not buried does not matter. Their souls live on. In the Army, each company clerk files a daily report, but in combat, forget it. In those days, we had the "Articles of War" which didn't cover many things about combat. They were written so that we would be nice soldiers. We made up our own rules. When a soldier was missing for two weeks, more or less, I signed a report that he was KIA whenever I could get around to doing it. None of us filed an MIA (Missing in Action) report. This saved many families from grieving over the unknown. If a soldier was reported alive in a POW camp in Germany, that was a blessing.

Soldiers always had to stand in long lines waiting for shots in the arm, waiting for pay, waiting to load on ships, waiting for everything. Always, some soldier would say, "When I have a son or daughter, they will ask me, "Daddy, what did you do in the war?" Then I will tell them, "I stood in long lines waiting for some blankety-blank officers to get their act together."

During the winter of 1943-44, the weather was terrible. There was snow, sleet, mud, rain, and cold winds in the mountains. As we fought during the days and nights, we tried to out-flank the Germans and they tried to out-flank us. Battle lines in the mountains are not straight; they zigzag because of the ups and downs of the terrain. There were some gaps at ridges. One night, the Germans attacked our company and the company next to us. Their main objective was to penetrate our line by following a ridge that separated our two companies. We had two soldiers dug in on the ridge, and the rest of us formed a thin line facing our front because we were shorthanded.

One of the two soldiers protecting our flank on the ridge went down during the first enemy assault. There was a cold steady rain coming down. The remaining soldier had to crawl out of his foxhole and lay flat down to have a clear firing position and he was the only one that could return the enemy fire along the ridge. We couldn't reach him in the night and besides, we were all busy stopping the Germans in front of us.

That soldier lay there in the cold rain all night killing Germans every time they attacked. During some of the times when the firing stopped, we could hear him coughing. At daylight, the Germans had pulled back and we went over the gully to the ridge and brought the soldier back. He was in bad shape, coughing up blood and shaking. We got him to the medics, but never knew if he made it. All of these soldiers were heroes.

Sometimes, when things were quiet, I went down the mountain to our battalion headquarters to argue with our lieutenant colonel. Every outfit must have at least one soldier who was a good scrounger. They were called "Gold Bricks," "Yard Birds," "Foul-Ups" and the like. I always had one or two of them go with me to the headquarters. While I begged the lieutenant colonel for more men and everything else, my scroungers loaded our empty packs with all sorts of things. Several times, they confiscated some bottles of whiskey and sometimes they would find new field jackets. We received mail irregularly. I wrote letters home and to Rosette sometimes. Once, I received a box of Whitman's Sampler that had been mailed to my old address at the military police company in Tunis. The box of chocolates was crushed, but I could still eat the pieces.

Four replacement soldiers came up the mountain to our company. One of them talked about seeing a notice at regimental headquarters saying that the air force needed pilots. Eligible combat infantrymen could apply and if selected would be returned to the U.S. for training. The other replacements said they had also seen the notice. After hearing this, I hastened down to talk to the lieutenant colonel about it. At first, the lieutenant colonel didn't believe there was such a notice. His sergeant called and confirmed that there was a notice signed by a general on General Clark's staff. Then the lieutenant colonel said, "All platoon sergeants and platoon lieutenants in the infantry have been declared essential and cannot be released. Since you are a platoon sergeant, you cannot apply."

I replied, "Sir, I am an acting platoon sergeant and when we don't have any officers, I am an acting captain, but I can quit "acting" at any time." We talked back and forth and I was getting desperate. I said, "Sir, with all due respect, when I was a cadet in the CMTC (Citizens Military Training Corps.) we were taught that a soldier could file an appeal to the Inspector General as provided by The Articles of War and the commanding officer was required to provide proper assistance with the correct forms and procedures." I was partly bluffing. However, the lieutenant colonel seemed concerned and said to his sergeant clerk, "Look that up." The sergeant got a copy of The Articles and read the appropriate parts and said, "Sir, Sergeant Houston is correct."

The lieutenant colonel told the sergeant to fill out a pass and a release for me to go and apply for aviation cadet training. I borrowed a jeep and went to our rear echelon division headquarters and filled out an application. I was informed that I would receive orders in a few days. After returning to Battalion Headquarters and leaving the jeep, I went back up the hill.

In a few days, orders came. About two hundred of us assembled in Naples and were flown to Bizerta. We pitched our pup tents and prepared to be interviewed. There were still many airfields in Africa and the air force assembled a review board of senior officers in Bizerta. Things moved fast. There were no written tests. Applicants had to be between certain ages. My age (twenty) was just right.

One question was, "What is our approximate Longitude and Latitude?" My response was, "We are East of Greenwich about 9 degrees Longitude and about 35 degrees North Latitude." One of the officers said, "Do you know what Latitude that would be in the United States?" I replied, "Sir, that would be about Cape Hatteras in North Carolina." and that really clenched it.

After the written questions, they asked for comments. I told them about my friends in the three Eagle Squadrons in the Royal Air Force; how I had parachuted through the bomb bay doors of Wellington Bombers; how I knew the people at Maxwell Field and how I had flown an ME-109 from France to England. By then, the officers were smiling and nodding their heads and I knew the interview was over and I had passed. They kept me longer because they wanted to know more about the early days of the "Battle of Briton" and more about the officers at Maxwell Field during the 1930's.

We were ready to be flown to the United States in C-47's by way of the ocean-crossing route from Dakar in French West Africa to Brazil. Then it happened. An order from on high came that canceled this program and ordered all infantrymen to return to their units immediately. There were so many casualties in Italy that all infantrymen were needed. I was snake bit again. The Army ordered all replacements in Repo Depots to be issued rifles and sent to the infantry. It didn't matter if they were trained to be medics, clerks, artillerymen, armored, truck drivers, cooks, mechanics or whatever. There was great consternation. These soldiers had never fired a rifle. My heart was heavy as I returned to my company.

Words can't express the brutality of the fighting and living conditions. Italy had surrendered after Sicily was captured. The days and nights were like weeks, the weeks like months, and the months like years. Some of the Italian soldiers fought with us and some fought against us. The "Stars and Stripes" had an article about soldiers from some forty nations that fought together against the Germans in Italy. The Japanese American Battalion was assigned to the 34th Infantry Division. There were British soldiers from the United Kingdom, Americans who were black, white, yellow and red-skinned, Americans of Mexican, Irish, Italian, German, Polish or other descent. There were Canadians, New Zealanders, French, South Africans, Greeks, Arabs, Jews in the Jewish Brigade of the 8th Army, Brazilians, Porto Ricans, Poles, Palestinians, Dutch, Senegalese, Sikhs, Belgiums, Gurkhas and others. These men of different races, nationalities and religions fought as brothers against a common enemy. This was absolute proof that people throughout the world can live together in peace and harmony if they have the will to do so. Again, it is evil leaders who cause strife between nations and people.

As the battles went on and on, some soldiers were so weary that their minds would give up. Then they became careless and took too many chances. One soldier in our company started sticking his legs up in the air out of his foxhole while the Germans shelled us. He was willing to give up his legs to get it over with. Sometimes soldiers joked about "Dear John" letters. These were letters from girl friends or wives at home. They usually started like this: "Dear John, I have found someone else that I love -----." Soldiers were affected by these letters depending upon the closeness of the relationship.

We could tell when one of these letters was serious by the expression on the soldier's face. In cases such as this, the soldier's mind would give up and he was more likely to get killed. We attacked a German position and were forced to drop back. A soldier who had received a "Dear John" letter didn't drop back. He continued forward firing his rifle until he was dropped.

Italian refugees, consisting of old men, women and children, came through the German lines and then our lines. They were headed south to get out of the battle areas. Sometimes German soldiers would demand sex from the women and sometimes-Allied soldiers would do the same thing. Most us of looked upon this in disgust and shame. If one of my soldiers even thought about it, I would start cursing at him.

Now and then, each company would go back down the mountains for a few days to regroup, get new clothes, weapons and supplies. One day, while my company was down from our battle line, a captain in the Jewish Brigade came by to see me. He had a list and said that after the war the Jewish Brigade would form a small army and they needed volunteers. He knew that I had been trained by the British and they needed volunteers who had the same training as the Jewish Brigade because they would use the British system in their army.

Before World War II and after, Palestine was a British Protectorate and many people thought the British would leave after the war. The captain explained that if I volunteered, I would start with the rank of captain and be an instructor. There would be increases in rank and pay as the size of the army increased. Anyway, just think about it. I told him the war was not nearly over, but I would think about it.

One of the worst things that happened in the Italian Campaign, happened to my friend, Roy Palmer. When I heard about it, I was sad and angry at the same time. One night, a German Komando Unit penetrated the headquarters of the 34th Infantry Division and captured the commanding general, carried him away and killed him. All of the high ranking officers in Division Headquarters were surprised and didn't realize the Germans also had Komandos. They looked around to find someone to blame. They had full colonels, lieutenant colonels, majors, captains, first lieutenants, second lieutenants, and all kinds of noncommissioned officers. They blamed Private Roy A. Palmer for the entire failure to protect the general.

The high-ranking officers had a problem. What specifications and charges could they use to court-martial Private Palmer? They tried to fabricate charges such as disobedient, uncooperative, sullen, and all kinds of charges not in the regulations. The truth is, in war you win some and you lose some. This was not anyone's fault and the enemy liked to create these situations. When other soldiers heard about this, they were angry and cursed the officers. All charges against Roy were dropped, but they had destroyed the best soldier I ever knew.

Another irony of this happening was the fact that Roy had been awarded a medal, the "Legion of Merit" previously. He refused the medal and all promotions. This was an unusual medal for an infantryman. The medal was awarded because he carried many wounded soldiers down the mountains while under shellfire. One time, he and a medic were carrying a wounded soldier on a stretcher when a Screaming Meemie hit beside them. The medic was wounded, so Roy dropped his rifle, pack and gear, and then carried both of the wounded men down the mountain.

It required the combined forces of many Allies to capture Cassino and the Abby on the mountain and destroy the Gustav Battle Line. Different units captured Cassino, then would be driven back. The Allies continued assaults on the Abby. There were U.S. Divisions of the U.S. 5th Army, the old ones and the newer ones, such as the 85th Infantry Division and the 88th Infantry

Division. There were British units including New Zealanders and Free French units. The Abby was finally captured by Polish troops. There were German snipers and booby traps everywhere. The Germans destroyed everything whenever they moved back, including shooting holes in barrels of vino.

As I have written before, our minds became hazy with so much fighting. Some nights we prayed for daylight. Some days we prayed for the cover of darkness. My night patrols continued alone while sweating out ambushes, mines, flares, fire fights, mortars, and German patrols in no-man's land. We needed information and so did the enemy. All of our scouts hunted for river crossings, trails, Kraut outposts, weak points, and strong points. We did this in all kinds of weather.

Our lieutenant colonel kept telling me to train others to go on patrol. He was right, but I knew it was dangerous. I started taking, one at a time, some of our better men on patrol. The lieutenant colonel said I should take some ninety-day wonders on patrol when we received them. As he pointed out, they did have to learn. Most of the ninety-day wonders were good, strong, intelligent young men. What they needed was combat training. The instructors for the Officer Candidate School at Fort Benning were telling the newly commissioned second lieutenants to watch and listen to the experienced soldiers. Dress like a soldier and act like a soldier. Don't show any brass for a sniper to shoot at.

So, every now and then, and one at a time, I took a ninety-day wonder on patrol. One time, two ninety-day wonders came up to our company at the same time, which was unusual. We went on patrol. After crossing no-man's land, the first sound of trouble was the sound of a shell hitting the bottom of a mortar barrel. I whispered, "Down." We dropped as a flare lit up over us. Somehow, we had been heard or seen because a machine-gun in ambush behind us in no-man's land opened fire. I shouted, "Run." We were in single file with the two ninety-day wonders following me. The second one was hit by the machine gun bullets and went down. The two of us ran until we found some bushes and rocks. In the bushes and rocks, we crawled further away until we found some overhanging rocks to squeeze under. It started raining and became pitch black dark.

We heard the Germans searching for us, then they stopped in the darkness. For us to move in the darkness would be foolish. The only thing we could do would be to go sideways; that is, parallel to the battle line to find a ridge after daylight. Then head to our line while staying down in the gullies to the side of the ridge.

We moved a short distance sideways until we saw a Kraut patrol. They were all around us searching. A patrol to our rear saw us. The only thing we could do was to outrun them through no-man's land to our battle line. We made it to the bottom of a hill out of sight of the German patrol following us. Stopping to catch our breath, I said, "We can't stay here. That patrol will get us. If we can get over the ridge, our guys can help us. The problem is, we will be exposed to their Screaming Meemies before we get over the ridge." After that, we took a deep breath and ran as hard as we could up that hill. The only thing I remembered was the world was spinning around and upside down.

SUCK A ROCK 41: Somewhere in Italy

Winter & Spring 1944

Everything was vague and blurred. It seemed that I was in a Station Hospital. Then it took a while to realize I was on a cot in a General Hospital in Naples. One of the things I could see was a ceiling. I mean a real ceiling; not a canvass tent. A wounded soldier from my company was brought to the hospital. He told me what had happened. A patrol went out after dark and picked up the second lieutenant and me. The second lieutenant was killed by shrapnel. At first, they thought I was dead. My leg was bleeding, but my heart was still beating. I had been bounced.

When I was able to talk enough, the doctors and nurses wanted to know my medical history so they could prepare a medical file. They examined me all over and asked about the scar on my left arm. I noticed my right leg was bandaged. I also noticed a strange thing. My Canadian-British dog tags were gone and my bottom U.S. dog tag was gone.

I said, "My tonsils were removed in England, Christmas, 1941; the scar on my left arm was caused by a bullet during a commando raid in France; the scars on my right foot and great right toe was from shrapnel in Tunisia; the scars on my lungs were from pneumonia in Tunisia. I had malaria and amebic dysentery in Africa, and what is wrong with my right knee?"

The doctors and nurses were silent. Then I heard a nurse, somewhere in the background, say, "Oh my God, he has malaria." They immediately started the malaria routine, taking blood samples every hour, wearing out my fingers, and then using my ear lobes. My body and mind were in bad shape. My body weight kept on dropping. The chills and fever came, not as bad as before. All I wanted to do was sleep. Then the bad dreams came. A doctor talked to me and told me that the malaria had shown up again and they had confirmed some medical reports.

The nurses were kind, helpful and hard working. All Americans should know how tough it was in the battle zones. The wounded arrived at all times, day or night. One morning, a nurse woke me up and told me to go to the day room. The day room was a small room on our ward with a table and some chairs. When I went into the day room, I saw a cake with candles; all the nurses said "Happy Birthday!" I was stunned. It was my twenty-first birthday and I hadn't thought much about it. After I thanked the nurses, they cut the cake up and handed out pieces. It was very rich compared to K-Rations, but I ate a small piece. There must have been some wheeling and dealing for a cook to get materials to bake that cake. So, I found the cook and thanked him. He said, "It's not every day that an old soldier has his twenty-first birthday."

There was another important thing about nurses and ward boys (medical assistants). If you wake a combat infantryman by touching or shaking his head, arms or shoulders, he'll come up swinging his fists. Nurses and ward boys were injured doing that. We soldiers had to teach them to touch their feet. Combat soldiers had spent a long time sleeping for two hours and then watching for two hours. We would wake each other up very quietly by tapping on our boots or helmets. Any other way, we would think the enemy was upon us.

A doctor came to see me. He said he was a Doctor of Psychiatry and was Chief of Psychiatry for the Mediterranean Theater. He explained that he visited all of the hospitals and met with the doctors to teach them about treatment for combat personnel. During his visits, he also wanted to talk with soldiers who had been in combat over long periods of time.

There were not enough Medical Doctors so the army had many Doctors of Psychology. Explaining further, he said Doctors of Psychology had a four-year degree in Psychology and no medical training. A Psychiatrist had to become a medical doctor first and then train to be a psychiatrist. There were only a few psychiatrists at that time. All combat soldiers, no matter what wounds they had, were also "tagged" with "Combat Fatigue."

That is why we were called "psycho." The real problem was what combat did to our bodies and minds. We didn't go to combat with mental problems. The doctor warned me about psychologists in the army who played games with soldiers' minds. We talked a long time while he made notes in his record book. He told me that I had been in combat too long and probably when I had an interview with a board of doctors, I would be Z.I.'d.

A bunch of us boarded a hospital ship and were carried to a station hospital in Algeria in the boondocks. It was located somewhere near Phillippeville, Bone or Constantine. I was never sure because we unloaded at night and never saw anything. The hospital ship had to hurry back to Italy. The doctors, nurses, and all the crewmembers on hospital ships did a fantastic job, especially at Anzio. They loaded the wounded while the Germans were shelling the docks and had to start immediate treatment of the seriously wounded.

At the station hospital, there were some buildings that had machine gun bullet markings on them. There was a large tent for meetings or whatever. Some wards were in the buildings and there were smaller tents that held about a dozen soldiers each. My first ward was a large one in one of the buildings. It was jam packed with cots and small aisles in between for walking. This was a terrible place. Soldiers had bad dreams and screamed. Everyone woke up every two hours, staggered around and then returned to sleep.

There was a soldier who was very sensitive about being "goosed." Another soldier (a nut) thought it was great fun to get back of him, then "goose" him so that he would hit anyone in front of him with his fist. The sensitive soldier asked some of us for help. We agreed to do the "goosing" whenever the nutty soldier was the one standing in front. It happened that I was the one that had the chance. I "goosed" and the sensitive soldier flattened the nut. The nut got up with his nose bleeding. He was ready to fight. I said, "O.K., let's go outside." The nut started making excuses and backed down. The others told him, "If you ever goose again, we'll break your arms, whether you want to fight or not."

When I found out who some of the good guys were, we started scheming to get a small tent. We wanted to get out of that ward and protect ourselves. Using some gentle persuasion, we got a tent and hid our contraband. The tent had a small stove in the center for heat. Taking the stovepipe loose, we lifted the stove over and dug under it. After wrapping our stuff in a shelter half, we buried it. Our inventory included: two combat knives, one loaded Luger, one carton of morphine, and two hand grenades. Some of the wounded arrived at hospitals still wearing their uniforms and whatever they had in their pockets. They would gladly give whatever they had to other soldiers before the medics stripped them down and burned their clothes. As a matter of principle, we never took money, but we wondered what happened to the money soldiers were carrying.

A young airman was brought to the hospital by some guys in an Air Force jeep. He had been found walking along the Mediterranean beach. He could not remember anything, not even his name. There was no feeling in his right arm. It just hung there limp. No one knew how he got to the beach. My thought was, his bomber went down in the Mediterranean Sea during the night and he managed to jump. I told the doctors (psychologist) to look at his back and shoulders. Sure enough, there were red marks made by parachute straps. This I learned during commando training. Unbelievably the doctors put cigarettes out on his arm to see if he was faking. This angered me, but I couldn't afford to do anything about it.

Everyone had their turn to be interviewed by a medical board. The board decided if a soldier could be returned to combat or be sent to the Zone of Interior (Z.I. United States). The medical board held their interviews in a small tent containing a large table and chairs. Of course, we could hear every word outside the tent. The doctors looked over the patient's file (many files were not complete) and after discussion, the patient was called in. Usually, the first questions they asked were: "Which one of your parents do you hate? Your father or mother?" Usually, the patient would reply, "Sir, neither one of them." But the doctors continued to hammer away about parents and sometimes a soldier would agree just to get it over with. Then I knew that the psychiatrist had told me the truth. Most, if not all, of these doctors were psychologists and they were determined to find some mental illness they could write about or do something with after the war.

I was outside of the tent when they interviewed an unusual combat infantryman. He had a great name that was something like Oscar J. Wellington, Jr., from the Smokey Mountains. When the doctors asked for his name, he stood tall, saluted, and said, "Oscar J. Wellington, Jr., Sir. I be from the mountains." When the doctors started their usual questions, he would reply, "My teeth are gone, Sir, when do I get my "China Clippers"?" More questions. Oscar replied, "I'm hungry, Sir. Can't eat, when do I get my "China Clippers?" Finally, one of the doctors said, "Private Wellington, do you hear noises?" Oscar replied, "Yes, Sir." The doctor said, "What kind of noises?" Oscar replied, "String music, Sir."

The doctors never asked him what had happened. We knew he was bounced by a Screaming Meemie which knocked his teeth out, scrambled his brain and he still had slivers of shrapnel in his head. One of the doctors said, "We'll get you some China Clippers." He lied. There were no dental services. A surgeon did grind the bottoms of my two front teeth smooth. They were damaged when my nose was broken in the bayonet fight at Hill 609.

During my interview with the medical board, they started out with their questions about hating my parents. I had to keep from showing my anger, or I would be in trouble. I stared into the eyes of each one of them and said, "Sir, I love my parents and my brothers and sister. I am not mentally ill. When I was in the hospital in Naples, the Chief of Psychiatry for the Mediterranean Theater came to see me because I have been in combat so long with the Canadian Army, the British Army, and the U.S. Army. I have Combat Fatigue and for years I have not had enough sleep, rest, food or water. That is why I keep loosing weight."

It was a good thing that I had told the doctors in Naples my medical history because these doctors were looking at it. One of the doctors said, "Does malaria still bother you?" I replied, "Yes, Sir, I don't ever know when it will hit me because it comes and goes." They had the papers filled out by the clerk for me to be sent to the Continental United States.

The soldiers who were going home had to wait for transportation. One time, I happened to finish chow early and returned to my tent. In the tent next to ours was a black soldier bent over sitting on his cot. When I went in he looked up and he was crying. I asked him what was the matter. He said, "These soldiers won't leave me alone. They keep cursing me and tricking me." I said, "When they come back, I'll talk to them." He replied, "It won't do any good." I said, "We'll see."

My anger was building up. He told me he was born and raised in a place called "North Montgomery" in Alabama. That did it. When the other soldiers in that tent returned from chow, I started talking to them. I told them, "You've been messing with this soldier and you will stop right now." At first, they were belligerent. One of them said, "What do you care about a nigger?" They had assumed that I was from New England or somewhere like that because of my accent.

I replied, "I care about people. You are a damn bunch of cowards. You know he can't whip all of you. If you aren't cowards, then you'll fight me one at a time." They were mumbling, but no one accepted my offer. One of them said, "Where're you from?" I said, "Not that it matters, but to make things clear to you foul-ups, I'm from Montgomery, Alabama, and if you don't stop messing up, I'll get every one of you with my Luger and grenade."

That night, I moved the stove and got my Luger and one grenade. That evening, I heard a conversation between some soldiers in the other tent and some from my tent. A soldier from my tent said to them, "When the old Sarge gives you an order, you better do it, he is commando and he has put officers, sergeants, and others down. He has commanded companies and saved many soldiers in Africa and Italy. There is a soldier over there in the big ward from his battalion. Go talk to him."

The cowards stopped harassing the black soldier and I started asking the black soldier to go to chow with me. We enjoyed talking about Montgomery and he told me about things that had happened in the years I was gone. There were many interesting things in North Montgomery; the stockyards, the pickle factory, the cotton mill, the gravel pits from mining in the plains of the Alabama River, the old Alabama State Fair Grounds, Kilby Prison (the main prison in Alabama), and the Municipal Airport, which became Gunter Field when the Army Air Force obtained it during the war.

Many wounded, sick soldiers arrived at this Station Hospital from time to time. Some would stay on their cots and not move. The nurses asked for our help. Those of us who could picked them up and with two of us supporting each one, walked them to the latrine and to eat. Their legs would wobble and their sense of balance was gone. Gradually, we got them walking again or they would have starved. These soldiers were not faking. Their minds and bodies were worn out. The good doctors in Italy and Africa told us we were bound to have arthritis from living on the ground and being wet and cold for so long.

There wasn't any telephone service or Postal Telegraph or Western Union service from the hospital to Tunis. There wasn't any chance of getting a pass and if I did there was no transportation to Tunis. When I wrote to Rosette, I tried to explain everything to her and gave her the address of the Station Hospital. Anyway, by the time we could write to each other, I'd be gone again. Postage was free to and from military personnel, including the French.

Late Spring & Early Summer 1944

A bunch of us soldiers, who were scheduled to return to the United States, boarded a hospital ship. No one would ever tell us where we were going, so we thought, this is it. We're going home! Our hopes were high as the hospital ship headed west in the Mediterranean Sea with all lights on. This was a great sight for me, after living in the darkness for years. I slept some and then I'd go walk the decks just to see the lights. Again, all of this was too good to be true. After traveling about 500 miles, I went on deck when I felt the ship slow down and change course. We were docking in the harbor at Oran, which I recognized. After docking, we boarded lines of ambulances and some 6x6 trucks and were transported to a huge "Hospital Row" outside of Oran. These were all General Hospitals housed in tents.

The trials and tribulations for us were repeated. The hospital ship had to return to Italy after taking on supplies. This was another stopping place on the long journey home. There were several hundred of us. We were assigned to different General Hospitals. There were a great number of wounded soldiers from Italy in these hospitals. Most of the doctors in these hospitals were psychologists and some of them were determined to prove that some of us were psychotic or psychopaths and that is why we were there. The doctors gave some of the soldiers shots of the so-called "Truth Serum," Sodium Pentobarbital. We called the shots "Walkie-Talkies." When one of the doctors talked to me about having a shot, I replied, "Hell no, and if anyone does give me one, I'll kill them one way or another." After that, they didn't bother me and my mind was ready to challenge them if they asked any more stupid questions while playing their games. The truth was, psychologists were not qualified to treat soldier's minds or bodies. I would have told them this, plus they needed to talk to the psychiatrist that I had met.

The "Truth Serum" did not work the way it was shown in the movies. In the movies, a person would be given a shot and immediately start talking. These doctors gave soldiers shots in the mornings and the soldiers were ready to be "interviewed" in the afternoons. One morning, they gave a shot to a man in our tent. We had observed how the shots worked. We "encouraged" this man by telling him what a rascal the first sergeant was. During the day our man started chasing the first sergeant and throwing rocks at him. The first sergeant kept on finding hiding places, but the soldiers in all the tents were watching. When the first sergeant hid, the soldiers quietly told our man where he was. Our man flushed the first sergeant out of hiding over and over again, then chased him while hitting him with rocks. The first sergeant was worn out by the time our man was "interviewed" by the doctors.

During this period of time, my mind was working on a "Hypothesis" involving the "Modulus of Elasticity" in order to explain the true meaning of "Combat Fatigue" which was called different things in different wars. "Modulus of Elasticity" means "the capability of a strained body to recover its size and shape after deformation (stretching or pulling in tension)." My mind included in this meaning the word "Strength." This was obvious. To demonstrate this "Hypothesis" think about the words springiness, resilience and a spring. A rubber band can be stretched and then return almost to its original size. The longer it is stretched, the longer it gets. If it is stretched far enough, it will break. If a spring is stretched too far, it will either break or become useless because it will not return to its original size or shape in order for it to do its job.

SUCK A ROCK 42: Somewhere in Italy, North Africa, The Atlantic Ocean & Virginia

Another illustration. When the metal in an aircraft (or other things) has been subjected to vibration (stretching or springing) over a long period of time it will fail. This is called "Metal Fatigue." This "Hypothesis" would also apply to animals. When a racehorse goes as fast as he normally can and then some, he has been winded and can't race anymore. His entire body has been extended (over stretched).

Therefore, my mind has proved what happened to me and the other soldiers. My "Hypothesis" is correct. We all had "Combat Fatigue" using the above definition. How far can a soldier walk carrying a heavy load? How long can a soldier endure being wet and cold or hot? How far and how fast can a soldier run without food, water, or sleep? Our brains and bodies were stretched too far. Whenever a combat soldier fails, he is dead.

The weather was the same everyday. No rain and desert hot in the barren land outside of Oran. No trees and not a single blade of grass or weeds. The evening chow was at 1700 hrs. (5:00 P.M.), which was the hottest time of the day. We went to eat in the mess tent. The food wasn't good, but that was not the fault of the cooks or anyone else.

The drinking water was hung in canvas bags supported by tripods. They were called "Lister Bags" and they were placed in front of all the tents. The "Lister Bags" had many teats on them. To fill a canteen or a canteen cup with water, you placed them under a teat and pushed. The reason for many teats was at times many soldiers had to load their canteens at the same time. This was standard operating procedure (S.O.P.) at all headquarters back of battle lines.

For the evening meal, we had powdered lemonade mixed with water from the "Lister Bags." The water tasted bad with so much chlorine in it. In addition, we were sweating in the120-degree temperature, drinking 120-degree lemonade. The evenings were our worst times. There was a Red Cross tent that had a small radio, magazines, old Readers Digests and newspapers in it. However, the well-paid Red Cross lady in charge closed the tent every day at 5:00 P.M. because she had a date with an officer. Every evening after she left, we opened the tent back up. The articles in the Readers Digests were mostly lies. They told about how every soldier received all these good things; such as chlorine tablets and food during the African Campaign. I enjoyed reading the old newspaper advertisements about the prices of cars and farmland. You could buy some farmlands for $10.00 an acre. We listened to the short-wave radio broadcasts from B.B.C. London, Axis Sally, and Lord Ha Ha from Berlin. We found a dictionary and carried it back to our ward. To relieve our boredom, we played a game with the dictionary. One of us looked in the dictionary, picked out a word and asked the others to spell it and explain its meaning.

When the Red Cross lady discovered that we were going into "HER" tent in the evenings, she blew her stack to the colonel in command. Since we soldiers were good scouts, we listened outside the colonel's tent. She was in a rage and called us ugly names; some kind of dogs to be exact. The colonel tried to calm her down, but failed. Finally, he said, "Dammit, shut up, after all, the damn tent is for our patients." This was another strike for the Red Cross.

One day, we received some mail and another soldier noticed that I had a letter from Montgomery, Alabama. He asked if I was from Montgomery. I said, "Yes." Then he told me he was from Montgomery and his name was Spencer Longshore. We didn't know each other in school because he went to Starke's Military Academy. We discussed different people that we knew and when I mentioned Sarah Box's name, he said, "That's odd, we're engaged." Sarah and I were friends at Baldwin Junior High and at Lanier High. Spencer said, "I've heard about you. You're that crazy guy that volunteered in Canada before the war."

SUCK A ROCK 42: Somewhere in Italy, North Africa, The Atlantic Ocean & Virginia

In our ward there was a Hollywood star. He was a redheaded good guy named Sterling Holloway and he had acted in cowboy movies. He was unpretentious. Just worn out and tired like the rest of us. When some people found out he was there, they came to see him day and night to talk, get his autograph and the like. He didn't want to see or talk to anyone and asked for our help. When people came to see him, we told them he had been moved. If someone came inside our tent, Sterling would lay down beside his cot and one of us dropped a blanket over him. Sterling told us that all he wanted to do was to get home, find a cabin in the mountains and never go back to any city.

One day a soldier in our tent started having stomach pains. He went to see the doctor. The doctor told him there wasn't anything wrong, the pain was in his head and it would go away. During the day and that night, the pains increased. Late that night he was screaming and some of us continued to go over to the doctors' and nurses' tents to beg them to help him. We left our carton of morphine and other stuff under the stove in the other hospital because we thought we were going home. If we had the morphine, we would have put him out.

At dawn, the soldier whimpered and died. We had seen shrapnel scars on his stomach and believed there was some shrapnel left in him. All of us were angry enough to kill. We went over to the doctors' and nurses' tents and talked real loud saying things like, "The soldier whose stomach was O.K. has died from the pain in his head. The great doctors have declared him psycho and we didn't know being psycho would kill us. Even an animal shouldn't die with that much pain. We wonder how his death report will be filled out?"

After that, the doctors and nurses would not look into our eyes. The nurses were not to be blamed because they can't do anything without a doctor's order. Maybe something good came out of this, because two days later thirty-two of us received orders to board a ship in Oran, which was going to the United States. We were issued musette bags to carry our few belongings in. We had already been issued small blue, cotton, drawstring, and Red Cross bags for our shaving kits and the like.

I was called over to the headquarters tent. The first sergeant gave me all of our medical files to carry and an order signed by the colonel to report to the commanding officer of a hospital in the United States and deliver the files to him. The colonel was there, but neither of us wanted to speak. It was understood that they wanted to get rid of us because we knew too much.

The ship we boarded in Oran was a fast, new, United States Navy Transport. She was not an ordinary troop or supply ship. It seemed that she carried VIPs (Very Important Persons), dispatches and other high priority items. She had many nice cabins in different secured areas. The thirty-two of us were bunked together in some sort of ward or conference room. Probably the only reason we were onboard was because this space was available. We were issued the usual life jackets and tags for meals and lifeboat stations. One of the things people were not told, including those on ocean-liners, was the fact that when a ship is torpedoed, ordinarily she will list (go down) on whichever side the torpedo hits. The ship may have enough lifeboats, but because of the list, half of the lifeboats (those on the high side) cannot be launched without crashing against the hull.

For this reason, all United States ships carried large life-rafts lashed down, on a slope, to the ships rigging so that when they were untied or the lines cut, they would slide into the water. When I was on a ship, I always memorized my lifeboat station and then selected a life raft on the other side for a backup.

The ship didn't stop at Gibraltar and traveled fast without a convoy. Most, if not all, German submarines in the Atlantic had been destroyed by the summer of 1944. The Allies had invaded and were fighting in Europe. The German Navy was no longer a factor in the war. The U.S. Navy used blimps for submarine patrols, covering thousands of square miles of the Atlantic. The blimps could stay out for much longer periods than long-range aircraft.

The only medics onboard were the ship's doctor and some Navy corpsmen. We met a few officers and crew, but never saw people in the cabins. There were a few wounded U.S. Army Infantry officers on board. I talked, now and then, with one of them who had lost a leg.

Our ship arrived off the coast of the United States during the night. We could see lights. There were lights on a Ferris wheel at some park. What a sight after years of darkness. After daylight, we were in the channel approaching other ships and docks. I recognized this place. It was Naval Operations Base (N.O.B.) Norfolk, Virginia. It seemed to be a lifetime since I was here.

During the day, the ship was unloading and there was activity everywhere. All we could do was to stand at the rails and watch. We wondered why we couldn't unload. On the wharf were two Red Cross ladies dispensing coffee and doughnuts to those passing by. We really wanted some. We called to the ladies, but they ignored us. This was another strike for the Red Cross.

There were railroad tracks on the wharf and as soon as it was dark, and all the people were gone, a hospital train backed up alongside the ship. It had six hospital cars for thirty-two of us. A petty officer came to us and instructed us to board the train. The cars had beds with sheets on them. It had been a long time since I had slept on sheets. In the hospitals, we had blankets, but no sheets except when I had malaria. The windows were locked and were covered by heavy drapes so we couldn't see out; or were they covered so people couldn't see in? It slowly but surely began to sink into our addled brains that people in high places didn't want anyone to see us. That would be bad for morale, seeing America's finest as a motley bunch of soldiers.

At the crack of dawn, the train stopped and we got off. There was a convoy of ambulances waiting for us. This was not a railway station it was the middle of nowhere without any buildings or people. We rubbed the sleep out of our eyes and looked at each other with apprehension. We were home, but what else could our country do to us? Our instincts were correct. We would face many more tribulations.

.

SUCK A ROCK 43: Somewhere in Virginia

Summer 1944

The place where the train had stopped was next to the Appalachian Trail through the Blue Ridge Mountains. This place was near Waynesboro, Virginia. Our destination was a new hospital located on the northeast side of the highway between Waynesboro and Staunton, Virginia. The hospital was named Woodrow Wilson General Hospital because Woodrow Wilson was born in Staunton. It was hastily built a good way back from the highway. The construction was wood framed buildings connected together by long corridors. It's primary purpose was to receive some of the thousands of wounded soldiers returning from Europe. These things we learned later.

The medic, in charge of the ambulance convoy, was a staff sergeant. I told him that I was in command of the detail and was carrying all the files. I rode in the front seat with him in the lead ambulance. The main reason was for me to see where we were going. We drove through the gate when the civilian guards waved us through. Up the hill, every person in that hospital, except the W.A.C. patients was standing in front of the headquarters building waiting for us. We were the first combat infantrymen that they had ever seen.

The sergeant stopped the ambulance close to the crowd. I told him to drive on and form a line about 100 yards away from all these people. The soldiers got out of the ambulances, looked around and started shaking with anger. The crowd was gawking at us like we were some kind of circus freaks. Of course, we looked terrible, but it wasn't our fault. Talking to them softly, I formed them in a single line facing the crowd. We were wearing our new style boots, which we got in Italy. They had leather uppers which strapped around our pants and legs. We were wearing them without the straps fastened; which made them flop around as we walked. This was just one of the things that made us look crazy. The truth was, the straps were not fastened because we didn't have any pants or socks. We were wearing pajamas which were too short. Our pajama tops didn't fit very well either. In the hospitals we had been through, we were issued black cotton bathrobes with red letters on the pocket. The letters were U.S.M.C. (United States Medical Corps). Some of the people thought we were marines when they saw the letters.

There was a real fear in me that one or more of these soldiers would go wild with this humiliation. Continuing to talk softly, I told them to put on their steel helmets to be proud that they were American Soldiers, to drop their musette bags and carry them by their straps when we marched forward to report. Standing in front of the line, I gave the orders: "Detail Attention." After I did an about face, I ordered: "Detail Forward March."

After marching about sixty yards, I gave the order: "Detail Halt." I saluted and said, "Sir, I have orders to report to the commanding officer of this hospital and to deliver the files of the soldiers in this detail." By stopping short, the colonel had to leave the crowd and walk out to meet me. I handed him the files, did an about face, and gave the order: "Detail Dismissed." After the crowd gawked some more, some medics came and guided us to our ward. A sergeant showed us the latrine and said, "Breakfast is ready. Soon as you wash up, I'll take you to the mess hall." Our last meal had been the noon meal on the ship the day before. The Red Cross doughnuts and coffee would have been a blessing.

In the mess hall, we were astounded, it was very large and all of the personnel had already eaten and had cleaned up. There were several tables with chairs in one area. The tables were loaded with food; milk, cereals, coffee, juice, fruit, toast, biscuits, pancakes, syrup, butter, eggs, bacon, sausage, ham, pork chops, gravy, and they even offered to cook a steak if anyone wanted it.

We were introduced to some ladies in nurses' uniforms. They were not nurses. They were specially trained people called "Dietitians." There was one of them seated at each table. They wrote down the name of each soldier at their table in their notebooks and explained that they were doing a study and wanted to write down how much and what kind of food each one of us ate. Of course, we wanted to eat some of all of it, and as much as we could hold. Gobbling it down fast, all of that rich food hit our stomachs. One after another, we ran to the exit door and threw it all up. We didn't know if this wrecked the dietitians' study or not. As for me, the only rich food that I had for a long time was my Whitman's Sampler chocolates, but I had sucked slowly on each piece and made them last a long time.

After breakfast, we were taken to the P.X. (Post Exchange) which had been opened just for us. They gave us anything we wanted. We didn't have any money anyway. I tried some ice cream. That stayed down. I tried a Coca-Cola and lost it. We returned to our ward and were issued clean pajamas, bathrobes, towels and such. We showered, shaved and dressed in the clean clothes. Yep, they gave us new socks. They assigned each of us to a hospital cot and we rested. The nurses arranged our medical records, took our temperatures, blood pressure and all the things that nurses do.

At lunch, we ate only a little bit, although we were very hungry. Later in the afternoon, I was scouting around and discovered a W.A.C.'s (Women's' Army Corps) ward. When I went in, I was greeted royally by a bunch of beautiful women. They were all trim and fit, except for injuries, because of their training and hard work. The mean nurse they had did not allow them to go out with the crowd that morning to meet us. They gathered around me and had so many questions I couldn't answer them for a while. As I stood there, I remembered the victory parade in Tunis where I met Rosette Attelan and the others. These ladies sure did look and smell good. One of them in a wheelchair said, "Bend over." When I did, she reached up, pulled my head down and gave me a long, real kiss. My face turned red as a beet. Later, when the other soldiers found out the W.A.C.s were there, they started visiting them also.

That evening, after chow, the P.X. was opened and we were told to go there. At the P.X. we were informed that the telephone company had arranged for us to make a free phone call home. They had long-distance operators on duty at the P.X. and at their switchboards in town to help us. We couldn't talk but about five to ten minutes because there were thirty-two of us. When my call was made, my mother, Callie, answered the phone. I was shocked because she had such a strange accent. Lord, all of the things I had forgotten. I kept telling her I was all right. I hadn't lost my arms or legs. Some malaria came back sometimes and the wounds in my leg had healed. She was crying. I said, "Momma, I love you, let me speak to Daddy and give him my new address." I told my father I would write and I didn't know when I could get leave to come home, because we had just arrived at the hospital.

The days and nights dragged on and on. The doctors of psychology interviewed each of us, now and then. The medical records were kept in a closet with a padlocked door. We didn't open the padlock. We used a dime to take the screws out of the hasp and read our files when the night duty nurse went to eat. The diagnosis by the group of doctors depended upon how I answered their questions. They had several diagnoses that they liked. One of them that I remember was an "anxiety complex."

After reading my file, I changed my answers at the next interview and sure enough, they changed my diagnosis. Anxious I was, because all I wanted was a discharge. Whenever I mentioned this, the doctors came up with excuses. They even said, "You can't get a discharge because you are regular army, you weren't drafted, you enlisted."

After this, they kept insisting that I should go to Fort Benning, Georgia, and be an instructor at the Infantry School and O.C.S. They said that I would be at least a staff sergeant and could have a commission if I wanted it. Always, my reply was, "Sirs, my strength is gone, I can't run around the Benning Hills. I need a discharge." The next time I read my file, I saw that the jerks had called a senior officer at Fort Benning and told him I was a commando and the officer replied that they needed me as soon as possible.

In the meanwhile, one of our soldiers, we called him "Blackie" because he had worked in a Pennsylvania coal mine before the war, was having a tough time. In Italy, Blackie carried a wounded soldier down to the medics. While he was there, he had what soldiers called a "fit," rolling around on the ground and foaming at the mouth. A real doctor saw him, gave him some morphine and tagged him "Combat Induced Epilepsy."

The doctors would not give a pass to Blackie, not even to go to town. Naturally, Blackie became more and more upset. He had never had epilepsy before. Finally, he asked the doctors when could he go home. After some mumbling, a doctor said, "We don't know when you can go anywhere because you might have another seizure." Blackie attacked, he was strong, vaulting over the table, he used his fists and boots on the doctors. None of us saw this, but a medic described it to us. We did see some doctors and medics with broken noses, broken arms and one of them had a ruptured spleen. A bunch of medics wrestled Blackie into a straight jacket, put him on a gurney and locked him in a padded cell.

All of us were frustrated and saddened. Blackie was a good guy and he was not at fault. The hospital personnel were afraid to go into that cell. There was a trap door to push food in and feces out. Blackie stopped eating. Our group of soldiers took turns going to see him. One of us would go to the mess hall, get food and go eat with him.

Our original detail was being disbursed, one at a time, to other places and what happened to Blackie, we never knew. All of us had become killers. We were the ones who killed the enemy. Now we were supposed to go back to being nice people, stop cursing and all of this in a short period of time. During the nights, we talked softly as we remembered the soldiers we left behind. Those soldiers needed us and we felt guilty because we were sleeping on sheets and they were dying in the valleys and mountains. We were not the strangers; the strangers were the people round and about us.

Another soldier in our detail, "Cajun," from Louisiana, always stuttered except during the nights. He was buried alive in combat when a Screaming Meemie hit some artillery shells near him and the explosion caused a landslide. Other soldiers dug him out. He had a great singing voice. Because he had been on guard duty so much like the rest of us, he would wake up automatically every two hours during the night. At these times, he would sing some great songs softly. Some of us joined in singing or humming.

Before any of us got a leave to go anywhere, we were issued uniforms. The procedure was to get a pass (leave) then go to Waynesboro or Staunton and upon return take your uniform off and put on your pajamas. Our uniforms were hung in a closet with a lock on it. Instead of hanging mine in the closet, I folded it neatly and placed it under the mattress on my cot. That kept my uniform neatly pressed and I stopped asking for a pass so I could go out whenever I wanted to.

The gate and guardhouse were a joke. Busses ran between Waynesboro and Staunton. One of their stops was at the hospital. Whenever we were on the bus leaving the hospital, we had to show our passes to the guard at the gate. The joke was, there were no fences in the rear, sides or front of the hospital. It was simple to walk around the fence, board the bus on the road or hitch a ride.

At last, I was given leave to go home to Montgomery. I loaded my musette bag with my stuff, caught the bus to town and boarded a train. This was a small mountain railroad. In the afternoon, I left the train in a small mountain town. The station was very small. The ticket agent told me that the mainline train from Washington, D.C. would pick me up at midnight when it made a quick mail stop. The train from Washington went to Atlanta, Montgomery, Mobile and New Orleans. I went outside and sat down on the sidewalk to wait for midnight.

After a while, a string of cars passed by. One of them stopped, turned around and came back. The man driving said, "Soldier, we are going to a square dance. Would you like to come with us?" I replied, "I have to catch the midnight train to Montgomery. Thanks, anyway." He told me they would bring me back by midnight. The ticket agent said, "I'll keep your bag for you. I have to come back to meet the train." I got in the car with them. They noticed my different kind of boots, my ribbons and my 5th Army patches. I can't remember where I got the ribbons; they were just a few of the ones that I would receive later. One was Canadian and one was British. I was no longer assigned to the 34th Infantry Division, but I was still assigned to the 5th Army in Italy.

They asked many questions. The dance hall was a wooden pavilion with porches and windows around it similar to the one in Oak Park in Montgomery during the 1920's and 1930's. This one was located several miles from the small town in some kind of park. The family I rode with introduced me to others. There was a good crowd and I was the only young man there. Everyone had someone in their family gone to the war their sons, brothers or husbands. Some of the young girls were married and some were single. They wanted to ask questions about the war, but were hesitant.

Because I was from Montgomery, they thought I could square dance. I explained that I had seen square dancing, but I was exposed more to ballroom dancing. Country folks called ballroom dancing "round dancing." Anyway, they said they would show me. Someone said, "Hank Williams is from Montgomery, did you know him?" Hank Williams had become a great star while I was gone and this was the first time I heard about it. I replied, "Yes, I knew him for a short time in Junior High School. He and I are the same age, born the same month and year. He was born in Georgiana, Alabama, a small town south of Montgomery."

The band started playing and we started dancing. Every now and then, one of the men asked me to join the men outside. All of us sipped some moonshine and they told me it was not rotgut whiskey. It was the best "White Lightening" and they knew it because they made it. After several trips outside, I began to think I was a great square dancer. It was the ladies who guided me and it was a great physical work out. The dancing was over after 11:00 P.M. and the entire convoy of cars returned to the railroad station. When I got my musette bag, one of the men placed a jug of White Lightening in it and said, "Son, you may need this."

As we waited the few minutes for the train to arrive, the people got out of their cars. The ladies hugged and kissed me with tears in their eyes. Some asked the Lord to bless me and some told me they had already received the message, "I regret to inform you." Those were the messages from the President saying their loved one was K.I.A.

These people were "The Salt of the Earth," and my heart understood they would never see the bodies or the graves of their loved ones. That is one of the reasons combat personnel didn't want to talk about it. Sailors had no choice; they had to bury the dead in the sea. In all branches of the military, there were dead. Their bodies were gone and there would not be a grave marker.

As the train was stopping, the people started blowing the horns in their cars. The people on the train looked out of the windows. The train stopped and the conductor opened a door, placed his step stool down and I boarded as people all around me said goodbye. The sounds of the horns got louder. This is what I remember. The conductor on a train is in command of that train. At night, they signaled the engineer the commands by lantern light. Whistle and bell signals always have a certain meaning. I think the conductor gave the signal to proceed and use the whistle, or maybe the engineer did it on his own. As the train left the station, the bell was ringing and the whistle was sounding the longest blast I have ever heard.

During the war, all passenger trains were fully loaded. Some civilians could travel on them, but military personnel came first. Everyone on this train was awake because of the commotion. The conductor offered to get me a seat. In the back of a passenger car was a group of soldiers and W.A.C.s sitting and lying back on their packs and gear. I said, "This will be fine, thank you." I slept until daylight.

After daylight, I watched things through the windows. Then I went to the dining car to eat because I had a military meal ticket. The soldiers and W.A.C.s were reluctant to talk at first because they hadn't figured out who I was. There were no stripes on my sleeves and the lowest rank for an infantryman was P.F.C. (Private First Class, a single stripe). I never did make P.F.C. or get a good conduct medal and I refused the Purple Heart twice. After I told them I had returned from Italy to the hospital and was on my way home on leave, they relaxed.

A W.A.C. said, "How long have you been gone?" I replied, "Since 1939." At first, they thought I was kidding, or lying, until I explained. The train rumbled on and I was getting more nervous every mile. I removed the jug of White Lightening from my bag and offered them some; warning them that it was over 100 proof and to just sip it and cut it with water. One of the soldiers had a bottle of bourbon, so we had some of that also. The soldiers and W.A.C.s were going to a camp in Louisiana. My jug of moonshine was left with them. As the train neared Montgomery, I wondered what all had changed.

SUCK A ROCK 44: Somewhere in Virginia, Alabama
& Florida

Late Summer 1944

Before I left on the train, I sent a telegram to my parents telling them when my train would arrive. The train stopped at the Union Station on the south bank of the Alabama River in Montgomery. There were many people at the station because this was a major railway terminal. As I stepped off the train, I saw my mother and father. My brother, Howard, and his wife, Dea, were with them. Howard had recently been discharged because he had been blinded in one eye. We all hugged and kissed. The soldiers and W.A.C.s got off the train to speak to my parents.

We went home. My mother had cooked and cooked, southern style. She had prepared things that I hadn't seen in years; chicken and dumplings, sweet potato soufflé, pone corn bread, her own fig preserves, pickled peaches, jellies and jams, and of course fried chicken and apple pies. She remembered the song, "Mom, I Miss Your Apple Pie," that was in the B.B.C. broadcast from the Eagle Club in London.

My leave was short because in those days, traveling to and from anywhere took a long time. The people that I grew up with were gone to different places around the world. Clifford Dunn was in Europe. Jack Whittle and Fred Martin were in the Navy. Don Meredith was in the Merchant Marines. Frank Gordon was a major in the infantry in Burma. There were many others. Some had been K.I.A. I slept a lot and then it was time to return to the hospital.

Things at the hospital were about the same. Some of our first group of soldiers were gone, and some new ones had arrived. Rosette and I continued to write each other. Sometimes nurses or others saw my letters from Rosette. It didn't matter, they couldn't read them because they were all in French. Some of the W.A.C.s and us slipped out at night and went to our secret camp deep in the woods in the rear of the hospital. We had beer, blankets, food and a good fire to sit around. We ate, drank, sang songs, talked, and sometimes were just silent.

Many civilians and military people thought the W.A.C.s were dumb, ignorant, and poor white trash. The opposite was the truth. Many of these W.A.C.s had college degrees and were above average in knowledge. The women who flew multi-engine bombers from the factories to the Air Force, for the Air Transport Command, were certainly smart and skilled people. Most of the ones in this hospital had been injured while driving 6x6 trucks, jeeps, weapons carriers and such, during army maneuvers in the Carolina mountains. They were members of trucking companies and supply units. They lived in harsh conditions, wearing the same uniforms as the infantry. For example, the W.A.C. in the wheelchair owned property in Miami Beach, Florida, and was ready to restart her real estate business. Two of the W.A.C.s owned beach houses in California and were on the Board of Directors of a foundation that awarded college scholarships. They offered me a scholarship whenever I was discharged from the army.

Five of the W.A.C.s asked me if I would escort them on a shopping trip. They didn't like to go out without a male escort because some people made snide remarks to them. One morning, we caught a bus to Charlottesville. They went into about every store in the downtown area making purchases every now and then. Using a list, they purchased some items to take back to the others. We had lunch in a nice restaurant and in the afternoon they said, "We would like to buy you a gift." I said, "O.K., I need a good pocket knife, let's go to Sears & Roebuck." After picking out a knife, I said, "I could use a screwdriver." One of them said, "Why do you need a screwdriver?" I explained about the lock on the records room door. They burst out laughing so hard that everyone in the store started looking at us. They bought me a screwdriver and another for themselves.

173

I looked at the rifles. One of them said, "Do you want a rifle?" I replied, "No, just looking; I have one at home just like this one." I was holding a bolt-action, rim-fire, Winchester 22. My oldest brother, Ray, gave me one for Christmas when I was about nine or ten years old. It took me a long time to file the front sight down so thin I could light a kitchen match stuck in a fence post by shooting the head.

There was a nice lady that I met with some friends. A soldier was dating a friend of hers. She lived in Waynesboro and we went to U.S.O. (United Service Organization) dances there and sometimes we went swimming at the city swimming pool in Staunton.

Some physical therapists came to the hospital and set up a room with weaving looms, saws to make wood whatnots and the like. We were told to go there; it would be good for us. Within minutes the soldiers had the threads in the looms all tangled up. I picked up a piece of wood and was cutting it up into little pieces when a therapist said, "And what are we making?" I replied, "Sawdust, and when I'm finished, I'm gonna paint it red." She went away mumbling. After that, none of us had to go back. The U.S.O. arranged for Al Jolson to do a show at the hospital. He put on his black face and sang "Mammy." None of us were impressed and we left before it was over.

The doctors kept insisting that I go to Fort Benning and I kept insisting that I wanted a discharge. Finally, they gave me leave to go home for a few days and orders to report to the Infantry Rest Center in Miami Beach, Florida, on a certain date. They could have done this earlier, but didn't. I was given a train and meal ticket to Montgomery, but not to Miami. When it was time to leave Montgomery to go to Miami, I went to Maxwell Field to bum a ride on an aircraft to Miami. After showing a captain in operations my orders, he went over the list of scheduled flights and told me that a squadron of Piper Cubs (L-5s meaning Liaison) would soon be leaving on maneuvers going to Tallahassee, Florida. These were the same small aircraft used for artillery spotters, army scouting and pilot training. They had two seats, fore and aft, high wings, and flew slow and low.

The captain said, "You look like you can fly in one of these small "Paper Cups." I quickly replied, "Yes, Sir." He issued me a seat type parachute, the same kind fighter pilots wear, because there is not enough room to wear a chest or back type. As I signed for the parachute, he told me to turn it in at any air force base. On the flight line, I met all the pilots. They were all buck sergeants, except the squadron leader was a master sergeant. They looked at my strange uniform, but there was not much talk because they were busy getting ready to leave. They strapped down my bag in the second seat of one aircraft and the master sergeant said, "You will fly in my second seat."

The squadron moved out to the runway and did all the final warm-ups and checkouts and were ready for take off. An order from the control tower canceled take off. A flight officer (F.O.) needed a ride. We waited and waited. Each aircraft had an intercom between the two seats because that was the only way to hear each other. Also, each aircraft stayed on the same radio frequency to talk to each other. During the wait, I heard all about F.O.s. They were called other things. They were not commissioned officers; they were warrant officers. During these transmissions, the pilots asked if I would vomit. I replied, "Don't think so. I knew the sergeant pilots in the three Royal Air Force Eagle Squadrons that helped me land in England when I was flying an ME-109 out of France. Squadron Leader, Gus Damon, was a special friend. Some of the pilots transferred to the U.S. Army with me in England."

SUCK A ROCK 44: Somewhere in Virginia, Alabama
& Florida

Two of the aircraft were ordered to taxi back to the flight line to pick up the flight officer and his bag. It is not certain whether by accident or otherwise, the intercom and radio were not working at the seat the flight officer was flying in. The pilots talked about him and he didn't know it. The squadron took off, flying low over South Alabama through the rural areas. Flying about 20 feet high over cow pastures made cows run. In the tall pine forests, we flew through them by using gaps in the trees. The maneuvering in the forests was tricky. When the gaps closed, the pilots had to go full throttle, bank sideways to swing around the trees or climb out. I enjoyed it and followed through on the stick, rudder pedals and throttle.

Soon, we landed in Tallahassee, Florida. After picking up my bag, I thanked the pilots, said goodbye and went to operations to find a flight to Miami. A BT-11 (Bombardier Trainer) had landed to refuel and whatever. The destination was an air force base near Fort Myers. Fort Myers is fairly close to Miami via Alligator Alley. There were four people in the crew. The pilot and co-pilot were lieutenants. Another lieutenant flew in the nose blister, which was used for bombardier training, and a major flew in the cockpit in the navigator's position. This was a twin engine aircraft with aluminum bench seats running fore and aft in the cabin similar to a C-47. There was another passenger in the cabin with me; a lieutenant in the quartermaster corps.

The route from Tallahassee to Fort Myers was over the eastern Gulf of Mexico, near the west coast of Florida. After passing the Tampa area, one of the engines starting running away. It took three of the crew to feather the prop and shut the engine down. The quartermaster lieutenant got up and started pacing up and down. He was nervous. The pilot turned the aircraft to head straight to the coast; which could be seen on the horizon. In a few minutes, the other engine started losing power. The major told me that the pilot wanted to see me. The pilot said, "We're losing altitude. We'll have to jump. As soon as we reach the coast, undog (open) the door. When I yell "go," push that lieutenant out; the rest of us will jump right behind you." I tried to calm the lieutenant as I tightened his chute straps and explained what to do. In a few moments after I undogged the door, the pilot hollered and the crew was right behind me. The quartermaster lieutenant grabbed the doorjamb and I hit him with a shoulder block and pushed him with my hands. I went out with him. The crew made it out just before the aircraft banked and started down.

In the fall of 1944, the west coast of Florida had very little development. We had jumped over the low coastal plains, mostly covered with palmettos. All of us, including the nervous lieutenant, landed safely. As I was dropping, I kept swinging around to see where the others would land. It was fortunate that we landed as close together as we did. The greatest distance between any of us was one-half mile. While we were walking to get together, a farmer drove up in his truck to pick us up. The farmer and his wife and children saw the aircraft when it hit and exploded. Then they saw some parachutes. The farmer carried us to his house. We met his family and had some cake and coffee. The farmer was really a rancher. They grew some vegetables, but their main livelihood was growing cattle. At this time, Florida had an open range law; which meant no fences so there were large cattle ranches in South Florida, complete with cowboys and rodeos in the old days.

The pilot had called in a mayday just before he bailed out. While we were standing around talking, a fighter aircraft came in low, banked to see us and the downed aircraft. We waved and the pilot said, "He must be from MacDill in Tampa." The rancher carried us to a small town to use the telephone because he didn't have one. The major called the base in Fort Myers. We thanked the rancher and he returned home as we waited for a truck from Fort Myers to pick us up. While we waited, there was a lot of good-natured kidding going on, especially with the quartermaster lieutenant. The others asked him if he didn't want to transfer to the air force. Since I was the only one in the group that was not a commissioned officer, I left the kidding to them.

They asked me where I'd been and where I was going, things like that. I told them some of the things about my travels. It was late at night when the truck picked us up and carried us to Fort Myers. Everyone at the base was nice to me. There was good food and they gave me a bag, shaving kit, and such. My bag went down with the aircraft.

The next afternoon, I caught a bus to Miami, arriving there at 4:00A.M. the next morning. By now, I was late arriving to report to the officer in command of the Infantry Rest Center. When I went to the headquarters, the duty sergeant gave me a paper to check in at my assigned hotel and a meal card to eat in any restaurant of my choice. He told me that everything was paid for by the U.S. Army.

The sergeant also told me to report to the commanding officer later in the day. The commanding officer was a brigadier general. After he returned my salute, he said, "Soldier, sit down and explain why you are late arriving here. Most soldiers are eager to get here to enjoy the wonders of the world famous Miami Beach." I explained. The brigadier general said, "That's the damndest excuse for being late, I've ever heard. How do I know you're not shooting bull?"

I replied, "Sir, may I remove my shirt?" He replied, "Of course." Removing my shirt and undershirt, I turned my back around and said, "Sir, those are chute marks." The brigadier started laughing, louder and louder. He called out for his staff to come in and said, "Look at this soldier's back. Those are genuine parachute marks. This soldier jumped out of an aircraft to get here." His staff was also laughing.

I said, "Sir, now I have a real problem. The parachute was issued to me at Maxwell Field and I was supposed to turn it in at the Air Force Base in Fort Myers. Now, it is long gone. If the cost is deducted from my pay, I'll never have any money." He replied, "Son, don't worry about it. I'll handle it." I thought I would be dismissed, but the brigadier wanted to talk. He was a nice older guy. He was transferred from a field command to command the Infantry Rest Center when it was established for all returning infantrymen to rest and relax. He asked about my travels. After our conversation, he said, "Is there anything else bothering you?" I replied, "Sir, I have malaria and this place is too hot." It was September or October, but Miami was hot. The brigadier said, "I'll see what I can do."

There were some good restaurants on Collins Avenue where most of us had our meals. I went swimming and went deep-sea fishing on an army boat. We caught barracuda, snapper and grouper. The master sergeant in command gave the fish to a local hospital. After several days, I received train tickets, meal tickets and orders to report to Fort Indiantown Gap, Pennsylvania. When I was shown my railway car at the station by the conductor, I was amazed. My car was an air-conditioned Pullman with rooms and bunks and I was the only person in it. As the train pulled out of the station, I went forward to see the car in front of my car. The railway car in front of mine was something I had never seen. It was a United States Military Troop Carrier. It was crammed full of WAVES (Women in the Navy) It looked like a "Toonerville Trolley" with all the windows opened and heads sticking out.

As I stood there in the midst of all these girls, a chief petty officer (a girl, of course) reached me and said, "I am in command and what in the hell are you doing here?" I replied, "Chief, it seems that you forgot to salute. I have commanded as an acting Captain in the Infantry, companies of infantrymen in Africa and Italy, United States Marines and United States Navy personnel at N.O.B. Norfolk." There was a reason for this. Knowing the rules and regulations for at least two major military powers, I would not allow anyone to overpower, out talk or con me. The chief and the WAVES under her command were hot, tired, needed a bath, and were afraid because they didn't know where they were going.

The chief said, "Sorry, Sir, you see our conditions." I replied, "Yes, that's why I'm here. I have an air conditioned Pullman car with private compartments and rest rooms. I need only one compartment you and your personnel are welcome to use the others. Calm down, everything will be O.K." She said, "Oh, thank you. We can certainly use the other compartments, especially the restrooms. We are tired and dirty. Sorry I sounded off; it was uncalled for." The WAVES left the train during the night at a stop somewhere in Virginia. I stuck my head out of my door to say goodbye when I heard some of them shouting, "Thanks and good luck."

The train stopped in Washington, D.C. I was supposed to change trains to go to Fort Indiantown Gap. Reading my orders again, I noticed that there was four more days before I had to report. It was 4:00 A.M., still dark, but I started hitchhiking anyway to Waynesboro, Virginia, to see my friends.

Fall 1944

My first ride from downtown Washington, D.C. to the outskirts of the city was in a milk delivery truck. The trip to Waynesboro was uneventful. After spending two nights and a day there, I caught a train to go to Pennsylvania. To reach Ft. Indiantown Gap, I had to change trains twice. Because I was carrying a military ticket, the conductors didn't care what trains I rode on.

At the Fort, I was sent to a wood frame two story barracks. There were some soldiers there like me. No one in command seemed to know where to assign them. Some had been sent to California and back. Everyone was tired of riding the rails. While we waited for orders, some of the soldiers shot dice and played poker to pass the time. Now and then, one of them would get orders to report to some unit.

Some days passed before I received orders. My orders were to report to ARMY SERVICE FORCES, Third Service Command, Pennsylvania District, Harrisburg Sub-District, Military Police Detachment, Harrisburg, Pennsylvania. I knew Harrisburg was the capitol of Pennsylvania, but my orders were a mouth full of military jargon. The above units had occupied the Pennsylvania State Police Barracks and Training Center. The barracks were located on a hill. In the distance, the railroad marshaling yards could be seen. Harrisburg had a large railroad system. There was only one street that led into and out of the Military Sub-District and Military Police Detachment. Harrisburg is about 20 miles from Ft. Indiantown Gap.

After I reported to the captain in command of the military police detachment, the first sergeant went with me to introduce me to my platoon. There were a number of buildings at the police barracks. One building contained the offices of the military sub-district and mess hall. Another one was the headquarters and weapons armory for the military police detachment. There were some barracks and latrine buildings which had been added, including a guardhouse and stockade for prisoners. The food was very good. The army hired civilian ladies to do the cooking and they liked to see us eat. The military police were on duty for 12 hours, then on standby for 12 hours to eat, sleep, wash clothes and the like; then they were off duty for 12 hours. For this reason, the cooks worked in shifts to coordinate with the military police schedules. The main meals were at 6:00 A.M., 12:00 noon, 6:00 P.M. and 12:00 midnight, with snacks in between.

The military police duties were many and varied. They were on duty at the railway station and other places where they might be needed. Also, they did guard duty at the stockade and transported prisoners. Railway officials requested that military police be on duty on their passenger trains. The trains were loaded to full capacity with civilians and military personnel and the conductors could not handle the rowdy ones and those who had too much to drink. The trip was unusual and interesting so I did it several times. Two of us would board a train in Harrisburg while two M.P.s from Pittsburgh got off. The conductor showed us our reserved Pullman compartment and then one of us started patrolling forward and the other one started aft. These were long main line trains. Most of the times, we could calm down the rowdy ones by talking to them. Also, the conductors called us when they spotted trouble.

A few times, a soldier, sailor or marine wouldn't calm down. They were cursing and wanted to fight. The civilians, mostly women, were moved out of the way. In these few cases, we had to use our Billy clubs, put them down and handcuff them. The conductors then called a station ahead of us to have military police ready to remove them from the train.

In Philadelphia, we left the trains and boarded ones for Chicago to return to Harrisburg. All trains in the United States were vital to the war effort. The crews on all of them worked long, hard hours. The ability for the U. S. railway system to deliver military personnel, the tons of military supplies and equipment to shipping ports on the Atlantic and Pacific Oceans and the Gulf of Mexico astonished the Axis Powers.

One time, I was off duty and was hitchhiking into downtown. A nice lady named Margie gave me a ride. She had a high civilian position in the military sub-district headquarters. She said, "Aren't you the soldier that was recently transferred here to the M.P. Detachment?" I replied, "Yes." She said, "I have heard about you. When your records came in, even the colonel was shaking his head. It is amazing what you have done." We talked some more and then she said, "Do you know that none of the officers and men here have ever been overseas except for three soldiers who were overseas for a short time. They were wounded and returned." I replied, "Yes, I have figured that out and they are all scared, including the captain, that they will be shipped out."

Maybe I shouldn't have said that, but when she smiled, I knew she wouldn't rat on me. We became friends. Margie had a college degree and was a member of the country club and things like that. She took me to the country club and introduced me to her friends, mostly women, and some older men. At my age, older men were those over thirty-five.

We played bridge and golf. Card games, such as bridge and poker, consist mainly of memory and then odds. I did get the hang of it. Margie was a member of a book review club. Most of the members were her friends from college. The book club was going to review a book that was written about the South and Margie asked me to meet with them. This was early winter in the last days of 1944. People in the North and South still had gross misunderstandings about each other. The Yankees had the impressions caused by books and other news media that the Southern Rebels sat around drinking mint juleps and going to and from parties. This was all depicted in the novel Gone With the Wind.

When asked, I explained that we were very much the same people. I was born and grew up in South Alabama, in the city that was the first capitol of the Confederacy. Montgomery had the same type of descendants of emigrants as Pennsylvania. There were some differences mainly caused by weather, such as food. Basements or cellars were rare in South Alabama. There are some beautiful places and nice people in Penn's Forest.

Someone in our platoon knew the owners of a ski lodge in the mountains up the Susquehanna River. It seemed that everything from Harrisburg was either "up" or "down" the Susquehanna. During the war, there were no tourists and the lodge was vacant. Arrangements were made for the members of our platoon to have a party there at little or no cost.

The soldiers who were married arranged for their wives to come by train or bus to our barracks. Other soldiers invited their girlfriends. The married couples received reduced rates at a hotel downtown. It was not Christmas, but it was December 1944, and everyone helped. Even our captain helped. He authorized the use of our military vehicles to go to the lodge. The lodge and everything around it was covered with snow. All of it was beautiful. My friend, Margie, came with me as my guest. The main great room of the lodge contained a huge stone fireplace, a dining area and a dancing area. The fireplace had huge logs burning in it and bear skin rugs to sit on and watch the fire. The best thing I remember was the method used to have cold beer. A mountain stream was piped in and out of a huge trough that contained all the different kinds of bottled beer, ale, lager and malt. This was a self- serve trough. Records were played. These were

179

the great old spinning music records by the great bands of the 1940's. We danced, had great food, watched the fire and best of all created friendships.

One of our officers, 1st Lieutenant Bowen, had never been in combat and had never served far from home. He was married and his family were well to do people that owned a funeral home or things like that, down the Susquehanna. He had been trying to get a date with Margie before I got there. When he found out that Margie and I were friends, he went to her office in headquarters and made some threats. Margie warned me. He started sly remarks, calling me old soldier and why did I quit fighting. It was time for all of us to go to the short firing ranges. Short ranges are for pistols, grenades and Thompson Sub-Machine guns. We took turns firing old G.I. Brownings and Colts.

When it was time for us to fire Tommy guns, Lt. Bowen continued his chatter about me. He was trying to influence my mind. He said, "Now we'll see what Commando Houston can do. He lies about his combat and was sent back because he's psycho." After so much of this and slowly thinking about it, I replied, "Sir, I don't have to lie. While you were sitting on your butt, I was killing the enemy with this weapon." That turned him on, he had taken the bait. He said, "You smart-ass, are you afraid to bet on which one of us is the best shot?" I replied, "Sir, as you know, I don't have much money, but I will accept a bet." He said, "How about $100?" I replied, "Sir, I accept, but I don't have $100, you'll have to take all of my two-months' pay." The targets were on wood stakes, short range for Tommy Guns which were short-range weapons. The wood stakes were mounted so that they would rotate by pulling on ropes, running through a pulley, to expose the target. The range officer and his crew pulled the ropes to expose the targets for a certain number of seconds while the shooter fired and then they pulled them so that the only thing showing was the stake. Speed and accuracy were needed to hit the target.

The lieutenant and I each had a turn firing. He fired long bursts which made the gun move off target for his final rounds. My bursts were always three to four. The range officer counted our hits and the result was inconclusive. We fired again with the same result. I suggested that we fire at the stakes without our targets exposed and the first one to cut the stake off would be the winner. That was agreed and the range officer would give the order to fire and cease fire with the timing of six seconds. Lt. Bowen and I stood next to each other and when the order to fire was given, I used three round bursts and cut my stake off. Sure enough, the lieutenant held his trigger down and the muzzle of the gun raised off target. He did hit his stake with the first round, but didn't cut it off. I won and this made him madder.

The next exercise was to throw hand grenades. I asked our captain if he would like for me to give grenade instructions. He replied, "Of course. You were in the infantry and should know all about grenades." Starting out, I explained how the Mills Hand Grenade was developed in World War I by the British Army. None of them knew that. Explaining how the timing was set, I started taking one apart. They ran. The range officer and the captain made everyone come back with them.

I didn't change the timing, but showed how, plus anyone using hand grenades might kill themselves if they didn't understand the timing. Once the cotter pin is pulled and the lever released, it is armed and will explode within the seconds according to the timing. After I demonstrated the different ways of throwing grenades, I threw some using the Houston method. Then each one took turns throwing. It seemed that the soldiers were understanding that I was helping them, but I was probably crazy. To prevent accidents, the grenades were thrown over a protective barrier.

The new stockade, which the army built at the Police Barracks, was surrounded by double fences on all four sides. Between the fences on all four sides, war dogs were placed and the M.P.s on guard duty strolled on the outside of the fences. Meaning, four guards and four war dogs were on duty at all times. I was assigned to guard duty. I was strolling along the fence one night, armed with a riot gun (12 gauge auto-load shotgun) loaded with 00 buckshot, and I started thinking about whether or not I would shoot an escaping soldier. Most of the prisoners were there because of minor infractions, such as A.W.O.L.

Prisoners of war, who would kill you if they had a chance, were not treated this badly. Neither were civilian criminals. Having decided this was not the right thing to do, I went into the guardhouse. The sergeant of the guard and a few others were there. I asked the sergeant for permission to speak with the officer of the guard. When the sergeant opened the door to the back room, I caught a glimpse of Lt. Bowen, the officer of the guard, standing over a seated prisoner with a rubber hose in his hand. The sergeant closed the door and in a few minutes the sergeant and Lt. Bowen came out. I said, "Sir, I request to be relieved of guard duty. I cannot shoot any of these soldiers." Surprisingly, the lieutenant agreed, but I knew he would keep trying to get me. I went to my barracks and slept. The next morning, I went to the first sergeant and told him I needed to go on sick call. The M.P. Detachment didn't have a military doctor. They used a civilian family doctor whose office was downtown. Using an M.P. car, I went to his office. He was an elderly gentleman and knew I was a combat soldier with malaria and such. He said, "Son, I wish I could help. You should be discharged." He wrote an order for me to report to the hospital at Ft. Indiantown Gap. After reporting back to the first sergeant, I went to the hospital. The doctors ran the usual tests, particularly for malaria. After a few days, I met with their "board," but again, they said they could not authorize my discharge. I returned to the barracks in Harrisburg.

It was not openly called "punishment," but it was. Because I wouldn't perform guard duty, I was ordered to clean the weapons in the armory. The armory was built like a huge vault, by the State Police, to contain weapons for the entire State Police because this was their headquarters. The only opening was a huge metal door, which had to remain open when anyone was inside. The armory was nice. No one could watch me, but I could see out through the door opening whenever I wanted. The walls were lined with racks holding weapons and the other areas had heavy weapons. Since no particular progress was required, my counter-attack was prepared sitting down way in the back. Some of the weapons were; pistols, M-1 rifles, M-1 carbines, Springfield 03s, Thompson Sub-Machine guns, 12 gauge auto-load shotguns, grenades, 30 caliber light machine guns, 50 caliber machine guns and mortars. The 30 caliber machine guns had mounts for jeeps and the 50 caliber machine guns had mounts for half-tracks. The M.P. Detachment had these weapons plus vehicles to carry them, including half-tracks.

Did the powers that be expect the Axis Powers to attack or did they expect the civilians of Harrisburg to attack? These were my thoughts and still are. The armory was in the same building as our headquarters, near the first sergeant's office and the captain's office. Taking different weapons apart, I started some cleaning, but the different parts sort of got mixed up. Every now and then, I sprinkled some graphite down a barrel and carried it to show the first sergeant how dirty it was. He said, "You're doing a great job." Opening cases of ammunition, I loaded some weapons to see if they worked O.K. Some grenade parts I left lying about. When I was near the door and someone walked past, I aimed my finger at them and said, "Bang." Soon rumors were flying around about this. One of the clerks told a soldier who was one of my friends that he overheard the captain talking to our doctor about me. The doctor told the captain that Pvt.

Houston is a long time combat infantryman with malaria and should have been discharged. If anything happens in that armory, or if he gets a fever, captain, you are responsible.

That night in our barracks, my friend told me about this. There were many friends among the soldiers, but they couldn't say anything that would get them in trouble with the officers. The next morning, I went back to the armory and continued my cleaning duty. About an hour later, the first sergeant told me that my weapons cleaning was over and I would be assigned other duties.

The author with 1939 Buick

Winter 1945

Occasionally, when I was off duty, I went downtown and walked around. The state capitol and many state buildings were there. Like a tourist, I visited many places and spoke to people. They were all very nice. In the multi-story downtown parking garage, I met the two owners and operators. They owned a major car dealership but, during the war, there were no new cars to sell. Their problem was, they couldn't hire enough good drivers to park and bring down cars on the circling up and down ramps. The lead man said, "Can you park cars and do you have a driver's license?" I replied, "I can drive and park anything, including half-tracks, full tracks, and whatever has an engine. I have a British "Class 3," Internal Combustion qualification, a U.S.M.P. Driver's License and an old Alabama Driver's License which I got when I had my Model "T" Ford."

He said, "You want a job?" I laughed and replied, "I haven't thought about that." That's how I started parking cars sometimes when off duty. The pay was small, but it sure helped. My army pay in the U.S. was $50.00 a month. The army should have been paying me an extra $10.00 a month for my Combat Infantry Medals. They did pay me several years later. My new boss and I became friends and I asked him to find a good used car that I could buy. One day he told me he had found one. We went to see it and met the lady owner. She told us that it belonged to her son who was K.I.A. and the car had been in her garage since he went overseas. She opened the garage door and there it was! It was a 1939 Buick convertible with a rumble seat and a straight eight Buick engine. It was set up on wood blocks. This was one of those long, black beautiful cars. I wanted it! The lady said, "Would $800.00 be too much?" My car dealer friend said, "That would be a fair price." I told the lady, "I will call my father to see about getting the money. It will take a while." The lady replied, "That's all right, I'm in no hurry."

While I was in the Canadian Army, half of my pay was deposited in the Chase National Bank, with my parents listed as the next of kin so they could withdraw it at any time or if I was K.I.A. I called my father and asked him to withdraw the money from the bank and send it to me. I told my father about the car and he said, "That's a good car. I bought a new 1912 Buick that lasted many years." When I received the money, I bought the car and the dealer friend had one of his mechanics check it out. He wouldn't let me pay for anything. When I drove my car to my barracks, the soldiers wanted to see it and hear it run. I asked a State Trooper about the old tag and my old driver's license from Alabama. The Trooper told me not to worry; military personnel were exempt from buying new tags or driver's license.

It was cold in Pennsylvania during that winter. The Buick would be covered with ice and snow in the mornings. The moisture on the brake linings would freeze. The rear brakes could be broken loose by starting the engine and putting it in gear. Sometimes the front wheels would slide on the ice with the brakes still frozen. Pouring hot water on them would free them.

One afternoon I was on stand-by, doing chores and such, and decided I would try to find out why the Buick was running hotter than it should. I drove it around for about five or ten minutes to heat the engine so I could check the hoses and connections for leaks. As I was returning to park in front of my barracks, I saw Lt. Bowen in an M.P. car, with a sergeant driving, in back of me. When I parked, I opened the hood and started looking.

The M.P. car stopped, Lt. Bowen and the sergeant got out. The lieutenant asked me what I was doing and I explained. Lt. Bowen said, "You've been A.W.O.L. Don't you agree

183

sergeant?" I looked in the sergeant's eyes and I knew what he had to say, but he didn't agree. The sergeant said, "Yes, Sir." The problem with my Buick was the radiator needed cleaning.

Lt. Bowen filed a charge against me for being A.W.O.L. for at least two-hours. The charge, together with a specified time and date for a summary court martial (company), was delivered to me. In preparing my defense, about twenty soldiers signed to testify that I was doing what everyone usually did and there was no way that I could have been A.W.O.L. I had showered and washed my clothes as they did only minutes before the specified time in the charge.

All of us carried a Military Police authorization card to arrest any member of the Armed Forces, complete with photo, physical characteristics and right thumb print. On the back of this card was a Class "A" Pass for the bearer which allowed me to be up to 50 miles from post when not on assigned Military Police duties. Mine is still in an old cigar box. This card created a grave problem for Lt. Bowen. It was time to counter-attack. The grapevine was loaded with rumors. All officers, noncommissioned officers and enlisted knew what was happening; including the colonel and others in the Third Service Command, Pennsylvania District, Harrisburg Sub-District. Lt. Bowen wanted to get me.

Lt. Bowen had assumed that I would accept company punishment. The only court-martial I would accept would be a general court-martial with a J.A.G. attorney representing me as provided by the Articles of War. As these rumors continued, how could an embalmer, with sadistic tendencies, be commissioned an officer in the Military Police Corps so he could beat soldiers? All of this was getting to our captain. Naturally, he wanted to protect his position and record.

The first sergeant sent word that he wanted to talk to me. In his office, without anyone else present, he told me the captain wanted to make a deal to settle this matter. If I would agree, there would not be any court-martial. If I would accept company punishment to spend two weeks in the stockade at Carlisle Barracks, the captain would guarantee there would never be any record of any of this; and further, when I was released from the stockade, there would be orders already prepared for me to report to Fort Meade, Maryland for an Honorable Discharge.

Thinking about the offer, I could stay in the army and fight, or get out. I told the first sergeant I would agree, but someone such as the colonel in the headquarters would have to know about the agreement to make certain there were no hang-ups. The first sergeant said, "A private meeting between you and a lieutenant will be arranged to go over the details." I replied, "O.K."

The meeting with the lieutenant went well. He was sympathetic because he knew this situation should not have happened. He asked me when did I want to go to the stockade. I replied, "Right away." He made the arrangements. I placed all my gear in my Buick and locked it. I carried my shaving kit with me. Lt. Bowen must have been sent on leave because no one saw him. Two of my M. P. friends carried me to Carlisle in an M.P. car. The old U. S. Indian School, with the great Jim Thorpe, was located in Carlisle, Pa. At the stockade, we met the first sergeant in command. It was unusual to have an M. P. prisoner in a stockade. My friends reminded the first sergeant to take care of me and to let his guards know that I had many M. P. friends in Harrisburg where they went on leave.

I was never placed under arrest, handcuffed, or searched. The first sergeant guided me into the cellblocks and allowed me to carry my shaving kit and whatever else I had. As soon as the first sergeant left, the prisoners gathered around to talk. Lo and behold, they already knew, through their grapevine, that I was coming and the things that had happened. I was some kind of hero for sticking up for the prisoners and they hated Lt. Bowen's guts anyway.

In prison, the routine was in the mornings the cells were unlocked; we went to the latrine; ate breakfast; went on work details with guards; returned to prison for lunch; went on work details with guards; returned to prison for dinner; shaved and showered; stayed in the open area until time for lights out; returned to our cells for lock down and then lights out. Some of the work details consisted of removing ashes from the furnaces that heated the boilers that supplied heat to the buildings; then carry the ashes out in garbage cans and load on trucks. After that, carry coal and re-stoke the furnaces. This was hard work because it was winter, January 1945

During the first week, I managed to do the job, then chills and fever started, just enough to make me weak. I could have gone on sick call, but I was determined to finish the two weeks. There was another prisoner there who still had yellow in his eyes. He had served with Merrill's Marauders in Burma. There was a movie made about that. Many of the prisoners had been in civilian prisons and were paroled to serve in the U.S. Army. They had goofed and were now serving time in the stockade. They were young and strong and I preached a little bit to them because they now had an opportunity to straighten out and have a clean record. I loaned them my small knife to cut their nails, my razor and single edge blades, shaving cream and the like. Otherwise, they had to ask the guards for a razor and then return it with the blade. There was a popular cowboy song, "Don't Fence Me In," which was appropriate to our situation.

One day, on a work detail, I became so weak I couldn't hoist a garbage can of ashes into a truck. A guard came and said, "I'm going to report you for malingering. Pick up that can and load it on the truck. Immediately, we were surrounded by prisoners. One of them picked up the can and loaded it on the truck. Another one said to the guard, "You snotty nose jerk, you're trying to make points so you won't be sent to the combat infantry. If you report anything, we'll take care of you and you will go to the infantry." The guard was shaking and said, "I meant no harm, just doing my duty." Another prisoner said, "That's a lie. This prisoner has done the killing for all of us. You can talk to your first sergeant about this or shut up." He did shut up.

It was my final few days and I was on the same kind of work detail. At Carlisle there was also a school for training of newly commissioned second lieutenants to be medical administrators in the U.S. Army Medical Corps. My fever made me hot so I stripped down, taking off all my outer clothes. When I carried out a load of ashes, my boots slipped on the ice. I fell down flat. A group of second lieutenants happened to be passing by. They ran over to me, helped me up, and one of them said, "You're sick. We'll take you to a doctor." I replied, "Thank you, Sirs, I am a prisoner and it is illegal for you to speak to a prisoner. Somehow, I'll make it." My fellow prisoners came to help me. The second lieutenants left, talking about what a disgrace.

The two weeks were completed. Two of my M.P. friends came to carry me back to our barracks in Harrisburg. It was work hours, but the first sergeant made arrangements to have all prisoners confined in the prison so I could tell them good bye. I thanked them and they thanked me. We shook hands. I thanked the first sergeant and his other sergeants and we shook hands. It does pay to be a good soldier and do your best.

When I arrived to the Harrisburg Barracks, I went to the first sergeant's office. I got my orders and train tickets to go to Fort Meade. Many of my soldier friends wanted to talk. I told them that my "company punishment" was over and I was going to get my discharge. They said they would take care of my Buick and my gear. During these times, it was difficult to write to my parents and Rosette. I did write to them to tell them I was O.K. My parents and Rosette never knew I was in a prison.

Trains carried me to Fort Meade. Upon arrival, I reported to headquarters as ordered. The officers and clerks were not prepared to handle my discharge. One problem was they only had a temporary service record for me. They asked for my serial number. One of the clerks said, "They ain't none like that. I know all of 'em." I removed my dog tag from around my neck and showed it to him. He shook his head and said, "Yaw'l look at this. It's lower than the regular army. It shore ain't no draft number." Then he wanted to know why I had only one. I said, "Because I woke up in a hospital in Italy and this is the only one I had left. My other army dog tags were gone also."

They were confused. I said, "Just listen and I'll explain." I explained that I was a volunteer with service in the Canadian and British Armies and after the United States entered the war, I enlisted in the U.S. Army on September 3, 1942, at a British depot at Thursley, Surrey, England. That is why I had a different serial number. They asked for my home address. I replied, "General Delivery, Los Angeles, California." I did this because they were supposed to give me travel pay according to mileage either to place of enlistment or my hometown. This required another conference. With each new development, the clerks called the captain in and the captain would call the colonel.

The colonel told the captain he would call the Finance Department in Washington for a ruling because they had not had a question like this before. I had to wait two days for someone to decide. The ruling arrived from Washington. The ruling was stated like this. When anyone was discharged from military service they would be sent to the military base nearest their home, then paid mileage to their home. This rule applied in the Continental U.S. If they had enlisted in any territory of the U.S., such as the Philippines, Panama Canal or Puerto Rica, and further, if those places were their homes, they would be transported to those places by the military and discharged there.

My case was unusual because England was not a U.S. territory. The ruling for me was for me to receive travel pay to the nearest P.O.B. (Port of Embarkation). The nearest P.O.B. to England was New York, New York. My travel pay to New York was ten dollars and some change. Over and over again, I was shafted by our great U.S. Army. The clerks kept twittering about. The colonel came in and said, "Quit messing around, fill out the damn papers and give the soldier his discharge." I stood up, saluted and said, "Thank you, Sir." The colonel replied, "It's not your fault. The army screwed up your records."

With my discharge in my hands, I returned to Harrisburg to get my Buick and other stuff. My friend, Margie, was still furious about what had happened. We said our good byes. Through our grapevine, I found out approximately when Lt. Bowen would go to the mess hall. All of my preparations were made so that I could leave immediately after seeing Lt. Bowen. In the mess hall, I ate and waited. Lt. Bowen came in and sat down at a table to eat. I moved and sat down at his table straight across from him. I stared into his eyes. Neither one of us spoke. The mess hall became quiet. I leaned over the table, grabbed his shirt with my left hand and with my right hand hit him just above his collar brass in the throat. He and his chair went over backwards to the floor. He was gasping for breath. I walked out. There were soldiers outside that patted me on the back and we shook hands. I drove away going to Alabama.

SUCK A ROCK 47: Somewhere from Pennsylvania to Alabama

Winter 1945

Alabama was a long way. There were no Interstate Highways. It was February and a blizzard had moved in. My Buick needed gas and I didn't have gas coupons. The U.S. had rationed gas and people needed gas coupons to buy any. Anyway, I didn't have much money. I went to the service station that supplied gas to our military vehicles by military contract.

The people at the station had filled my Buick and the cars owned by other M.P.s when we used them to go on stake- outs as ordered by our captain. The owner of the station came out and I told him I didn't have coupons. I had a discharge and I was going home. He filled my gas tank and wouldn't let me pay

After searching for a route home, using road maps, I selected one that would get me out of the blizzard and head south. Taking the Pennsylvania Turnpike west I turned south on U. S. Highway 11. The Turnpike was open, but snowdrifts were forming. With the radio on, the announcer said a lady with some children perished when trapped in a snow bank.

On U.S. 11, the snow was piling up. I stopped at a small rural gas station. When I asked the elderly gentleman the condition of the road going south, he said, "The snow plow passed going south about an hour ago." I said, "Do you think I can make it through to the south?" He replied, "Maybe, if you go fast and make it to Hagerstown. You're welcome to stay here until this thing blows over."

All I could think about was going home. Heading south, I throttled up. The snow was piling up so much that I drove on the centerline of the highway and at times barreled my way through the drifts. Again, the Lord was with me. The great blizzard missed Hagerstown, Maryland. Stopping in Hagerstown, I went to a café to go to the bathroom and drink a cup of coffee.

Reading my highway maps, my route was the old U.S. Highway 11. When I reached Waynesboro, Virginia, I stopped to tell my friends goodbye. They talked me into staying two days and nights. The first night we went to a dance at the U.S.O. Some of the girls were about my age and some were older. Some of the married ones had received "We Regret to Inform You" notices from the President while I was gone.

The second night, they had a farewell party for me at one of their homes. Me thinks, they just needed to have a party. They cooked all kinds of food, even hot dogs and hamburgers. We talked, snacked and drank beer. They insisted that I tell them everything that had happened since the last time I was in Waynesboro.

Three of the widows husbands had been killed in Italy. One was a sergeant in the combat engineers, another one was a sergeant in the artillery and the third one was a captain in the infantry. The captain was commissioned a second lieutenant at V.M.I. (Virginia Military Institute). They wanted me to tell them every detail about combat in Italy. This was a difficult thing to do. Leaving many details out, I tried to explain things without adding to their grief. These were nice people. Many of them had college degrees and they liked to play tennis and other sports.

It was sad saying goodbye, but they knew I was anxious to get home. There were lots of hugs and kisses. One morning I was driving on a good four-lane highway in the Carolinas. Wanting to reach Montgomery non-stop, I floor boarded the accelerator. After a while, there was a clunking sound. The engine threw a rod or something. Driving very slowly, I turned off on a side road that had a sign indicating a small village. Fortunately, there was a small one-man auto shop on that road.

After the man checked the engine, he told me he could fix it and have it ready to go about noon tomorrow. The cost would be $26.00. I said, "OK, I'll be back then. Which way is the town?" He gave me instructions. I walked out to the highway to thumb a ride. In a few moments, there were two cars with girl drivers headed my way. They were racing each other, skidding and sliding across the highway. They saw me as they barreled past. They braked and did a 180-degree skid around and raced to see who could pick me up first.

When they stopped, I explained that I needed a ride to the city (I've forgotten which town or city) to stay there while my car was being repaired. While going into the city with one of them, they kept up their racing. We had lunch in a café downtown and we talked. The two girls were cousins and lived next door to each other. It turned out that they lived on farms in the country and next door was a mile away. They both had brothers who had gone to war. Sort of kidding, I said, "You girls drive like you could run shine. Do you have extra heavy springs to keep your cars from sagging when your trunks are loaded?" They laughed. One of them said, "Oh, so you noticed. Do you have fast cars in Alabama?" I replied, "I think there are fast cars and drivers throughout the South." They wouldn't let me pay for the food. They talked about a dance somewhere that evening and they would be happy if I would go with them, so they would have someone to dance with.

They insisted that I go to the dance and in the meanwhile, we would go to their homes so I could meet their parents. Their parents welcomed me and one of them insisted that I spend the night with them after the dance. Their boys were gone and it would be a pleasure to have a young man in the house. One of the fathers noticed my military police insignia and sort of frowned. When one of the girls mentioned that I was discharged and going home to Alabama, he smiled. It turned out that they were related to the county sheriff. I told them that my grandfather was the sheriff of Covington County, Alabama, when he was killed.

The dance was at a large honky-tonk on a highway outside the city. The girls knew everybody and were kidded about picking up a lost soldier. A good time was had by all. The next morning there was a huge breakfast. Seeing the eyes of the lady of the house, I could tell she was thinking about her sons. After breakfast, one of the fathers said, "Son, do you need any gas?" I replied, "Yes, Sir, I sure could use some, but I don't have any coupons. He said, "That's all right, we get extra gas for our farm equipment. After you pick up your car, come on back and we'll fill it up." The girls carried me back to the auto shop. I paid the man and thanked him. When the girls saw my Buick, they "oooohed and aaaaaded" and wanted to trade. After getting some gas, I was on my way again.

Reaching Atlanta, I was getting tired, but I was determined to continue to Montgomery about 200 miles away. The roads in those days were narrow and winding through the mountains and hills. It was necessary to stay alert. One afternoon, before I reached Atlanta, I was going through a town and had to stop at a crosswalk at a factory. It was time for the workers at the factory to change shifts. As I waited, about a hundred girls and women passed. They whistled and made me a lot of good offers.

About 4:00 o'clock in the morning, I stopped at a café in Opelika, Alabama. It was the only place open. I ordered a cup of coffee and really wanted some breakfast, but I had counted my money and all I had left was $1.13. There were some other customers there. Some of them wanted to talk so I told them I had been discharged, was going home to Montgomery and I was just about out of gas.

A deputy sheriff said, "Follow me, I have a farmer friend who will give you some gas." The lady cook looked at me and served me a plate of eggs and such. She said, "Soldier, you need to eat, it's on the house." A long distance truck driver spoke up and said, "I have double tanks of gas and you're welcome to fill up." We all went outside. I moved the Buick next to the fuel tank on the truck. The deputy moved his car to shine his lights and spotlight on the tank. Someone came up with a siphon hose and used it to fill my tank. With all the evil people in the world, there are still many good people.

When I arrived home after daylight; it was February 1945. My mother had my room ready. I ate some and slept a long, long time. My long journey was over and my life was changed forever.

Afterword

Many things had changed while I was gone. Wandering around Montgomery, I saw some of the people that I used to know. There were certain things I had to do. My memories and dreams would always remain. I had to stop using vulgar language. Ninety-eight percent of the people in the military that I was with used vulgar language constantly. It has been my purpose to leave out vulgar words in this book.

I had to tell Rosette that there was no way I could go back to Tunisia. I had not realized how sick I was; my weight and strength were down. Even if I had enough money, there was no civilian transportation to Tunisia, and if we married, how could we return to America? Rosette would not be a war bride. The military would not help us.

It took several years for me to learn how to eat. I applied for a job with an insurance company, but I was turned down because I couldn't pass the physical exam with malaria. An editor, whom I knew, gave me a job as a cub reporter writing obituaries for the Montgomery Advertiser. My salary was $35.00 per week.

There was an electrocution scheduled at Kilby Prison so the Associated Press (A.P.) and United Press International (U.P.I.) sent their reporters to our office to wait for the correct time to go to the prison. They were supposed to witness the electrocution and then file their reports. They started drinking and drinking because they didn't want to go. At first, they each offered me $10.00 to go for them. When they drank some more and couldn't make it, the offer increased to $20.00 each, plus $5.00 each to have my suit dry cleaned. I accepted. When the switch was pulled, all of the prison lights dimmed. The smell of human flesh burning was the same as I remembered when tanks were hit and the crews were burned alive. Most of the witnesses vomited. When I walked out of the death chamber, I could hear the prisoners in their cellblocks softly singing gospel songs. After I returned to the Advertiser office, I gave the reporters the exact time of the electrocution and other information for their stories. My typing was poor and slow, so I got another job with an insurance company.

Something else I had to do was to detrain myself from being a commando. As Ernie Pyle had written, we were trained to be instinctive killers. My greatest fear was that I would kill someone that moved or touched me the wrong way. We had learned to kill fast and silent. One second would do it. The British had a program to detrain when the war was over. It is a terrible thing to know that millions of men, women and children wanted to kill me and would have if they could. My feeling was to kill them. I liked to kill them. Our enemies started it and I wanted to finish it.

Some of the girls that I had known in Montgomery had married and some were engaged. When I visited Lanier High School, all the students that I had known were gone. I was now twenty-one years old and in the older days, we had football players that old. When the football coach heard I was there he came to see me. He wanted me to play football and told me that I was still eligible. I told him to forget it.

There was a strange feeling at Lanier. The students were all girls except for a few young boys. When I visited my beloved geometry teacher's class, Miss Kirk, she explained that all boys were drafted at eighteen years old. She introduced me to her class of girls and said, "Collier can teach this class maybe better than I can."

Afterword

I looked at the textbooks and they were still the same. It is true, I was showing off. I said, "Miss Kirk calls this "Gee-O-Me-Try." If you will turn to the last page in your books, there will be on the right hand page the Pythagorean theorem. These textbooks saved me in so many ways. The principles are used for aiming weapons and navigation."

Miss Kirk invited me to have lunch in the cafeteria with her at the teachers' table. I remembered when I didn't have enough money to eat in the cafeteria. Many teachers that I had known sat with us for lunch. The principal of Lanier High School came in. He was the same principal that I had at Baldwin Junior High. He joined us at our now large table. He welcomed me and told the others that I was one of the two best students he had ever had. The other one was Cannie Morris Turnipseed.

It was in my memory bank that in special classes the teachers allowed us to debate. At Baldwin, we took some I.Q. tests (intelligence quotient). We both had high scores, something like 150's or 160's. Both of us were selected to go to a special school and classes. My parents did not agree. The only reason I write about this is because I saw a picture and an article about Cannie Morris in a "Life" magazine when I was in a hospital somewhere. She was doing great things in New York and I wish her well.

The principal had read about the new G.I. Bill passed by Congress to help returning veterans complete their education. He wanted me to start back to High School. I decided I would take the college entrance exams; which I did later.

There was a beautiful little girl that lived next door to my parents. She was seventeen and a senior at Lanier High. She was only twelve when I went to the war. We started dating and became engaged. Her father told her that she didn't love me, she loved my Buick. Anyway, we cut grass for her father to get enough money to buy a marriage license. Dorothy Lamar Smith and I got married and at the last count, we have been married for fifty-six years. We have two sons, Daniel Collier Houston, Jr., and Walter Lamar Houston. We have two grandsons, Daniel Collier Houston, III, and George Parrish Houston. Our only granddaughter is Dodie Marie Houston King. We also have one great-grandson, Collier Jordan King.

When we married, we immediately moved to Opelika, Alabama, where I was employed by an insurance company. Opelika was a small town about seven miles from Alabama Polytechnic Institute (now Auburn University). Dorothy got a job as a legal secretary for Roberts Henry Brown, Attorney. Roberts Brown was in private practice and also a state representative, Speaker of the House of Alabama, Trustee of Auburn, and District Attorney for Lee County, Alabama. Roberts was a glider pilot during the war and landed his glider in France during the Normandy Invasion.

About two months after Dorothy and I married, I had a serious attack of malaria. It was fortunate that we were visiting our families in Montgomery when the attack occurred. Many people helped as I went into high fevers and then chills. My mother, Dorothy's mother, and Dorothy's sister, Helen Ruth Smith Dill helped. Her husband, Dick Dill, was somewhere in France in the infantry. A friend, who was in our wedding, Dorothy (Dot) McKemie Miree, came down from Birmingham to help. Her husband, Reggie Miree, was a marine air-gunner somewhere in the Pacific. In those days some of the older people were familiar with tropical fevers. My mother was born about a hundred miles from the Gulf of Mexico and had typhoid fever when she was a child.

In the past, tropical fevers had wiped out all of the people in the settlements of Pensacola, Port St. Joe, Apalachicola and St. Augustine. Some of the medical personnel from the new

Veterans Administration Hospital in Montgomery came and offered to take me to the hospital. I couldn't stand even thinking about going into another hospital. My recovery was slow and I never knew how long I would be sick.

The Veterans Administration awarded me 60% disability for malaria, combat fatigue and other general physical disabilities dating from the date of my discharge in 1945. I never remember asking for it. In 1947, the V. A. cancelled all of this award because I had no "Proof of Medical Records" to send them. Of course, the V. A. had massive medical records on me and I didn't have any.

In the 1970's I filed an appeal to the V. A. No one, including the State of Georgia veterans representative thought I would get anything. It took several years. Whenever I was notified that my appeal was denied, I continued to appeal higher up. Finally, I was approved to meet with the V. A. Board in Atlanta. One of the board members, a lady doctor, asked me why I waited so long to appeal. I replied, "Mam, I have been able to make a living, now I am getting older and I need medical help". I was awarded 40% disability, 30% for combat fatigue and 10% for sinus. My sinus problems were caused by my broken nose in Africa. Now after two operations they are worse than ever. In the 1990's I filed an appeal to no avail. Currently, I have had an appeal on file since April 2001 for arthritis.

Roy Albert Palmer (sometimes I called him "RAP"), my friend, came to see us in Opelika. The German Army surrendered in the Alps near Brenner Pass. Our U.S. 34th Infantry Division captured the German 34th Infantry Division. They fought each other all the way to the north in Italy. Members of the 34th Infantry Division were told they could go home if they could get transportation. Roy managed to get a ride on a bomber. In order to cross the Atlantic Ocean, the bomber flew to Dakar in French West Africa, then to Brazil, then to Guiana, then to Puerto Rica and then to Miami. He was discharged in Georgia and went to my parent's home in Montgomery by train. He spent a few days with my parents and he liked my mother's cooking so much that she fixed him a parcel of fried chicken and such to carry with him. Roy stayed with us about two weeks before he headed for Alaska. He was so bitter about the army (all of us were) that he didn't want to see anybody except us. It would be two more years before he returned to his home.

At Alabama Polytechnic Institute, I took the college entrance exams. My brother Howard's wife, Dea, worked for the Veterans Administration in Montgomery and said that I made the second highest score on the exams in the State of Alabama. The good thing about my score was the Veterans Administration approved me under the rules of the G.I. Bill to study for any degree that I wanted. I chose the second oldest profession, Architecture (the oldest profession being the "Ladies of the Night"). Architecture is the smallest profession because it takes so long and hard work to make it. I started at Auburn with the largest class in history. It was September 1946 and most of the veterans had returned.

During the 1930's some students at Auburn formed an orchestra called "Auburn Knights". They played at many colleges, universities and large nightclubs up and down the East Coast. They were a great orchestra and one of the songs that they played was, "Stars Fell on Alabama". Now you know why I like this song. In later years one of the vocalist was a beautiful lady from Montgomery. Her name is Tennille and after she graduated from Auburn she was the vocalist on the television show, "The Captain and Tennille".

Most of the students were girls and a few boys. The tradition required all freshmen to buy and wear "rat caps," then report to the main gate. At the main gate, the football team was

192

waiting to paddle all of the rats before they could pass through the main gate. The veterans overwhelmed the football players, pulled their pants down and paddled them. There were many talented students in my classes. None of them had been gone from schools for the many years as I had been. It was necessary for me to catch up.

Auburn has many different schools. One of the degrees in the School of Engineering is Aeronautical Engineering. That is the reason Auburn produced, in later years, the "Auburn Astronauts"; the only complete team that went into space together from the same university, plus the mission commander in Houston was from Auburn.

The students in Architecture went to many other schools for math, surveying, physics, English grammar, literature, economics, welding, machine tooling, sheet metal, woodworking and others. When I went to the Dean of the School of Engineering to apply for pilot training, he said, "Of course, I will schedule your training with your other classes. The G. I. Bill will cover all the costs." Alabama Polytechnic Institute (now Auburn University) owned and operated the local airport. The head professor of Aeronautical Engineering was in charge and we had the greatest instructors in the world. They were all former flight instructors for the U.S. Army Air Force that had been discharged and were now students at Auburn.

The aircraft used for training were Piper Cubs that the Air Force used for basic training and they were given to Auburn. The instructors gave me the full military training with stalls and spins above 7,000 feet, wearing parachutes. To be honest, I really liked the training. Airsickness is like seasickness and I have never suffered from either.

In the late 1940's, the airport at Auburn had short runways. The airport was on a hill, but it was surrounded by tall southern pine trees. This required using the sideslip landing method in order to use the entire runway. We went around the airport in the old box pattern at 200 feet to read the windsock. After side slipping below the pines at the end of the runway, we would make a 90-degree left turn onto the runway. I was issued a Student Pilot Certificate and Solo Permit by the Civil Aeronautics Administration on March 19, 1946. My Pilot Flight Record and original Log Book is from the Auburn School of Aviation.

One morning, while I was in a class at Auburn, I received a message to go to the President's Office. At the President's Office, I was told to call Roberts Henry Brown, the attorney that Dorothy worked for. When I called Mr. Brown, he told me that it was important for me to drive him to Phenix City, Alabama, and to bring my shotgun and pistol. Also, I was to tell no one where I was going. Trouble had been brewing in Phenix City for years. The city was controlled by organized crime, with wide open gambling, prostitution, and illegal whiskey. Whenever anyone won too much gambling, they were killed and their bodies were usually dumped in the Chattahoochee River. Many of the patrons were soldiers from Fort Benning.

A judge in Phenix City formed a group of good citizens to stop the criminals. Roberts Henry Brown was the attorney for this group because he was the District Attorney for Lee County. The judge, Mr. Brown and the others were threatened with death. Mr. Brown had to be extra careful whenever he went to the courthouse to meet with the judge and the others.

Taking back roads, I drove Mr. Brown to the rear door of the courthouse, let him out, then I parked. Wearing my pistol concealed, I casually walked around inside the courthouse asking different questions about taxes and such in different offices. When the meeting in the judge's office was over, one of them gave me a nod and I drove my car to the back entrance and picked up Mr. Brown. This time, the trip was uneventful. Later on, the judge was gunned down on the courthouse steps. After that, the home of Roberts and Sara Brown, in Opelika, was fire bombed during the night. They barely escaped through a window. People in Alabama and Georgia were outraged and angry. Phenix City is located just across the river from Columbus, Georgia, and next to the part of Fort Benning on the Alabama side of the river.

The Governor of Alabama ordered out the National Guard and declared martial law for the city. The Attorney General of Alabama was ordered to establish law and order with the power of the National Guard. The F.B.I. and U.S. Marshals, who had tried for years to get the organized criminals, moved in because U. S. soldiers had been murdered. It was good that the federals were involved. It was also fortunate that Roberts Brown had evidence from the judge regarding certain people. This gave law enforcement trails to follow. There was a movie made about all of this. It was named "The Phenix City Story."

The U.S. Army, Navy, Marines, and Air Force had great R.O.T.C. (Reserve Officers Training Corps) programs at Auburn. In the past, Junior R.O.T.C. was required by all males. The military was having a tough time trying to recruit veterans into Senior R.O.T.C. Veterans were exempt from Junior R.O.T.C. Two friends, Jay Gaston Golson and Joseph Crenshaw Martin, and I debated whether or not to become Senior Cadets. Joe Martin and his wife, Sara Hudson Martin, were from Montgomery. I met Sara Hudson at Baldwin Junior High School. Both Jay and Joe served in the U.S. Navy during the war.

There was an incentive. Senior Cadets were paid $28.00 a month. We needed the money, so we signed up. Officer's uniforms and whatever we needed were issued to us and we started classes in Military Science and Tactics, plus Corps of Engineer training to be Combat Engineer and Construction Engineer Commanders. We also had drill once a week. The Senior Cadets were the officers for the Junior Cadets. After two years, we had final exams. All three of us flunked our final exams because we thought we could get out. Our unit instructor, Captain Shepard (a nice guy) called us to his office and said, "What are you guys trying to do to me? You will take the exams over." This time we aced them.

We were sent to the Engineer School at Fort Belvoir, Virginia, for summer training. I was commissioned a 2nd Lieutenant in the U.S. Army Corps of Engineers at Auburn in March 1950. Yes, I remembered Lt. O'Farrel and Staff Sergeant McDonald of the Corps of Engineers during the days of Kasserine Pass. An unusual thing happened when I was issued a new military serial number. This was my fifth serial number; now, I can only remember three of them.

A degree in Architecture requires about six academic years, and since I had another year to go after I was commissioned, my assignment was to an Active Reserve Engineer Battalion Headquarters in Opelika. After the colonel in command read my officer's 201 file, he appointed me to be one of his four staff officers with the acting rank of major. He said, "With your experience, this is where I need you. Also, you are a sixth year senior in architecture and we don't get many of those."

After I completed my thesis, I graduated with a degree in architecture. Strangely enough, I was awarded a high school diploma, dated November 29, 2000, by the State of Florida. The state passed a law awarding diplomas to veterans who went to war before completing high school. As soon as I received my degree, Dorothy and I moved to Albany, Georgia, with our first son, Daniel Collier Houston, Jr. Dan was born at Drake Infirmary, on campus, on July 7, 1950. There wasn't a hospital in the City of Auburn at that time.

My oldest brother, Walter Ray Houston, was a banker in Albany, and he sent me membership cards (which he paid for) in the American Legion, Post 30, Albany. He became the Commander of Post 30, and exactly fifty years later, our second son, Walter Lamar Houston, became the Commander of Post 30. In Albany, my military assignment was to an Active Reserve Combat Engineer Company. Also, there were enough high-ranking engineer officers in the Albany area to form an Advanced Engineer Officer's School.

From time to time, we went to Fort Benning, Fort Jackson, and other places for training. It was required to keep up with skills in firing weapons and so forth. I was the Weapons Training Officer many times. One time, while at Fort Benning Infantry School, I jumped twice from the parachute tower, wearing my genuine Corcoran Jump Boots. You don't really jump from the tower; you are picked up high with the parachute open and then released.

After I passed the N.C.A.R.B. (National Council of Architectural Registration Boards) exams and became a Registered Architect, I started my own architectural practice in 1953. It became increasingly difficult to practice architecture and perform military duties. I discussed this with the commanding general of the Third Army. He made me many great offers if I would become a regular army career officer. The Commanding Officer of Turner Air Force Base asked me to transfer to the U.S. Air Force and become the Post Engineer with the rank of lt. colonel. Not wanting a military career, I did the only thing I could do to get a discharge. I refused any further promotions and let my three-year commission expire.

There is an irony regarding the men and women who served in the military during World War II. We were had and discriminated against by the United States Congress. When the U. S. Congress amended the Social Security Act, it included a provision that all persons born in the years 1918 through 1926 would receive less money than all other persons. The persons born during these years lived through the "Great Depression" and then they served in the war. To this date, the U.S. Congress has refused to correct this "Age Gap" atrocity.

The American Red Cross was created by an act of the U.S. Congress. It is difficult to criticize the Red Cross because there are so many good volunteer workers. However, it is my duty to write some things on behalf of the many veterans both living and dead. The Red Cross DISTRIBUTES the items given to it by people, companies or the government. They do not pay for anything. They DISTRIBUTED cigarettes to us in the war and SOLD us coffee, lemonade, donuts and such. I still have my American Red Cross Cigarette Card from London, England. The Red Cross LOANED soldiers a few dollars to buy a bus ticket or something in an emergency. Then they harassed the soldier and his or her family to get paid back. The point of all of this is where do the billions of dollars given to them go? Do they receive any money from Congress? Is the Red Cross ever audited? The only reasonable answer is, the money goes for salaries for the full-time employees and officers. It is now November 2001, and the Red Cross has just announced that it has destroyed thousands of pints of donated blood because it cannot store it. By the way, they also sell the donated blood. Soldiers in the Middle East, Africa, and Europe knew that the Red Cross forced the military to accept them as the one and only relief agency in those areas.

Jeff Newell, a Fort Walton Beach Daily News staff writer, interviewed me and wrote a special report about the" Battle of Kasserine Pass, Fifty Years Later." The report was published in the "Daily News" on Monday, February 15, 1993. After that, a lady living in Destin, Florida, came to see me and brought some of her deceased husband's notes and momentous. He was a young soldier in my division, the 34th Infantry Division, and was captured at Kasserine. The lady had one of his shoulder patches, the Red Bull or the Skull Division, as the Germans called us.

Afterword

The soldier described in his notes the terrible journey from Kasserine to Germany where they were used as slave labor, repairing the railways as the Allies blew them up. I regret that I have misplaced his notes and mementos.

Dear Reader, please do not think that I was the good guy during the war years. I cursed and sinned as much as anyone else. I remember stealing a rabbit out of a snare on the South Downs of England. I was going to cook it and eat it whenever we stopped, but we didn't stop, and the rabbit spoiled; the owner of the snare and his family went hungry.

It is still a wonder to me why people argue and kill each other over religion. I was baptized as it is written in the Bible. For centuries, only a few people could read and had access to Bibles and other religious books. So, all of the other people knew only what they were told by other men. Strangely enough, the major religions are not that far apart. The main differences are traditions and what men wish to impose on others.

Please read all of the religious texts and you will see that we should love each other and not judge each other. <u>There are no Holy Lands, Places, Buildings, or things</u> on this earth. As it is written, the Lord is the one and only judge and the Lord has promised us that He will destroy the earth and everything on it on Judgment Day. Why would the Lord want to destroy anything that was Holy?

ISBN 1-55369375-2

9 781553 693758

Manifest in an Hour

A coloring book to manifest your life

Rose Kelly

Manifest in an Hour

by Rose Kelly

Breathe
Slow down
Peace is here

My
time
is a
gift

THE POWER OF PLAY AND SELF-CARE IN MANIFESTING YOUR DREAM LIFE

In the hustle and bustle of daily life, it's easy to lose touch with the deep, primal wisdom that resides within you—a wisdom that knows exactly how to manifest the life you've always dreamed of, full of abundance, time, energy, and joy. As a mom, your days are often consumed with caring for others, leaving little room for your own needs, desires, or dreams. But here's the secret: your ability to manifest the life you want hinges on your connection to your primal inner being, and that connection is nurtured through play and self-care.

RECONNECTING WITH YOUR PRIMAL SELF

Your primal self is the part of you that is instinctual, beautifully intuitive, and deeply connected to the rhythms of nature and your soul's true desires. It's the part of you that knows how to rest when you're tired, play when you're stressed, and seek out joy as naturally as you breathe. This primal wisdom is your guide in manifesting the life you envision, but in order to access it, you must create space in your life to listen to it.

One of the most effective ways to reconnect with this inner wisdom is through play. As adults, especially as parents, we often forget the importance of play in our lives. We're so focused on being productive and responsible we overlook the fact that play is not just for children —it's a vital part of our well-being. Play opens up a channel to your primal self, allowing you to tap into creativity, joy, and a sense of possibility.

ROSE KELLY

simple joys

THE ROLE OF PLAY IN MANIFESTATION

ROSE KELLY

When you allow yourself to play, you're not just having 'wasting time'; you're aligning with the energy of abundance and possibility. Play puts you in a state of flow, where time restrictions disappear and your mind is free from the usual constraints of daily life. In this state, your subconscious mind is more open to new ideas, solutions, and visions for your future. This is where the magic of manifestation happens.

For example, think about the last time you did something purely for the joy of it, without any agenda or outcome in mind. Maybe you danced around your living room, painted with your kids, or spent an afternoon in nature. How did you feel afterward? Energized? Inspired? More connected to yourself? That's the power of play. It raises your vibration, aligns you with your true desires, and makes you a magnet for the things you want to attract into your life.

THE VITAL IMPORTANCE OF SELF CARE

Self-care is often misunderstood as a luxury or an indulgence, but in reality, it's a necessity, especially for those who are juggling the demands of family life. Self-care is not just about bubble baths and spa days (although those are wonderful, too). It's about honoring your needs, setting boundaries, and making time to nourish your body, mind, and soul. When you neglect self-care, you disconnect from your primal self, leading to burnout, stress, and a sense of overwhelm.

To manifest the life you desire you need primal energy, soul clarity, and focus. All of which are fueled by self-care. When you take care of yourself, you're not just recharging your batteries; you're sending a powerful message to the universe that you are worthy of receiving abundance in all forms: money, time, energy, and love.

what is unfurling in your life?

today
I AM WORTHY
of beautiful
growth

today I only put my energy towards what makes my primal soul bloom

my heart
is free

PRACTICAL STEPS TO INCORPORATE PLAY AND SELF-CARE

1. Schedule Playtime: Just as you would schedule a meeting or a doctor's appointment, schedule time for play. This could be anything from a hobby you enjoy to trying something new and fun with your family. The key is to let go of any expectations and simply enjoy the moment.

2. Create a Self-Care Ritual: Find small pockets of time each day to engage in self-care. This could be a morning meditation, a few minutes of deep breathing, or a quiet cup of tea before bed. Make it a non-negotiable part of your routine.

3. Listen to Your Body: Your body is a powerful communicator, constantly sending you signals about what it needs. Tune in and honor those needs, whether it's rest, movement, nourishment, or connection.

4. Embrace Imperfection: Remember, self-care and play don't have to be perfect. It's okay if your self-care routine isn't Instagram-worthy or if your playtime is interrupted by the demands of motherhood. What matters is that you make the effort and give yourself permission to be imperfect.

5. Involve Your Family: Self-care and play don't have to be solitary activities. Involve your children and partner in activities that bring joy and relaxation to everyone. This not only strengthens your bond but also models healthy behaviors for your family.

this is the day *my*
life feels good

UNEXPECTED GOOD THINGS COME MY WAY TODAY

I am MANIFESTING abundance

I MEET all my own NEEDS

MANIFESTING ABUNDANCE THROUGH PLAY AND SELF-CARE

As you integrate play and self-care into your life, you'll find that your energy begins to shift. You'll feel more aligned with your desires, more connected to your primal wisdom, and more capable of manifesting the life you envision. The abundance you seek. whether it's financial prosperity, more time freedom, increased energy, or a happier family life, will naturally flow to you when you're in a state of joy, relaxation, and alignment.

Remember, your primal self knows the way. By honoring it through play and self-care, you're not just taking care of yourself; you're opening the door to a life of limitless possibilities, where your dreams can become your reality.

ROSE KELLY

my deepest love comes from **WITHIN**

read a chapter a day and use these
BOOKMARKS to save your place
ROMANCE BOOK CHECK LIST

Man Her Station ☐   THOSE LAST 10 POUNDS ☐

☐ Witchway To Romance

I am wealthy. I am happy, I am healthy.

Today
I am
manifesting
my
dream

ABOUT THE AUTHOR

Rose Kelly is an award-winning filmmaker and celebrated romance novelist known for her evocative storytelling and deep exploration of human emotions. With a unique talent for weaving intricate narratives, Rose has captivated audiences both on screen and in print. Her films have garnered critical acclaim, earning her a dedicated following. In addition to her achievements in filmmaking and writing, Rose is the creative force behind a successful YouTube channel where she shares insights on self-care, creativity, and personal growth. Through her engaging content, she has built a thriving community on Patreon, helping thousands of individuals reconnect with their primal inner beings and embrace their authentic selves. Rose's work is a testament to her passion for storytelling, empowerment, and the transformative power of art.

Rose is a passionate creator who thrives on crafting unique experiences that resonate deeply with audiences around the world. She empowers others to manifest their most authentic selves, encouraging them to embrace life's mysteries and joys with curiosity and courage.

with love,

Rose Kelly

Made in United States
Troutdale, OR
09/09/2024

22719888R00017